LEVELS OF LIVING IN A STATE SETTING

CESS RESEARCH STUDIES

Public Policy and the Rural Poor in India.

Public Policies for Rural Development in Andhra Pradesh: A Review of Research Trends.

Distance in levels of Living : Temporal and Spatial.

The working of the Andhra Pradesh State Road Transport Corporation.

Centre-state Financial Relations: A study in Levels of Development of States.

Levels of Living in a State Setting: The case of Andhra Pradesh.

CESS RESEARCH STUDIES 3

LEVELS OF LIVING IN A STATE SETTING
THE CASE OF ANDHRA PRADESH

R.RADHAKRISHNA
S.A.R.SASTRY
S.SUDHAKAR REDDY
G.K.MITRA

CENTRE FOR ECONOMIC AND SOCIAL STUDIES,
HYDERABAD

And

CONCEPT PUBLISHING COMPANY, NEW DELHI - 110059

ISBN 81-7022-202-8

First Published 1988

Published by
Ashok Kumar Mittal
Concept Publishing Company
A-15-16, Commercial Block, Mohan Garden
NEW DELHI-110059 (India)

Printed at
New Gian Offset Printers
495, DDA Complex, Shahazada Bagh
NEW DELHI-110035

Printed at
Taj Press
A-35/4, Maya Puri
NEW DELHI

CONTENTS

TABLES ON LEVELS OF LIVING

PREFACE

At the Centre for Economic and Social Studies, we have undertaken an intensive and wideranging study on Poverty Levels in Andhra Pradesh. The study is designed to assess Poverty levels within the sub-regions and construct comprehensive profiles of the poor. This study is based on the household data available in the consumption schedules (NSS) canvassed by the Bureau of Economics and Statistics, Andhra Pradesh during the 32nd round 1977-78. While the earlier monograph focussed on the distances in levels of living both temporal and spatial, this volume is a by-product of the processed data on levels of living at the districts level. We intend to share this data with larger audience in the hope that it would provoke fellow social scientists to look at the hard facts and make generalised characterisation of poverty. A brief introduction is provided to facilitate interpretation of the tables generated in the study. Summary figures on levels of living have also been provided at the beginning.

We are grateful to our colleague Mr. P. Satya Sekhar for sparing a great deal of his time for this project. Thanks are also due to Mr. K. Madhusudhana Charyulu, Jawaharlal Nehru Technological University, Hyderabad, for his involvement in the initial phases of the project.

A number of Institutions and Individuals contributed to the successful completion of the study. Among the former we recount the help rendered by the Bureau of Economics and Statistics and the

Electronic Corporation of India Limited (ECIL). Among the individuals our gratitude goes to Shri Lakshminarayana the Director and staff, Bureau of Economics and Statistics. Mention must also be made of the help by Sri PVGK Rao, Sri A. Hanumantha Rao, Sri T.K. Chari of ECIL. We are also grateful to Dr. KPC Rao and Dr. Annamalai both from All India Coordination Research Project from Dry Land Agriculture (ICAR), Hyderabad for improving our understanding of the sources of data regarding Income of Andhra Pradesh. We are extremely thankful to the administrative staff for valuable cooperation. But for their assistance this study could not have been completed in time. We add that the responsibility for all possible inadequacies in presentation rests with the authors.

AUTHORS

ONE

INTRODUCTION

The need for lessening the intensity of poverty in India has, of late, become one of the major objectives of development planning. It has naturally inspired many economists and as a result an extensive literature has evolved on welfare comparisons. The effects of these have been two-fold. On the one hand, a beginning has been made to measure the real income, inequality and poverty in a sound theoretical framework. Pioneering studies by Atkinson (1970) and Sen (1976 a, 1976 b) and the follow up studies by Gary Fields (1980), Kakwani (1980) and Osmani (1980) contain many important insights in understanding the welfare implications of GNP, Gini Coefficient, Head Count Ratio etc. On the other hand, empirical studies have laid focus on measurement of poverty and their determinants following the early studies of Ahluwalia (1978) Bardhan (1974) Dandekar and Rath (1971) and Minhas (1970).

A recurrent theme in much of the empirical work is that growth does not, in general, redress poverty. Much of the analysis is aggregative in nature and considers country/state as a unit of analysis and, hence, it is fraught with severe limitations. It is widely believed that levels of living and their determinants vary across regions and categories of sub-population even within a state. Comprehensive studies by Radhakrishna et al (1983) Sundaram and Tendulkar (1983) analyse the determinants of poverty in India by extending the regional disaggregation to sub-regions within a state.

This volume attempts to provide data on the levels of living in Andhra Pradesh at a disaggregated level and offers a wide scope for the analysis of the determinants of the inter-relationships between development and poverty. This study differs from other studies in two respects; first, it stratifies the population into narrowly defined occupational groups; and secondly it extends regional disaggregation to district. This is possible mainly because of the possibility of access to the abundant information available in the original schedules.

The principal source of data is the original schedules of the National Sample Survey (State Sample) canvassed by the Bureau of Economics and Statistics in their 32nd round for the year 1977-78. The survey covered 7,539 households in rural and 4,365 households in urban areas. Districtwise allocation of the sample is shown in Table 1.

Data collected from the original schedules is segregated by district and occupation. On the basis of the household type code and principal industry occupation given in the schedule, the households have been divided into four categories: (1) cultivator households, (2) agricultural labour households, (3) self-employed households, (4) employed households. The information available in the schedules permits only this classification. In the NSS Survey, the occupation of the household is defined as the one which fetches maximum earnings to the household during the last 365 days preceding the day of enquiry. It may be noted that there are differences between the concepts used by the census and the National Sample Survey. While individual is the basis for the former, household is the basis for the latter.

Households have been grouped into fractile classes on the basis of percapita total expenditure and for each fractile class the following estimates have been worked out:

1. Per capita monthly total expenditure
2. Per capita monthly intake of cereals (quantity and value)
3. Per capita monthly intake of pulses (quantity and value)
4. Per capita monthly intake of milk and milk products (value)
5. Per capita monthly intake of edible oil (quantity and value)
6. Per capita monthly expenditure on meat, fish and eggs (value)
7. Per capita monthly intake of sugar (quantity and value)
8. Average size of household
9. Size of the operational land holding of the house-hold.

TABLE 1: Sample households and estimated households and population (All Classes)

Districts	Rural: Sample House-Holds	Rural: Estimated** households (in lakhs)	Rural: Estimated* population (in lakhs)	Urban: Sample House-holds	Urban: Estimated households (in thousands)	Urban: Estimated population (in thousands)
Coastal Andhra						
1. Srikakulam (SKL)	493	5.10	24.31	197	68.65	334.37
2. Visakhapatnam (VSP)	461	5.53	23.84	387	182.83	853.75
3. East Godavari (EG)	561	6.57	27.78	312	162.94	757.69
4. West Godavari (WG)	419	5.27	21.81	211	130.24	545.71
5. Krishna (KSN)	413	4.83	19.87	407	188.97	903.18
6. Guntur (GNT)	474	5.68	23.89	363	192.27	880.50
7. Prakasam (PKM)	343	4.59	20.00	95	78.83	308.22
8. Nellore (NLR)	233	3.73	15.32	135	89.44	368.45
RAYALASEEMA						
9. Chittoor (CTR)	389	4.35	21.99	199	82.95	417.20
10. Cuddapah (CDP)	266	2.99	15.01	178	66.59	329.01
11. Anantapur (ATP)	343	4.19	19.94	174	84.46	486.58
12. Kurnool (KNL)	370	3.14	17.53	227	103.47	535.93
TELANGANA						
13. Mahbubnagar (MBR)	377	3.78	20.66	85	43.51	239.74
14. Hyderabad (HYD)	192	2.64	11.33	761	499.60	2397.91
15. Medak (MDK)	268	3.46	15.39	86	35.92	188.68
16. Nizamabad (NZB)	197	2.49	12.88	96	56.80	290.38
17. Adilabad (ADB)	272	2.92	12.57	125	64.72	284.18
18. Karimnagar (KRM)	417	4.10	19.74	110	69.72	329.74
19. Warangal (WRG)	374	5.58	18.29	144	80.87	354.21
20. Khammam (KHM)	257	2.43	13.80	84	50.29	261.59
21. Nalgonda (NLG)	420	3.77	19.32	46	45.25	214.50

* Estimated from the population of 1971 and 1981 census.

** Estimated by dividing population by sample average size of the household.

The information on levels of living has been presented for each district in 10 tables (8 for rural and 2 urban). A detailed analysis of the district-wise results is beyond the scope of the present volume, but we cannot resist the temptation of simple analysis of the data. We are curious of what the data reveals us on the inter-regional and inter-class variations in levels of living. This is what we have attempted in the next few sections.

TWO

OCCUPATIONAL COMPOSITION OF HOUSEHOLDS

The distribution of households by occupation is shown in Table 2. It can be seen that in Andhra Pradesh, of the 111 lakh estimated households in 1977-78, 87 lakh (78%) households are in rural areas and 24 lakh (22%) households are in urban areas. Further, of the 111 lakh rural households, 70 lakh 63%) households depend on agriculture for livelihood; 30 lakh (27% households belong to self-employed non-agricultural class and 11 lakh (10%) households belong to employed non-agricultural class. It is significant to observe that agricultural labour households constitute 54 per cent of the agricultural households. The occupational distribution of the households differs between rural and urban areas. In the rural areas, 76 per cent of the households depend on agriculture, 19 per cent are self-employed and 4 per cent belong to employed non-agricultural class. In the urban areas, as expected, a small percentage (11%) of households depend on agriculture; 57 per cent are self-employed and 31 percent belong to the category of employed non-agricultural class. It is worth nothing that urban agricultural households form nearly 4 per cent of the total agricultural households.

The occupational distribution of households in the three broad region of Andhra Pradesh viz. Coastal Andhra, Rayalaseema and Telangana is shown in Table 3. Two features are worth noting. First, the proportion of agricultural households varies marginally across the three regions but the composition of agricultural households varies significantly. Second, the percentage of agricultural labour household is the largest in the developed region i.e. Coastal Andhra.

TABLE 2: **Percentage distribution of households and population by occupation of the households for Andhra Pradesh**

	Households					
	Rural		Urban		Andhra Pradesh	
Occupational Classes	Estimated Households (in thousands)	Percentage distribution of house-holds	Estimated households (in thousands)	Percentage distribution of households	Estimated households (in thousands)	Percentage distribution of households
Cultivators	3080.90	35.00	116.27	5.00	3197.17	29.00
Agricultural Labourers	3661.00	42.00	155.72	7.00	3816.72	34.00
Agricultural classes	6741.90	77.00	271.99	12.00	7013.89	63.00
Self Employed	1639.00	19.00	1358.95	57.00	2997.95	27.00
Employed	333.00	4.00	747.38	31.00	1080.38	10.00
Non-agricultural Classes	1972.00	23.00	2106.33	88.00	4078.33	37.00
All Classes	8713.90	100.00	2378.32	100.00	11092.22	100.00

Contd.

(TABLE 2: Contd.)

Occupational Classes	Population					
	Rural		Urban		Andhra Pradesh	
	Estimated Population (in Lakhs)	Percentage distribu-tion of population	Estimated Population (in Lakhs)	Percentage distribu-tion of population	Estimated Population (in Lakhs)	Percentage distribu-tion of population
Cultivators	155.76	39.40	5.57	4.94	161.33	31.75
Agricultural Labourers	148.08	37.46	7.15	6.34	155.23	30.55
Agricultural Classes	303.84	76.86	12.72	11.28	316.56	62.30
Self Employed	76.64	19.39	64.66	57.31	141.30	27.81
Employed	14.84	3.75	35.44	31.41	50.28	9.89
Non-Agricultural Classes	91.48	23.14	100.10	88.72	191.58	37.70
All Classes	395.32	100.00	112.82	100.00	508.14	100.00

Table 3 : **Percentage distribution of households in 77-78 in the three regions of Andhra Pradesh**

	Coastal Andhra			Rayalaseema			Telangana		
	Percentage distribution of households			Percentage distribution of households			Percentage distribution of households		
	Rural	Urban	Coastal Andhra	Rural	Urban	Rayala-seema	Rural	Urban	Telangana
Cultivators	29.00	5.00	24.00	40.00	6.00	34.00	41.00	5.00	33.00
Agricultural Labourers	49.00	9.00	40.00	42.00	8.00	35.00	33.00	3.00	26.00
Agricultural Classes	78.00	14.00	64.00	82.00	14.00	69.00	74.00	8.00	59.00
Self Employed	18.00	56.00	26.00	14.00	61.00	23.00	22.00	57.00	30.00
Employed	4.00	30.00	10.00	4.00	25.00	8.00	4.00	35.00	11.00
Non-agricultural Classes	22.00	86.00	36.00	18.00	86.00	31.00	26.00	92.00	41.00
All Classes	100.00	100.00	100.00	100.00	100.00	100.00	100.00	100.00	100.00
Estimated Number of house-holds (in Lakhs)	41.30	10.94	52.24	14.67	3.37	18.04	31.17	9.47	10.64

TABLE 4 : **Composition of Rural Households by Occupation of Households in 1977-78**

Districts	Cultivators	Agricultural Labourers	Self employed	Employed	Agricultural classes (2+3)	Non Agricultural classes (4+5)	All Classes
1	2	3	4	5	6	7	8
Srikakulam	38.13	40.77	18.05	3.05	78.90	21.10	100.00
Visakhapatnam	40.13	38.61	18.66	2.60	78.74	21.26	100.00
East Godavari	18.54	60.07	16.40	4.99	78.61	21.39	100.00
West Godavari	19.33	52.03	21.48	7.16	71.36	28.64	100.00
Krishna	21.07	50.60	22.28	6.05	71.67	28.33	100.00
Gunter	27.64	46.62	22.36	3.38	74.26	25.74	100.00
Prakasam	43.44	42.27	11.37	2.92	85.71	14.29	100.00
Nellore	28.75	54.08	9.44	7.73	82.83	17.17	100.00
Chittoor	37.79	44.99	15.17	2.05	82.78	17.22	100.00
Cuddapah	38.72	37.59	16.54	7.15	76.31	23.69	100.00
Anantapur	44.90	38.48	11.96	4.66	83.38	16.62	100.00
Kurnool	34.86	42.43	19.74	2.97	77.29	22.71	100.00
Mahabubnagar	38.99	37.40	20.96	2.65	76.39	23.61	100.00
Hyderabad	41.14	37.50	17.19	4.17	78.64	21.36	100.00
Medaak	42.53	29.10	22.02	6.35	71.63	28.37	100.00
Nizamabad	49.23	29.45	18.27	3.05	78.68	21.32	100.00
Adilabad	44.48	34.93	18.02	2.57	79.41	20.59	100.00
Karimnagar	33.81	35.73	28.06	2.40	69.54	30.46	100.00
Warangal	42.24	30.75	23.80	3.21	72.99	27.01	100.00
Khammam	33.46	35.02	26.07	5.45	68.48	31.52	100.00
Nalgonda	38.33	31.91	24.76	5.00	70.24	29.76	100.00

TABLE 5 : **Composition of Urban Households by Occupation of Households in 1977-78**

Districts	Cultivators	Agricultural Labourers	Self employed	Employed	Agricultural classes (2+3)	Non Agricultural classes (4+5)	All Classes
1	2	3	4	5	6	7	8
Srikakulam	7.65	7.65	56.12	28.58	15.30	84.70	100.00
Visakapatnam	2.89	5.26	58.16	33.69	8.15	91.85	100.00
East Godavari	2.58	4.20	65.38	27.84	6.78	93.22	100.00
West Godavarri	4.78	17.70	53.12	24.40	22.48	77.52	100.00
Krishna	2.46	8.60	57.49	31.45	11.06	88.94	100.00
Gunter	2.49	8.29	54.97	34.25	10.78	89.22	100.00
Prakasam	10.53	33.68	42.11	13.68	44.21	55.79	100.00
Nellore	8.89	5.93	42.22	42.96	14.82	85.18	100.00
Chittoor	4.65	10.47	59.88	25.00	15.12	84.88	100.00
Cuddapah	4.57	9.71	56.00	29.72	14.28	85.72	100.00
Anantapur	7.39	10.79	59.66	22.16	18.18	81.82	100.00
Kurnool	4.43	7.52	62.39	25.66	11.95	88.05	100.00
Mahabubnagar	7.14	14.29	54.76	23.81	21.43	78.57	100.00
Hyderabad	0.13	-	60.95	38.92	0.13	99.87	100.00
Medak	12.65	1.15	52.87	33.33	13.80	86.20	100.00
Nizamabad	22.92	11.46	43.75	21.87	34.38	65.62	100.00
Adilabad	2.42	12.90	67.74	16.94	15.32	84.68	100.00
Karimnagar	7.41	3.70	58.33	30.56	11.11	88.89	100.00
Warangal	5.76	7.91	59.71	26.62	13.67	86.33	100.00
Khammam	4.76	-	72.62	22.62	4.76	95.24	100.00
Nalgonda	9.30	9.30	20.93	60.47	18.60	81.40	100.00

The composition of rural households at the district level is presented in Table 4. The results reveal the tendency of the preponderance of agricultural labour households in developed districts and cultivator households in backward districts. For instance, agricultural labour households constitute 47 to 61 per cent of the rural households in West Godavari, East Godavari, Krishna, Guntur while cultivator households constitute 19 to 29 per cent. On the other hand in backward districts, viz., Anantapur, Warangal, Adilabad, Medak and Mahbubnagar, agricultural labour households constitute 29 to 38 per cent of rural households and cultivator households constitute 34 to 45 per cent.

Self employed class is the largest in size among the urban occupational groups in most of the districts of Andhra Pradesh (see table 5). But it is striking to note the high percentage of cultivator households in Nizamabad and agricultural labour households in prakasam.

THREE

LEVELS OF LIVING REFLECTED IN PER CAPITA EXPENDITURE

The total consumer expenditure of Andhra Pradesh in 1977-78 works out to Rs. 35,570 millions, of which rural areas account for 71 percent and urban areas 29 per cent. Per capita monthly expenditure is estimated as Rs. 58.18 in Andhra Pradesh (rural and urban together); Rs. 53.25 in rural and Rs. 75.49 in urban areas. Our estimate of per capita annual expenditure (Rs. 707.86) is in line with the estimate of per capita annual income (Rs. 1017.73) for 1977-78 provided by the Bureau of Economics and Statistics.

The district-wise per capita expenditure estimates are given in Table 6. The following features may be highlighted. In the case of rural areas, Krishna, Guntur, and East Godavari in Coastal Andhra, Nalgonda and Khammam in Telangana are at the top in per capita expenditure, while Srikakulam (Coastal Andhra) Anantapur (Rayalaseema) and Karimnagar, Warangal, Adilabad and Medak (Telangana) are at the bottom. It is significant to observe that the average per capita expenditure of the bottom districts is less than Rs. 50 per month; i.e. poverty line adopted in this study for rural areas. In the case of urban areas, Visakhapatnam of Coastal Andhra and Nalgonda and Hyderabad of Telangana are at the top; while Cuddapah of Rayalaseema; and Karimnagar, Warangal, and Adilabad of Telangana are at the bottom. Considering rural and urban areas together, Krishna, East Godavari, Visakhapatnam, West Godavari of Coastal Andhra, Nalgonda and Hyderabad of Telangana occupy top positions, while Srikakulam of Coastal Andhra, Anantapur of

Rayalaseema and Karimnagar, Mahbubnagar of Telangana gravitate towards the bottom.

TABLE 6 : **Consumer expenditure by districts**

District	Per Capita Monthly Total Expenditure (Rs. 0.00)		Per Capita Annual Expenditure (Rs. 0.00)	
	Rural	Urban	Rural	Urban
(1)	(2)	(3)	(4)	(5)
Srikakulam	44.20	72.43	530.40	869.16
Visakhapatnam	51.24	90.54	614.88	1086.48
East Godavari	60.91	72.74	730.92	872.88
West Godavari	56.71	68.80	680.52	825.60
Krishna	64.88	100.54	778.52	1206.48
Guntur	59.30	71.57	711.60	858.84
Prakasam	52.54	66.60	630.48	799.20
Nellore	54.16	78.46	649.92	941.52
Kurnool	50.59	71.32	607.08	855.84
Anantapur	46.60	70.74	559.20	848.88
Cuddapah	58.69	59.24	704.28	710.88
Chittoor	55.00	70.64	660.00	847.68
Hyderabad	48.94	80.27	587.28	963.24
Mahbubnagar	50.16	62.53	601.92	750.36
Medak	45.22	55.89	542.64	670.68
Nizamabad	58.13	56.76	697.56	681.12
Adilabad	43.92	63.91	527.04	766.92
Karimnagar	38.19	51.69	458.28	620.28
Warangal	43.75	57.36	525.00	688.32
Khammam	62.91	82.35	754.92	988.20
Nalgonda	72.45	98.44	869.40	1181.28

Since per capita expenditure is likely to be related to Gross Domestic Product (GDP), the available data on per capita domestic product along with total expenditure are presented in Table 7. The districts have been ranked on the basis of per capita GDP and per capita expenditure and grouped into three categories viz, top, middle and bottom. The top group comprises of the districts with ranks 1 to 7, middle group with ranks 8 to 14 and bottom group with ranks 15 to 21. Table 8 shows the grouping of the districts.

TABLE 7 : **Per capita expenditure and Gross Domestic Product by districts**

Districts	Per capita Annual expenditure rural + urban (Rs. 0.00)	Per capita Gross Domestic Product (Rs. 0.00)
(1)	(2)	(3)
Srikakulam	571.32 (17)	662.10 (21)
Visakhapatnam	739.20 (7)	963.71 (12)
East Godavari	761.28 (5)	1020.35 (10)
West Godavari	709.56 (8)	1271.50 (2)
Krishna	912.24 (1)	1133.72 (4)
Guntur	751.20 (6)	1036.95 (9)
Prakasam	652.92 (13)	1099.03 (7)
Nellore	706.32 (9)	1215.94 (3)
Kurnool	665.28 (12)	1103.11 (6)
Anantapur	615.96 (16)	992.87 (11)
Cuddapah	652.92 (13)	918.28 (16)
Chittoor	689.88 (11)	1085.55 (8)
Hyderabad	842.52 (3)	1423.38 (1)
Mahbubnagar	617.28 (15)	780.20 (19)
Medak	556.56 (19)	783.45 (18)
Nizamabad	694.44 (10)	1106.46 (5)
Adilabad	571.20 (18)	957.38 (13)
Karimnagar	481.44 (21)	927.78 (15)
Warangal	551.40 (20)	750.07 (20
Khammam	792.00 (4)	885.71 (17)
Nalgonda	900.48 (2)	936.11 (14)

Note: Figures in the brackets are ranks
The per capita Gross Domestic Product is obtained from Bureau of Economics and Statistics.

TABLE 8 : **Grouping of districts by level of development per capita expenditure**

Per capita GDP / Per capita Expenditure	Top	Middle	Bottom
Top	KSN, HYD	WG, NZB, NLR, KNL, PKM	
Middle	NLG, EG, GNT, VSP	CTR	ATP, ADB
Bottom	KHM	CDP	SKL, MDK, MBR, KRM, WRG

One can notice that the correspondence between per capita expenditure (PCE) and per capita Gross Domestic Product (GDP) is both in GDP and per capita expenditure, there is a good deal of reshuffling in the ranks of the top and middle groups (table 8). Clearly, Srikakulam, Medak, Mahbubnagar, Karimnagar and Warangal are grouped as the most backward districts in terms of both per capita expenditure and Gross Domestic Product. But Anantapur and Adilabad are in the bottom group according to per capita expenditure although they fall in the middle group according to per capita GDP.

Table 9 reveals the pattern of per capita expenditure of various rural occupational groups across districts. It is clearly observed that in the districts where per capita expenditure is higher, the levels of living of the various classes are also found to be higher. This implies that all occupational groups are sharing the benefits of development. When we shift the focus to the various rural classes across the districts, we notice that 'employed' non-agricultural class enjoys higher level of living followed by the cultivators, self employed and agricultural labour in that order. However, exception to this is noticed in Nizamabad, Visakhapatnam, Kurnool and Adilabad where the levels of living of the self-employed are found to be higher than those of cultivators. Only in the case of Guntur, the per capita expenditure of the agricultural labour class is coming closer to the self-employed. It is revealing to note that the 'employed' non-agricultural class enjoys a higher level of living than those of cultivators in a majority of the districts (14 out of 21). It must be remembered, however, that their incomes are exogenous and do not arise from the rural production system. A more significant observation is that the disparities between cultivators and agricultural labourers in the levels of living are wider in the developed districts as compared to the backward ones.

In the urban areas, it is revealing to note that the per capita expenditure of the employed are uniformly higher than those of the self-employed (Table 10). One significant observation is that the prosperous districts display greater distance in the levels of living between employed and self-employed groups compared to the backward districts. Nellore is the only exception where the per capita expenditure of both the groups are almost closer. Table 11 provides a summary picture on levels of percapita expenditure for the district as a whole by combining corresponding classes of rural and urban areas. By and large the pattern conforms to the preceding discussion.

TABLE 9 : **Expenditures of Occupational groups : Rural 1977-1978 (32nd Round)**
Per Capita Monthly Total Expenditure of :

Districts	All Classes	Agricultural Classes	Cultivators	Agricultural Labourers	Non-agricultural Classes	Self Employed	Employed
1	2	3	4	5	6	7	8
Srikakulam	44.20	43.05	49.10	35.93	48.66	47.61	53.39
Visakhapatnam	51.24	49.31	53.27	44.26	58.29	55.47	86.97
East Godavari	60.91	60.38	89.74	48.55	62.94	55.17	90.66
West Godavari	56.71	55.47	67.24	49.65	57.80	55.62	63.15
Krishna	64.88	61.38	73.47	55.33	70.73	64.37	95.12
Guntur	59.30	60.61	72.13	51.96	55.68	53.93	68.41
Prakasam	52.54	52.08	58.87	43.49	55.50	55.17	57.75
Nellore	54.16	53.83	59.97	49.94	55.76	52.91	57.98
Chittoor	55.00	54.09	61.23	46.09	58.13	53.11	94.47
Cuddapah	58.69	55.75	60.09	49.76	71.45	55.44	93.20
Anantapur	46.60	45.32	51.97	35.02	53.50	43.37	83.32
Kurnool	50.59	47.21	55.24	38.89.	62.33	59.99	78.97
Mahbubnagar	50.16	50.38	55.42	43.89	49.40	49.03	55.52
Hyderabad	48.94	48.88	57.11	37.33	49.16	48.38	52.33
Medak	45.22	44.50	47.61	38.21	45.60	43.60	52.30
Nizamabad	58.13	55.14	59.84	46.54	69.38	65.35	95.14
Karimnagar	38.19	38.46	45.71	30.70	37.56	37.37	43.34
Adilabad	43.92	40.97	46.40	33.09	55.26	51.50	80.51
Warangal	43.75	42.93	49.08	32.56	46.22	44.94	56.84
Khammam	62.91	61.29	73.66	47.78	66.92	64.91	78.50
Nalgonda	72.45	73.70	86.31	55.85	69.47	68.72	74.33

TABLE 10 : **Per capita monthly expenditure (Rs. 0.00) Urban classes in 1977-78**

District	All Classes	Self-employed	Employed	Cultivators	Agricultural Labourers
(1)	(2)	(3)	(4)	(5)	(6)
Srikokulam	72.43	71.81	78.56	68.84	56.60
Visakapatnam	90.54	87.45	105.68	62.49	64.90
East Godavari	72.74	68.85	83.41	96.55	44.43
West Godavari	68.80	66.31	85.46	73.40	52.09
Krishna	100.54	95.93	120.02	123.03	45.80
Guntur	71.57	64.28	86.07	84.09	57.17
Prokasum	57.36	55.32	70.15	68.57	48.74
Nellore	78.46	79.51	78.18	93.15	50.61
Chittore	70.64	67.55	79.28	78.89	50.66
Cuddapah	70.74	63.03	86.06	90.51	57.33
Anantapur	66.60	62.90	92.71	45.73	42.31
Kurnool	71.32	66.19	87.16	96.60	41.99
Mahabubnagar	62.53	58.66	77.68	58.80	49.00
Hyderabad	80.27	75.57	86.89	-	-
Medak	55.89	47.79	64.49	64.29	36.67
Nizamabad	59.24	59.65	69.85	58.36	41.50
Adilabad	56.76	57.04	61.70	84.43	43.55
Karimnagar	63.91	61.74	69.80	66.08	40.30
Warangal	51.69	45.40	58.58	62.85	69.79
Khommam	82.35	80.21	99.75	59.40	-
Nalgonda	98.44	84.09	116.96	49.94	59.41

TABLE 11: **Per capita monthly expenditure (Rs. 0.00) : Andhra Pradesh classes in 1977-78**

Districts	Cultivators Rural + Urban	Agricultural labourers Rural + Urban	Self Employed Rural + Urban	Employed Rural + Urban	Agricultural classes Rural + Urban	Non-agricultural classes Rural Urban
1	2	3	4	5	6	7
SKL	50.86	37.01	55.10	67.93	44.64	57.64
VSP	53.68	45.97	71.75	103.04	50.21	79.93
EG	90.23	48.38	61.54	85.10	60.61	66.22
WG	67.71	50.03	59.66	72.28	55.53	63.43
KSN	78.15	53.89	80.50	113.73	61.71	89.60
GNT	73.15	52.57	58.67	82.49	61.22	65.05
PKM	59.41	44.39	55.23	62.86	52.28	56.88
NLR	64.55	49.98	66.48	70.09	55.92	68.20
CTR	62.13	46.51	59.55	83.69	54.40	64.50
CDP	62.04	50.63	59.16	89.33	57.09	68.79
ATP	51.40	35.95	54.38	88.81	45.19	63.43
KNL	57.24	39.17	63.04	85.03	48.15	67.51
MBR	55.59	44.27	51.02	68.54	50.56	53.86
HYD	56.82	37.33	72.20	85.18	48.88	77.16
MDK	49.23	38.20	44.50	59.01	45.79	47.52
NZB	59.49	45.69	63.26	81.90	54.82	68.53
ADB	47.39	34.68	54.15	71.23	41.94	56.70
KRM	46.86	30.96	43.93	58.78	39.29	47.00
WRG	49.76	35.50	44.49	58.08	44.34	46.97
KHM	72.80	47.78	70.36	89.34	60.81	73.22
NLG	85.27	55.95	69.89	100.26	73.13	80.60

FOUR

RURAL AND URBAN DIFFERENTIALS

It is observed that per capita expenditure of urban areas is higher than that of the rural areas by 42 per cent. By and large this difference is higher. Even if we attribute 20 per cent of the differential to price variation, there is still substantial divergence between rural and urban areas. We have probed further into the sources of rural-urban variations by analysing rural and urban differences across districts as well as the rural-urban differences between the bottom 30 per cent and top 20 per cent. It is revealing that in Srikakulam, Visakhapatnam, Krishna, Hyderabad and Karimnagar the rural-urban dichotomy is more striking (column 1 of Table 12). In the above districts the per capita expenditure in urban areas is higher than in rural areas by 50 per cent. In general, rural-urban differentials are wider among the top classes than the bottom ones (columns 2 and 3 of Table 12). It is interesting to observe that in urban Visakhapatnam, the per capita expenditure of the top class is twice that of its counter-part in rural areas whereas in Srikakulam, Krishna, Hyderabad and Karimnagar the per capita expenditure of the top class is higher only by 70-80 per cent than that of their counterparts in the rural areas.

TABLE 12 : Rural Urban differentials in per capita expenditure in 1977-78

Districts	All Classes Urban/Rural	Bottom 30% Urban/rural	Top 20% Urban/Rural
(1)	(2)	(3)	(4)
Srikakulam	1.64	1.46	1.80
Visakhapatnam	1.77	1.49	2.06
East Godavari	1.19	1.17	1.22
West Godavari	1.21	1.17	1.34
Krishna	1.55	1.23	1.74
Guntur	1.20	1.11	1.34
Prakasam	1.09	1.17	1.12
Nellore	1.45	1.22	1.22
Kurnool	1.41	1.30	1.59
Anantapur	1.43	1.34	1.45
Cuddapah	1.20	1.27	1.17
Chittoor	1.28	1.25	1.22
Hyderabad	1.64	1.60	1.70
Mahbubnagar	1.24	1.22	1.22
Medak	1.23	1.10	1.49
Nizamabad	1.02	1.06	0.96
Adilabad	1.29	1.26	1.30
Karimnagar	1.67	1.70	1.76
Warangal	1.18	1.26	1.20
Khammam	1.31	1.26	1.31
Nalgonda	1.36	1.28	1.28

Note : Column (2) is obtained dividing the per capita expenditure of both 30 per cent of the per capita expenditure of urban areas by bottom 30 per cent of the per capita expenditure of rural areas.

Similarly Column (3) is obtained by considering top 20 per cent of per capita expenditure of urban areas by rural areas.

FIVE

POVERTY LEVELS

The first step in measuring the poverty level is to establish a minimum acceptable level of expenditure known as poverty line, which separates the poor from the rest. The persons with expenditure levels less than the poverty line are treated as poor and the extent of poverty is usually measured by Head Count, Poverty Gap, Sen's Poverty Index etc. Two approaches to the construction of poverty line have been explored in the Indian studies. Firstly, a number of studies chose the poverty line of Rs. 15 per capita per month at 1960-61 prices and adjusted it for price changes over time and region. In the second approach, calorie intake function (expressing calorie intake as a function of expenditure) is estimated from consumer expenditure data and the expenditure corresponding to a minimum level of calories is derived from it. Generally. a linear relation is postulated between per capita calorie intake (C) and logarithm of per capita expenditure (X), so that $C = a + b \log X$. Given a and b, one can arrive at the expenditure needed to ensure a given calorie consumption c by taking anti-logarithm of $(c - a)/b$. It is important to emphasize that establishing a correspondence between poverty line and calorie norm has led to an inconclusive debate and there has been no convergence of the view points.

In this study, the poverty line used is consumer expenditure of Rs. 50 for rural and Rs. 60 per person for urban areas for 30 days in 1977-78. It may be noted that the poverty line of Rs. 15 per person for 30 days at 1960-61 prices, when adjusted by the fractile class specific price index, works out to Rs. 47 at 1977-78 prices.

RURAL POVERTY

In rural areas of Andhra Pradesh 2.18 crore persons (0.87 crore in Coastal Andhra, 0.44 crore in Rayalaseema and 0.86 crore in Telangana) fall below the poverty line in 1977-78. In terms of households, it is estimated that in rural Andhra Pradesh, 44 lakh households (18 lakh in Coastal Andhra, 8 lakh in Rayalaseema and 18 lakhs in Telangana) are below the poverty line. The proportion of poor is seen to be 49 per cent in Coastal Andhra and around 60 per cent in Rayalaseema and Telangana.

It appears that the variation in rural poverty across classes is more pronounced than across the broad regions. Incidence of poverty is 69 per cent for agricultural labourers, 44 per cent for cultivators, 47 per cent for 'self-employed' non-agricultural class and 34 per cent for 'employed' non-agricultural population. Out of the estimated 218 lakh rural poor, a staggering 103 lakhs belong to agricultural labour class and 67 lakh to cultivator class; thus agricultural classes make up more than two-thirds of the poor. On the other hand, among the 40 lakh poor belonging to non-agricultural classes, more than 99 per cent are 'self-employed'. It is clear that poverty levels are low among the 'employed' non-agricultural class. This is not surprising since they are mostly employed in government organizations, banks, schools etc. However, what is surprising is the fact that this class is better off than cultivator class.

Class specific districtwise poverty magnitudes in the rural areas are shown in Tables 13, 14, and 15. The evidence supports the earlier observations that poverty levels are comparatively low in 'employed' non-agricultural class. Rayalaseema provides the most striking examples for class differences in poverty. In general, poverty magnitudes are higher for agricultural labourers both in developed and less developed districts. On the other hand, in rural areas, development appears to have made a dent on the poverty levels among 'cultivators' and 'self-employed' non-agricultural class.

We have given in Table 16 the districts with high poverty levels in various occupational classes by taking the observed rural poverty level (55%) as the cut off point. The table brings out that while the poor of agricultural labour population are spatially spread over the entire Andhra Pradesh the poor among the other classes are concentrated in less developed districts. It appears growth is effective in reducing poverty among 'cultivators' and 'self-employed' non-agricultural class, but it is still necessary to redress poverty among agricultural labourers. We want to emphasize that since agricultural labourers account for nearly half of the poor, growth by itself may not make much dent unless it is substantially higher than the rates presently achieved by the developed districts.

TABLE 13 : Poverty levels in rural Andhra Pradesh in 77-78

Districts	Percentage of persons below poverty line	Percentage of households below poverty line	Estimated number of persons below poverty line (in lakhs)	Estimated number of households below poverty line (in lakhs)
(1)	(2)	(3)	(4)	(5)
Srikakulam	71.93	68.76	17.49	3.51
Visakhapatnam	59.02	53.36	14.07	2.95
East Godavari	50.19	44.56	13.94	2.93
West Godavari	42.09	35.08	9.18	1.85
Krishna	37.11	32.93	7.37	1.59
Guntur	35.99	31.43	8.60	1.79
Prakasam	47.96	44.90	8.59	2.06
Nellore	47.84	39.91	7.33	1.27
Chittoor	52.04	49.36	11.44	2.15
Cuddapah	51.30	43.98	7.70	1.32
Anantapur	69.57	67.64	13.87	2.83
Kurnool	66.04	61.89	11.58	1.94
Mahbubnagar	64.00	60.21	13.22	2.28
Hyderabad	61.93	57.29	7.02	1.51
Medak	71.22	67.54	10.96	2.34
Nizamabad	41.71	41.62	5.37	1.04
Adilabad	74.60	65.80	9.51	1.92
Karimnagar	78.61	76.98	15.52	3.16
Warangal	72.80	69.79	13.32	3.89
Khammam	37.80	36.96	5.22	0.90
Nalgonda	29.93	27.38	5.78	1.03

Note : Poverty line : Rs. 50 per month.

URBAN POVERTY

In urban areas of Andhra Pradesh, 48 lakh persons (11 lakh households) comprising 42 (39) per cent of the population (households) are below the poverty line. Because of the low share of urban areas in total population and also due to lower level of poverty

TABLE 14 : Poverty levels of rural sub population and households in 1977-78

Districts	Cultivators		Agricultural labourers		Self employed non-agricultural population		Employed non-agricultural population	
	Percentage of persons below poverty line	Percentage of households below poverty line	Percentage of persons below poverty line	Percentage of households below poverty line	Percentage of persons below poverty line	Percentage of households below poverty line	Percentage of persons below poverty line	Percentage of households below poverty line
(1)	(2)	(3)	(4)	(5)	(6)	(7)	(8)	(9)
Srikakulam	58.45	55.32	90.63	84.57	65.94	62.92	73.02	60.00
Visakhapatnam	51.04	46.49	73.89	65.73	52.39	46.51	45.00	25.00
East Godavari	25.92	21.15	62.97	54.60	48.81	41.30	21.43	21.43
West Godavari	21.00	18.52	57.97	45.41	38.34	31.11	23.08	16.67
Krishna	23.00	20.69	47.52	40.19	31.60	28.26	30.38	32.00
Guntur	6.44	5.34	55.38	45.25	42.42	36.79	25.40	18.75
Prakasam	29.63	26.17	73.31	68.28	45.51	35.90	28.57	20.00
Nellore	35.29	31.34	61.70	50.00	32.26	22.72	27.54	22.22
Chittoor	34.80	32.65	72.34	65.14	52.72	47.45	27.02	25.00
Cuddapah	48.08	40.78	63.28	53.00	40.72	40.90	30.00	21.05
Anantapur	58.73	56.49	91.64	85.61	71.65	68.29	19.70	25.00
Kurnool	53.29	51.16	85.95	78.98	54.64	49.32	52.94	27.27
Mahbubnagar	57.85	55.10	71.30	66.67	67.32	60.76	41.46	40.00
Hyderabad	47.65	41.77	86.38	80.56	60.84	51.51	34.29	25.30
Medak	62.83	59.65	88.34	80.77	74.[illegible]4	69.49	60.87	52.94
Nizamabad	38.54	38.14	64.12	62.07	22.42	25.00	-	-
Adilabad	69.93	63.64	91.99	83.16	61.11	44.90	37.50	14.29
Karimnagar	68.52	63.83	90.70	87.25	77.28	79.49	75.51	80.00
Warangal	58.93	55.06	95.83	90.43	74.35	69.66	60.87	66.67
Khammam	30.46	27.91	55.85	56.67	28.35	26.87	14.03	14.29
Nalgonda	16.34	15.53	48.90	44.78	29.29	24.04	33.77	23.81

Note : Poverty line : Rs. 50 per month

TABLE 15 : Estimated number of rural persons and households (in lakhs) below poverty line in 77-78

Districts	Cultivators		Agricultural labourers		Self employed non-agricultural population		Employed non-agricultural population	
	Estimated persons below poverty line	Estimated households below poverty line	Estimated persons below poverty line	Estimated households below poverty line	Estimated persons below poverty line	Estimated households below poverty line	Estimated persons below poverty line	Estimated households below poverty line
(1)	(2)	(3)	(4)	(5)	(6)	(7)	(8)	(9)
Srikakulam	6.14	1.08	8.02	1.76	2.84	0.57	0.48	0.09
Visakhapatnam	5.30	1.04	6.02	1.41	2.52	0.48	0.22	0.03
East Godavari	1.60	0.26	9.60	2.18	2.80	0.43	0.13	0.06
West Godavari	1.04	0.19	5.84	1.23	1.85	0.37	0.45	0.06
Krishna	1.08	0.21	4.36	0.97	1.59	0.32	0.30	0.09
Guntur	0.49	0.09	5.54	1.21	2.36	0.46	0.19	0.03
Prakasam	2.87	0.53	5.64	1.35	0.96	0.18	0.16	0.02
Nellore	1.75	0.34	4.82	1.02	0.47	0.08	0.30	0.06
Chittoor	3.37	0.55	6.29	1.32	1.68	0.27	0.12	0.02
Cuddapah	3.41	0.50	3.24	0.63	0.80	0.16	0.25	0.04
Anantapur	6.02	1.05	6.06	1.36	1.65	0.36	0.15	0.06
Kurnool	3.65	0.58	5.76	1.09	1.92	0.27	0.24	0.02
Mahbubnagar	5.06	0.83	4.83	0.96	3.15	0.45	0.20	0.04
Hyderabad	2.45	0.47	3.16	0.82	1.24	0.20	0.17	0.03
Medak	4.76	0.91	3.32	0.84	2.62	0.48	0.32	0.11
Nizamabad	2.57	0.51	2.30	0.50	0.46	0.08	-	-
Adilabad	4.13	0.92	3.74	0.83	1.36	0.18	0.14	0.01
Karimnagar	4.93	0.92	6.11	1.34	3.90	0.89	0.14	0.01
Warangal	5.07	1.03	4.89	1.23	3.13	1.54	0.24	0.09
Khammam	1.57	0.25	2.61	0.52	0.99	0.13	0.07	0.02
Nalgonda	1.30	0.26	2.75	0.58	1.42	0.15	0.29	0.04

Note : Poverty line : Rs. 50 per month

TABLE 16: **Districts with high Poverty levels by Occupational classes in rural areas**

	Districts
Cultivators	SKL, VSP, ATP, MBR, MDK, ADB, KRM, WRG.
Agricultural Labourers	All districts except WG, KSN, NLG.
Self-employed non-agricultural class	SKL, ATP, MBR, HYD, MDK, ADB, KRM, WRG.
Employed non-agricultural class	SKL, MDK, KRM.

TABLE 17 : **Poverty levels in urban Andhra Pradesh in 77-78**

Districts	Percentage of persons below poverty line	Percentage of households below poverty line	Estimated number of persons below poverty line (in thousands)	Estimated number of households below poverty line (in thousands)
(1)	(2)	(3)	(4)	(5)
Srikakulam	43.04	38.07	143.91	26.14
Visakhapatnam	29.39	26.36	250.92	48.19
East Godavari	51.67	48.72	391.50	79.38
West Godavari	51.71	27.97	282.19	36.43
Krishna	25.95	25.80	234.38	48.75
Guntur	43.28	38.57	381.08	74.16
Prakasam	66.93	63.16	206.29	49.79
Nellore	37.05	31.11	136.51	27.83
Chittoor	37.41	30.15	156.08	25.01
Cuddapah	44.74	41.57	147.20	27.68
Anantapur	52.91	49.43	257.45	41.75
Kurnool	53.97	49.34	289.24	51.05
Mahbubnagar	55.72	41.18	133.58	17.92
Hyderabad	28.99	24.44	695.15	122.10
Medak	73.74	66.28	139.13	23.81
Nizamabad	64.97	59.34	188.66	33.71
Adilabad	72.06	64.00	204.78	41.42
Karimnagar	57.14	50.91	188.41	35.49
Warangal	79.15	57.64	280.36	46.61
Khammam	30.21	28.57	79.03	14.37
Nalgonda	28.43	21.74	60.98	9.84

Note Poverty line : Rs. 60 per month.

TABLE 18 : **Poverty levels of urban sub population and households in 77-78**

Districts	Cultivators		Agricultural labourers		Self employed non-agricultural population		Employed non-agricultural population	
	Percentage of persons below poverty line	Percentage of households below poverty line	Percentage of persons below poverty line	Percentage of households below poverty line	Percentage of persons below poverty line	Percentage of households below poverty line	Percentage of persons below poverty line	Percentage of households below poverty line
(1)	(2)	(3)	(4)	(5)	(6)	(7)	(8)	(9)
Srikakulam	51.51	37.50	60.37	61.54	45.65	40.18	30.28	28.57
Visakhapatnam	62.50	54.54	61.53	75.00	34.01	28.69	15.42	13.01
East Godavari		-	100.00	100.00	54.26	49.51	45.22	43.68
West Godavari	20.00	10.00	79.19	64.86	53.72	42.48	34.26	27.45
Krishna	24.44	22.22	81.56	74.29	26.52	25.00	12.48	14.50
Guntur	43.10	44.44	48.05	56.52	54.19	46.12	24.87	22.40
Prakasam	35.71	30.00	93.16	90.63	61.40	55.00	50.00	46.15
Nellore	6.12	8.33	90.62	62.50	36.24	29.82	36.99	32.76
Chittoor	8.88	12.50	90.14	73.68	34.40	27.13	33.49	23.26
Cuddapah	12.19	12.50	47.82	58.33	54.73	48.11	29.84	28.85
Anantapur	85.88	76.92	86.25	84.21	54.35	50.49	25.22	20.51
Kurnool	34.42	40.00	89.61	76.47	62.33	57.75	26.83	22.41
Mahbubnagar	48.88	50.00	88.89	91.67	64.26	56.52	28.68	23.81
Hyderabad	100.00	100.00			33.59	28.23	21.93	18.24
Medak	46.96	50.00	100.00	100.00	86.70	80.43	65.61	48.24
Nizamabad	58.06	54.54	100.00	100.00	79.60	69.05	30.09	23.81
Adilabad	60.00	66.66	77.27	75.00	75.57	66.28	50.00	45.00
Karimnagar	23.80	22.22	100.00	100.00	63.19	53.97	50.31	47.06
Warangal	63.15	62.50	94.59	90.91	82.32	70.79	72.67	69.44
Khammam	46.87	50.00			30.96	29.51	20.73	21.05
Nalgonda	75.00	75.00	68.75	50.00	31.58	18.18	13.49	11.11

Note : Poverty line : Rs. 60 per month.

TABLE 19 : Estimated number of urban persons and households (in thousands) below poverty line in 77-78

Districts	Cultivators		Agricultural labourers		Self employed non-agricultural population		Employed non-agricultural population	
	Estimated persons below poverty line	Estimated households below poverty line	Estimated persons below poverty line	Estimated households below poverty line	Estimated persons below poverty line	Estimated households below poverty line	Estimated persons below poverty line	Estimated households below poverty line
(1)	(2)	(3)	(4)	(5)	(6)	(7)	(8)	(9)
Srikakulam	17.86	2.67	11.20	2.35	88.23	15.94	26.61	5.15
Visakhapatnam	12.03	2.25	23.20	6.06	169.71	30.66	45.92	8.30
East Godavari		-	27.40	5.89	271.73	53.32	95.34	19.18
West Godavari	4.99	0.60	73.49	14.37	157.63	29.75	46.10	8.81
Krishna	5.08	0.97	53.41	10.18	139.71	27.55	36.21	8.80
Guntur	13.28	2.99	39.26	10.08	254.23	47.26	74.32	14.62
Prakasam	12.43	2.67	85.71	21.32	86.97	19.93	19.89	4.69
Nellore	1.99	0.66	19.23	3.22	54.98	10.99	60.31	12.96
Chittoor	1.92	0.54	30.85	5.01	88.18	13.83	35.17	4.86
Cuddapah	1.90	0.39	12.56	3.10	103.44	18.41	29.29	5.73
Anantapur	34.99	5.44	33.09	5.60	161.55	26.05	27.80	3.93
Kurnool	9.60	2.16	31.61	5.20	212.86	38.07	35.21	5.68
Mahbubnagar	11.39	2.12	24.85	4.65	78.22	12.49	19.15	2.89
Hyderabad	2.63	0.54	-		481.63	84.34	210.84	36.53
Medak	12.80	2.60	0.42	0.07	84.43	14.74	42.50	5.96
Nizamabad	42.57	7.82	31.33	6.13	94.64	16.06	20.11	3.11
Adilabad	4.70	1.19	26.64	5.89	155.18	30.99	18.29	3.75
Karimnagar	6.45	1.27	11.60	2.45	117.48	21.21	52.88	10.47
Warangal	13.86	3.15	20.38	4.46	173.28	34.04	72.71	15.86
Khammam	8.98	1.84	-		59.88	10.97	10.16	1.99
Nalgonda	18.93	3.99	11.56	1.77	12.63	1.53	41.27	3.11

Note : Poverty line : Rs. 60 per month.

in urban areas, the share of urban areas in the total poor population is very less; urban poor account for less than one fifth of the total poor. Poverty magnitudes based on Head Count are presented for twenty one districts at the poverty line expenditure of Rs. 60 in Tables 17, 18, and 19. It is revealing to note a lower incidence of poverty in Visakhapatnam, Krishna, Hyderabad and Nalgonda and high incidence in Prakasam, Medak, Nizamabad and Warangal. In general, it appears that urban poverty is more in less developed districts.

Just as in the rural areas, variations in poverty are much more pronounced across occupational groups as compared to inter district variations. It can be observed that the incidence of poverty is 20 per cent for 'employed' class, 43 per cent for self-employed, 40 per cent for cultivators and 79 per cent for agricultural labourers.

It is interesting to observe that poverty levels of agricultural labourers residing in urban areas are higher than their counter parts in rural areas; similarly, in a majority of the districts of Coastal Andhra poverty levels are higher for cultivators in urban areas than their counterparts in rural areas. However, the picture is mixed in other regions.

SIX

CONCLUDING OBSERVATIONS

The evidence provided shows the disparities in levels of living of various occupational classes. 'Employed' non-agricultural class enjoys a higher level of living both in rural as well as urban areas. As expected, agricultural labour class displays lower level of living in almost all the districts.

Our analysis suggests that poverty is concentrated among (1) the agricultural labourers in almost all the districts and (2) cultivators and self-employed in non-agricultural classes in backward districts viz., Srikakulam, Anantapur, Mahbubnagar, Medak, Adilabad, Karimnagar and Warangal.

Inter-district comparisons of the incidence of poverty in rural areas reveal that agricultural development in general reduces poverty among all the classes but the extent of reduction is not uniform across all the classes. It appears that agricultural development does not make much dent on the poverty of agricultural labour class who constitute the hard core of the poor.

There appears to be a systematic relationship between agricultural development and occupational composition of rural households. The size of agricultural labour class increases while that of the cultivator class declines with development. For instance, agricultural labour households account for as high as 60 per cent of the rural households in the agriculturally developed district viz., East Godavari while it accounts for only 29 per cent of the rural households in agriculturally backward district i.e. Medak. On the other hand, cultivator households constitute only 19 per cent in East Godavari while the proportion is as high as 43 per cent in Medak. The same tendency is reflected in the occupational composition of the districts (rural + urban).

The above analysis brings out the dual effects of agricultural development on poverty. On the one hand, it improves the levels of living of cultivators and 'self-employed' non-agricultural class and on the other hand it proliferates the agricultural labourers by diminishing the proportion of cultivators in the agricultural population. The total effect depends on which effect is stronger on balance.

It is possible that developmental effects may not be uniform for all the size class of cultivators. The fractile class data on levels of living given in this volume provides an opportunity for the researchers to enquire into the question of whether development results in stratification or polarization.

REFERENCES

Ahluwalia, M.S. (1978), "Rural Poverty and Agricultural Performance in India", *The Journal of Development studies.* Vol. 14, No. 3

Atkinson, A.B. (1970), "On the Measurement of Inequality", *Journal of Economic Theory,* Vol.2.

Bardhan, P.K. (1974), "On the Incidence of Poverty in Rural India in the Sixties", *Sankhya,* Vol.36, Series c, Pts. 2 & 4.

Dandekar, V.M. and N.Rath (1971), "Poverty in India: Dimensions and Trends", *Economic and political Weekly,* Vol. 6, Nos. 1 & 2.

Fields, Gary S. (1980), *Poverty, Inequality and Development:* Cambridge University Press.

Kakwani, Nanak (1980), "On a Class of Poverty Measures", *Econometrica,* March.

Minhas, B.S. (1970) "Rural Poverty: Land Distribution and Development", *Indian Economic Review,* Vol.5, No.1.

Mitra, G.K. (1984), "A note on suitability of NSS Consumer expenditure Survey data for district level poverty estimates (with special reference to 32nd round, 1977-78)," (Mimoo), Centre for Economic and Social Studies, Hyderabad.

Osmani, S.R. (1980), *Economic Inequality and Group Welfare,* Clarendon Press, Oxford.

Radhakrishna R.,Sastry S.A.R., Sudhakar Reddy S., and Gautam Kumar Mitra (1983), "*Distances in Levels of Living: Temporal and Spatial: A case Study of Andhra Pradesh*", (Monograph), centre for Economic and Social Studies, Hyderabad.

Sen A.K. (1976), "Poverty: An Ordinal Approach to Measurement", *Econometrica.* 44.

Sen A.K. (1976), "Real National Income", *Review of Economic Studies,* 43.

SRIKAKULAM

TABLE 1.1.1: Per capita monthly expenditure, average size of household and Household Operational Land Holding (acres)

Rural Srikakulam — All Classes

Fractile Classes	Monthly per capita average total expenditure (Rs 0.00)	Average size of house-hold	Household operational land holdings (in acres)
0 - 5	21.96	5.40	0.86
5 - 10	25.91	5.60	1.06
0 - 10	23.97	5.50	0.96
10 - 20	28.89	5.41	1.33
20 - 30	32.51	4.96	0.84
30 - 40	35.91	4.69	1.48
40 - 50	39.58	4.41	1.60
50 - 60	43.46	4.88	2.21
60 - 70	47.58	4.55	2.41
70 - 80	53.52	5.08	3.16
80 - 90	60.34	3.98	2.65
90 - 95	73.06	3.60	2.60
95 - 100	103.73	4.52	5.53
90 - 100	90.13	4.06	4.06
All Classes	**44.20**	**4.75**	**2.07**

Table 1.1.2 : Per capita monthly expenditure, average size of household and Household Operational Land Holdings (acres)

Rural Srikakulam — Cultivators

Fractile Classes	Monthly per capita average total expenditure (Rs 0.00)	Average size of house-hold (in acres)	Household operational land holdings
0 - 5	24.92	6.70	3.16
5 - 10	29.08	6.50	3.44
0 - 10	26.97	6.60	3.30
10- 20	33.30	5.53	3.14
20- 30	38.48	4.74	4.52
30- 40	42.64	6.00	5.16
40- 50	46.31	6.00	3.84
50- 60	49.96	5.61	5.45
60- 70	51.07	5.72	5.61
70- 80	58.80	4.95	4.73
80- 90	66.26	3.21	3.58
90- 95	80.20	5.40	5.58
95-100	94.24	5.10	8.01
90-100	87.02	5.25	6.80
All Classes	**49.10**	**5.36**	**4.61**

Table 1.1.3 : Per capita monthly expenditure, average size of household and Household Operational Land Holdings (acres)

Rural Srikakulam — Agricultural Labourers

Fractile Classes	Monthly per capita average total expenditure (Rs 0.00)	Average size of household	Household operational land holdings (in acres)
0 - 5	21.40	5.20	0.86
5 - 10	23.33	5.20	0.28
0 - 10	22.37	5.20	0.57
10- 20	26.25	5.15	0.57
20- 30	29.26	4.60	0.57
30- 40	31.68	4.30	0.16
40- 50	34.21	5.05	0.51
50- 60	36.37	4.25	0.50
60- 70	39.96	4.25	0.37
70- 80	44.54	3.95	0.13
80- 90	50.31	2.25	0.29
90- 95	57.80	4.10	0.12
95-100	70.53	2.80	0.09
90-100	62.97	3.45	0.10
All Classes	**35.93**	**4.25**	**0.38**

Table 1.1.4 : Per capita monthly expenditure, average size of household and Household Operational Land Holdings (acres)

Rural Srikakulam — Others

Fractile Classes	Monthly per capita average total expenditure (Rs 0.00)	Average size of household	Household operational land holdings (in acres)
0 - 5	25.52	6.00	0.80
5 - 10	28.57	6.33	0.67
0 - 10	27.09	6.17	0.73
10- 20	32.08	5.60	0.51
20- 30	36.56	4.00	0.07
30- 40	39.31	4.40	0.33
40- 50	42.39	4.90	0.39
50- 60	46.10	4.44	0.94
60- 70	51.94	4.40	0.20
70- 80	57.44	5.40	1.15
80- 90	63.90	2.80	0.20
90- 95	78.48	3.67	1.67
95-100	130.45	4.33	3.58
90-100	106.63	4.00	2.63
All Classes	**48.66**	**4.63**	**0.75**

Table 1.1.5 : Per capita monthly expenditure, average size of household and Household Operational Land Holdings (acres)

Urban Srikakulam <u>All Classes</u>

Fractile Classes	Monthly per capita average total expenditure (Rs 0.00)	Average size of household	Household operational land holdings (in acres)
0 - 5	30.37	7.00	0.83
5 - 10	36.12	5.60	0.00
0 - 10	32.93	6.30	0.41
10- 20	43.84	5.35	0.71
20- 30	50.42	4.45	0.14
30- 40	56.81	5.58	0.29
40- 50	64.88	5.68	0.18
50- 60	73.00	4.89	0.56
60- 70	81.57	5.15	0.27
70- 80	95.88	3.50	1.04
80- 90	112.79	4.00	0.45
90- 95	143.44	3.80	0.79
95-100	183.84	3.50	0.30
90-100	162.81	3.65	0.54
All Classes	**72.43**	**4.87**	**0.46**

TABLE 1.2.1 : Per capita monthly expenditure (Rs. 0.00) and quantity intake (Kgs) of major food items.

Rural Srikakulam — All Classes

Fractile Classes	Cereals		Pulses		Milk and Milk Proucts	Edible Oil		Meat, Fish and Eggs	Sugar	
	Q	V	Q	V	V	Q	V	V	Q	V
0-5	9.55	13.70	0.12	0.40	0.00	0.10	0.93	0.78	0.12	0.16
5-10	10.67	15.26	0.10	0.36	0.00	0.13	1.13	1.12	0.11	0.17
0-10	10.12	14.50	0.11	0.38	0.00	0.12	1.03	0.96	0.11	0.17
10-20	11.75	17.09	0.16	0.52	0.00	0.14	1.23	1.34	0.10	0.16
20-30	12.11	19.07	0.19	0.65	0.05	0.17	1.50	1.15	0.11	0.19
30-40	12.65	20.34	0.26	0.90	0.57	0.20	1.86	1.63	0.17	0.30
40-50	13.63	21.60	0.30	1.07	0.74	0.21	1.87	1.88	0.21	0.34
50-60	14.03	22.42	0.30	0.99	1.74	0.21	1.95	2.48	0.25	0.50
60-70	14.56	23.62	0.43	1.48	2.52	0.25	2.22	2.31	0.32	0.64
70-80	14.60	24.11	0.53	1.81	3.61	0.29	2.61	3.21	0.43	1.01
80-90	14.17	27.81	0.67	2.36	4.37	0.40	3.58	3.18	0.62	1.30
90-95	15.42	27.34	0.76	2.72	3.95	0.47	4.02	4.49	0.66	1.66
95-100	14.96	25.75	0.73	2.52	7.25	0.42	4.01	5.79	0.77	1.65
90-100	15.17	26.45	0.74	2.61	5.78	0.44	4.02	5.21	0.72	1.66
All Classes	**13.16**	**21.35**	**0.35**	**1.22**	**1.80**	**0.23**	**2.11**	**2.25**	**0.29**	**0.59**

Note : Q = Quantity and V = Value.

Table 1.2.2 : Per capita monthly expenditure (Rs. 0.00) and quantity intake (Kgs) of major food items.

Rural Srikakulam — <u>Cultivators</u>

Fractile Classes	Cereals		Pulses		Milk and Milk Products	Edible Oil		Meat, Fish and Eggs	Sugar	
	Q	V	Q	V	V	Q	V	V	Q	V
0-5	9.86	14.19	0.10	0.37	0.00	0.13	1.11	1.30	0.12	0.15
5-10	11.65	16.44	0.20	0.57	0.00	0.15	1.32	1.46	0.12	0.18
0-10	10.74	15.30	0.15	0.47	0.00	0.14	1.21	1.38	0.12	0.16
10-20	13.04	19.43	0.24	0.73	0.94	0.19	1.77	1.62	0.15	0.24
20-30	13.50	20.75	0.31	1.02	1.29	0.21	1.93	1.97	0.21	0.37
30-40	14.24	21.71	0.36	1.10	2.73	0.22	2.08	2.55	0.26	0.60
40-50	14.96	22.77	0.37	1.17	3.15	0.22	1.94	2.33	0.27	0.64
50-60	15.34	24.38	0.52	1.71	4.28	0.28	2.57	2.57	0.36	0.74
60-70	13.70	22.65	0.69	2.39	5.15	0.38	3.30	3.70	0.60	1.60
70-80	13.60	24.29	0.80	2.85	4.13	0.46	4.07	3.67	0.76	1.54
80-90	15.79	27.29	0.85	2.90	5.08	0.46	4.13	5.02	0.74	1.78
90-95	14.65	24.87	0.89	3.05	3.72	0.44	3.75	4.59	0.74	1.42
95-100	15.46	25.16	0.67	2.36	8.35	0.42	4.34	6.50	0.74	1.65
90-100	15.04	25.01	0.78	2.71	5.97	0.43	4.04	5.52	0.74	1.53
All Classes	**13.84**	**21.95**	**0.48**	**1.61**	**3.12**	**0.29**	**2.60**	**2.91**	**0.40**	**0.86**

Table 1.2.3 : Per capita monthly expenditure (Rs. 0.00) and quantity intake (Kgs) of major food items.

Rural Srikakulam — Agricultural Labourers

Fractile Classes	Cereals		Pulses		Milk and Milk Products	Edible Oil		Meat, Fish and Eggs	Sugar	
	Q	V	Q	V	V	Q	V	V	Q	V
0-5	9.70	13.77	0.14	0.48	0.00	0.11	1.02	0.65	0.17	0.25
5-10	10.62	15.29	0.09	0.30	0.00	0.09	0.83	0.86	0.08	0.10
0-10	10.16	14.53	0.11	0.39	0.00	0.10	0.92	0.76	0.12	0.17
10-20	10.50	14.95	0.12	0.39	0.00	0.12	1.03	0.89	0.13	0.21
20-30	11.97	17.91	0.15	0.53	0.00	0.15	1.33	1.18	0.13	0.21
30-40	12.17	19.35	0.18	0.66	0.00	0.15	1.42	0.90	0.11	0.20
40-50	11.80	19.62	0.24	0.86	0.00	0.19	1.77	1.33	0.14	0.24
50-60	12.64	20.67	0.24	0.85	0.02	0.20	1.82	1.51	0.17	0.29
60-70	13.88	22.83	0.30	1.07	0.53	0.21	2.00	1.70	0.23	0.37
70-80	14.70	25.64	0.35	1.41	0.15	0.24	2.05	2.03	0.28	0.36
80-90	14.01	25.79	0.44	1.67	0.00	0.30	2.63	2.30	0.33	0.46
90-95	14.61	23.75	0.28	1.04	2.01	0.25	2.14	2.89	0.20	0.38
95-100	15.11	25.79	0.14	0.52	0.00	0.18	1.60	2.89	0.21	0.22
90-100	14.81	24.58	0.22	0.83	1.20	0.22	1.92	2.89	0.21	0.31
All Classes	**12.42**	**19.93**	**0.22**	**0.80**	**0.17**	**0.18**	**1.61**	**1.44**	**0.17**	**0.27**

Table 1.2.4 : Per capita monthly expenditure (Rs. 0.00) and quantity intake (Kgs) of major food items.

Rural Srikakulam — Others

Fractile Classes	Cereals		Pulses		Milk and Milk Products	Edible Oil		Meat, Fish and Eggs	Sugar	
	Q	V	Q	V	V	Q	V	V	Q	V
0-5	10.56	13.98	0.11	0.42	0.00	0.16	1.37	1.67	0.05	0.08
5-10	12.89	18.79	0.09	0.35	0.00	0.11	0.95	1.08	0.03	0.04
0-10	11.76	16.45	0.10	0.38	0.00	0.13	1.16	1.36	0.04	0.06
10-20	11.59	17.69	0.15	0.50	0.20	0.14	1.21	1.36	0.12	0.20
20-30	13.39	21.73	0.17	0.56	0.00	0.14	1.28	1.31	0.06	0.10
30-40	14.45	20.59	0.25	0.98	0.68	0.21	1.71	2.00	0.18	0.30
40-50	13.17	20.27	0.11	0.41	1.12	0.17	1.41	2.23	0.12	0.18
50-60	13.29	22.62	0.42	1.48	1.25	0.25	2.22	2.78	0.36	0.61
60-70	14.80	24.37	0.32	1.20	1.78	0.20	1.66	3.28	0.41	0.86
70-80	13.15	23.34	0.56	1.90	4.40	0.29	2.67	2.85	0.44	1.05
80-90	16.39	26.87	0.45	1.61	3.57	0.32	2.99	2.01	0.54	1.13
90-95	14.68	27.59	0.84	3.03	5.32	0.48	4.27	3.52	0.59	1.84
95-100	11.77	22.65	0.69	2.58	9.46	0.46	4.31	5.02	0.83	2.05
90-100	13.10	24.92	0.76	2.79	7.56	0.47	4.29	4.33	0.72	1.95
All Classes	**13.06**	**21.30**	**0.31**	**1.12**	**1.94**	**0.22**	**1.98**	**2.31**	**0.27**	**0.60**

Table 1.2.5 : Per capita monthly expenditure (Rs. 0.00) and quantity intake (Kgs) of major food items.

Urban Srikakulam   <u>All Classes</u>

Fractile Classes	Ccrea,		Pulses		Milk and Milk Products	Edible Oil		Meat, Fish and Eggs.	Sugar	
	Q	V	Q	V	V	Q	V	V	Q	V
0-5	10.37	15.95	0.13	0.47	0.16	0.14	1.26	1.37	0.11	0.15
5-10	11.68	20.22	0.27	0.96	0.18	0.18	1.66	1.68	0.11	0.20
0-10	10.95	17.85	0.19	0.69	0.17	0.16	1.44	1.51	0.11	0.17
10-20	12.19	21.71	0.39	1.28	1.58	0.23	2.26	2.46	0.30	0.75
20-30	13.85	25.83	0.52	1.69	1.30	0.31	2.63	2.58	0.36	0.77
30-40	12.81	24.24	0.55	2.03	2.89	0.33	3.10	3.54	0.52	1.24
40-50	13.55	26.40	0.69	2.51	4.36	0.37	3.25	1.93	0.61	1.40
50-60	14.72	28.06	0.60	2.05	5.71	0.41	3.37	2.35	0.70	1.78
60-70	14.30	27.49	1.61	4.59	7.77	0.45	3.89	3.19	0.83	1.92
70-80	14.54	25.79	0.93	3.14	7.41	0.53	5.26	5.53	0.86	2.07
80-90	15.18	26.81	1.01	3.75	10.63	0.62	5.42	4.69	0.91	2.28
90-95	11.87	23.03	0.99	3.75	7.32	0.56	4.74	4.79	0.91	1.72
95-100	14.13	27.20	1.80	6.46	22.76	1.00	8.45	7.21	1.59	3.63
90-100	12.95	25.03	1.38	5.05	14.72	0.77	6.52	5.95	1.23	2.63
All Classes	**13.36**	**24.62**	**0.75**	**2.53**	**5.08**	**0.39**	**3.49**	**3.15**	**0.60**	**1.40**

VISAKHAPATNAM

Table 2.1.1 : Per capita monthly expenditure, average size of household and Household Operational Land Holdings (acres)

Rural Visakhapatnam — All Classes

Fractile Classes	Monthly per capita average total expenditure (Rs 0.00)	Average size of household	Household operational land holdings (in acres)
0 - 5	25.23	6.04	1.00
5 - 10	30.13	5.00	1.10
0 - 10	27.45	5.52	1.05
10- 20	33.76	4.60	1.18
20- 30	37.81	4.67	1.48
30- 40	41.95	4.70	1.32
40- 50	46.47	4.51	0.99
50- 60	51.12	4.46	1.29
60- 70	56.82	4.22	2.26
70- 80	63.98	3.69	1.98
80- 90	75.37	3.54	2.25
90- 95	91.66	3.26	2.04
95-100	138.34	2.74	2.78
90-100	112.98	3.00	2.42
All Classes	**51.24**	**4.29**	**2.71**

Table 2.1.2 : Per capita monthly expenditure, average size of household and Household Operational Land Holdings (acres)

Rural Visakhapatnam — Cultivators

Fractile Classes	Monthly per capita average total expenditure (Rs 0.00)	Average size of household	Household operational land holdings (in acres)
0 - 5	25.78	6.66	2.22
5 - 10	30.57	6.20	2.58
0 - 10	28.10	6.43	2.40
10- 20	34.82	4.52	2.71
20- 30	39.67	4.95	3.25
30- 40	44.32	4.72	2.77
40- 50	49.45	5.27	2.86
50- 60	55.08	5.05	3.17
60- 70	61.20	4.16	9.84
70- 80	68.93	4.63	4.25
80- 90	78.01	4.00	4.34
90- 95	93.56	2.78	2.73
95-100	118.34	3.11	5.31
90-100	106.65	2.94	4.02
All Classes	**55.27**	**4.66**	**3.95**

Table 2.1.3 : Per capita monthly expenditure, average size of household and Household Operational Land Holdings (acres)

Rural Visakhapatnam <u>Agricultural Labourers</u>

Fractile Classes	Monthly per capita average total expenditure (Rs 0.00)	Average size of house-hold	Household operatio-nal land holdings (in acres)
0 -5p+297X24.53	4.89	0.41	
5 -10	28.94	4.44	0.08
0 -10	26.63	4.66	0.24
10 -20	31.53	4.00	0.13
20- 30	35.52	4.72	0.27
30- 40	39.06	4.66	0.55
40- 50	42.27	4.05	0.49
50- 60	46.44	4.05	0.33
60- 70	50.10	3.44	0.25
70- 80	54.87	3.39	0.18
80- 90	60.61	2.88	0.57
90- 95	72.60	2.66	0.27
95-100	105.39	1.78	0.64
90-100	85.71	2.22	0.45
All Classes	**44.26**	**3.80**	**0.35**

Table 2.1.4 : Per capita monthly expenditure, average size of household and Household Operational Land Holdings (acres)

Rural Visakhapatnam <u>Others</u>

Fractile Classes	Monthly per capita average total expenditure (Rs 0.00)	Average size of house-hold	Household operatio-nal land holdings (in acres)
0 - 5	26.48	7.60	0.12
5 - 10	33.52	5.80	1.00
0 - 10	29.53	6.70	0.16
10- 20	36.15	4.40	0.32
20- 30	41.92	5.30	0.10
30- 40	46.09	4.70	0.03
40- 50	50.78	5.00	0.74
50- 60	56.11	4.78	1.55
60- 70	61.40	3.40	0.00
70- 80	73.25	3.60	0.19
80- 90	87.76	3.80	0.00
90- 95	131.38	3.40	1.40
95-100	189.74	2.60	1.70
90-100	156.67	3.00	1.55
All Classes	**58.29**	**4.45**	**0.45**

Table 2.1.5 : Per capita monthly expenditure, average size of household and Household Operational Land Holdings (acres)

Urban Visakhapatnam <u>All Classes</u>

Fractile Classes	Monthly per capita average total expenditure (Rs 0.00)	Average size of household	Household operational land holdings (in acres)
0- 5	31.57	5.26	2.29
5- 10	42.57	5.00	0.00
0- 10	36.93	5.13	1.17
10- 20	51.12	5.29	0.18
20- 30	58.91	4.95	0.05
30- 40	67.07	5.16	0.03
40- 50	75.60	4.53	0.03
50- 60	83.89	5.31	0.08
60- 70	96.54	4.60	0.09
70- 80	112.97	4.10	0.04
80- 90	138.62	3.60	0.18
90- 95	185.00	4.15	0.29
95- 100	309.59	3.42	1.42
90- 100	241.24	3.79	0.80
All Classes	**90.54**	**4.67**	**0.27**

Table 2.2.1 : Per capita monthly expenditure (Rs. 0.00) and quantity intake (Kgs) of major food items.

Rural Visakhapatnam <u>All Classes</u>

Fractile Classes	Cereals		Pulses		Milk and Milk Products	Edible Oil		Meat, Fish and Eggs	Sugar	
	Q	V	Q	V	V	Q	V	V	Q	V
0-5	9.78	12.75	0.29	0.98	0.52	0.08	0.60	1.21	0.06	0.10
5-10	10.51	14.75	0.31	0.87	0.13	0.19	1.70	2.38	0.06	0.10
0-10	10.11	13.65	0.30	0.93	0.34	0.14	1.10	1.74	0.06	0.10
10-20	10.71	16.91	0.26	0.94	0.55	0.27	2.22	2.11	0.11	0.25
20-30	10.95	17.78	0.42	1.33	0.74	0.30	2.47	2.64	0.12	0.32
30-40	11.96	18.76	0.51	1.54	1.52	0.35	3.09	2.86	0.19	0.49
40-50	12.02	19.16	9.55	1.65	1.64	0.43	3.41	3.15	0.20	0.51
50-60	12.92	20.65	0.62	2.03	2.01	0.44	3.70	3.79	0.23	0.59
60-70	12.73	21.30	0.71	2.25	2.53	0.54	4.77	4.16	0.34	0.91
70-80	12.83	22.63	0.99	3.16	4.23	0.70	5.28	4.47	0.42	1.16
80-90	15.14	25.92	1.11	3.64	6.05	0.71	5.90	5.06	0.49	1.26
90-95	14.74	25.73	1.53	4.59	7.81	0.94	7.52	6.75	0.81	1.98
95-100	16.62	28.30	1.40	4.64	7.84	0.98	7.93	7.87	0.63	1.57
90-100	15.56	26.86	1.47	4.61	7.82	0.96	7.70	7.24	0.73	1.80
All Classes	**12.23**	**19.74**	**0.64**	**2.02**	**2.36**	**0.45**	**3.66**	**3.48**	**0.24**	**0.66**

Table 2.2.2 : Per capita monthly expenditure (Rs. 0.00) and quantity intake (Kgs) of major food items.

Rural Visakhapatnam <u>Cultivators</u>

Fractile Classes	Cereals		Pulses		Milk and Milk Products	Edible Oil		Meat, Fish and Eggs	Sugar	
	Q	V	Q	V	V	Q	V	V	Q	V
0-5	9.91	11.01	0.43	1.30	1.13	0.25	1.78	1.18	0.11	0.18
5-10	11.48	13.97	0.36	1.06	0.45	0.26	2.17	2.18	0.10	0.16
0-10	10.27	12.44	0.40	1.18	0.80	0.25	1.97	1.66	0.10	0.17
10-20	11.26	17.55	0.27	1.07	0.50	0.23	1.98	2.33	0.07	0.20
20-30	12.38	19.01	0.57	1.76	2.34	0.28	3.57	4.58	0.14	0.60
30-40	11.71	17.78	0.54	1.82	2.66	0.37	3.29	3.44	0.20	0.54
40-50	12.94	20.82	0.69	2.31	2.19	0.45	3.56	4.01	0.24	0.63
50-60	12.47	20.59	0.73	2.39	3.84	0.54	4.88	3.94	0.39	1.01
60-70	12.58	21.54	0.79	2.62	2.70	0.54	5.31	4.94	0.42	1.14
70-80	14.68	24.66	0.90	3.16	6.22	0.55	4.90	4.47	0.39	1.30
80-90	15.56	27.69	1.10	3.80	7.73	0.71	6.24	5.22	0.61	1.49
90-95	15.65	29.68	1.59	4.85	8.98	0.92	7.99	7.47	0.65	1.98
95-100	15.72	29.85	1.29	4.39	7.33	0.59	7.46	7.93	0.45	1.80
90-100	15.69	29.77	1.44	4.62	8.14	0.72	7.72	7.70	0.53	1.89
All Classes	**12.70**	**20.36**	**0.69**	**2.30**	**3.35**	**0.44**	**4.05**	**3.95**	**0.28**	**0.81**

Table 2.2.3 : Per capita monthly expenditure (Rs. 0.00) and quantity intake (Kgs) of major food items.

Rural Visakhapatnam — Agricultural Labourers

Fractile Classes	Cereals		Pulses		Milk and Milk Products	Edible Oil		Meat, Fish and Eggs	Sugar	
	Q	V	Q	V	V	Q	V	V	Q	V
0-5	9.17	13.62	0.27	0.71	0.00	0.20	1.72	1.62	0.03	0.10
5-10	9.99	15.34	0.15	0.59	0.00	0.14	1.33	2.52	0.02	0.04
0-10	9.55	14.41	0.21	0.65	0.00	0.17	1.54	2.04	0.03	0.07
10-20	10.69	15.53	0.16	0.62	0.00	0.22	1.48	2.04	0.05	0.11
20-30	10.21	16.36	0.32	1.06	0.52	0.27	2.28	2.56	0.16	0.36
30-40	11.63	18.29	0.62	1.68	0.44	0.35	2.70	2.43	0.12	0.26
40-50	13.45	20.20	0.27	0.95	0.23	0.30	2.70	2.55	0.16	0.32
50-60	11.51	18.45	0.80	2.41	1.57	0.49	2.97	3.03	0.16	0.37
60-70	13.54	21.33	0.40	1.29	1.14	0.37	3.15	3.26	0.19	0.38
70-80	12.48	20.49	0.75	1.97	0.93	0.48	3.94	3.84	0.17	0.52
80-90	14.35	22.99	1.13	3.09	1.76	0.96	5.80	4.63	0.22	0.62
90-95	18.78	25.72	1.64	5.30	2.38	1.00	5.56	5.62	0.30	0.55
95-100	20.86	34.78	2.11	6.56	2.71	0.47	9.88	8.21	0.19	0.98
90-100	19.61	29.34	1.83	5.80	2.51	0.67	7.29	6.66	0.23	0.72
All Classes	**12.14**	**18.90**	**0.56**	**1.68**	**0.77**	**0.39**	**3.03**	**3.03**	**0.14**	**0.34**

Table 2.2.4 : Per capita monthly expenditure (Rs. 0.00) and quantity intake (Kgs) of major food items.

Rural Visakhapatnam <u>Others</u>

Fractilc Classes	Cereals Q	Cereals V	Pulses Q	Pulses V	Milk and Milk Products V	Edible Oil Q	Edible Oil V	Meat, Fish and Eggs V	Sugar Q	Sugar V
0-5	8.76	14.43	0.52	1.35	0.74	0.35	3.04	1.81	0.12	0.31
5-10	9.21	14.95	0.42	1.28	1.05	0.41	3.85	2.50	0.21	0.64
0-10	8.92	14.62	0.48	1.32	0.85	0.37	3.33	2.06	0.15	0.43
10-20	11.45	18.73	0.40	1.33	0.61	0.33	2.95	2.25	0.18	0.48
20-30	11.68	18.83	0.69	1.98	1.79	0.48	4.44	2.15	0.23	0.61
30-40	11.55	18.28	0.32	1.22	2.81	0.37	3.41	2.91	0.33	0.78
40-50	13.56	23.79	0.57	2.10	1.40	0.51	4.62	4.56	0.19	0.68
50-60	11.79	19.93	0.65	2.04	2.80	0.58	5.29	3.36	0.48	1.15
60-70	11.21	21.22	0.92	3.27	4.37	0.53	4.32	4.45	0.55	1.28
70-80	13.79	24.31	0.71	2.19	5.03	0.53	5.89	5.67	0.47	1.25
80-90	11.52	23.27	1.69	4.76	10.38	0.96	7.82	6.44	0.90	2.26
90-95	16.17	24.50	1.69	5.65	10.13	0.92	7.58	5.50	0.75	1.53
95-100	13.14	21.70	1.57	5.32	8.28	1.00	8.85	10.50	0.79	1.89
90-100	14.66	23.10	1.63	5.49	9.21	0.96	8.22	6.00	0.77	1.71
All Classes	**11.73**	**20.13**	**0.72**	**2.69**	**3.27**	**0.52**	**6.65**	**3.67**	**0.37**	**0.96**

Table 2.2.5 : Per capita monthly expenditure (Rs. 0.00) and quantity intake (Kgs) of major food items.

Urban Visakhapatnam

All Classes

Fractile Classes	Cereals		Pulses		Milk and Milk Products	Edible Oil		Meat, Fish and Eggs.	Sugar	
	Q	V	Q	V	V	Q	V	V	Q	V
0-5	10.56	17.86	0.25	0.75	0.13	0.23	2.23	4.05	0.18	0.43
5-10	11.10	20.62	0.37	1.23	1.38	0.32	2.88	3.73	0.24	0.58
0-10	10.84	19.28	0.31	1.00	0.77	0.27	2.56	3.88	0.21	0.51
10-20	11.22	19.81	0.56	2.06	2.62	0.49	3.68	3.31	0.35	0.80
20-30	10.30	19.86	0.66	2.49	4.28	0.49	4.18	4.67	0.45	1.06
30-40	11.39	21.25	0.64	2.42	5.15	0.73	4.34	3.87	0.58	1.46
40-50	12.07	22.84	0.87	3.38	8.40	0.67	5.27	3.82	0.68	1.56
50-60	11.97	22.63	1.04	4.07	8.23	0.75	5.93	5.01	0.90	2.19
60-70	13.00	25.49	1.05	4.09	7.58	0.69	5.96	5.52	0.78	1.76
70-80	12.38	24.27	1.22	4.78	11.75	0.85	7.02	6.74	0.98	2.55
80-90	11.67	22.48	1.25	4.77	11.77	0.76	6.80	6.31	0.89	2.36
90-95	13.13	28.59	1.69	6.36	20.38	0.92	8.68	6.64	1.19	3.02
95-100	11.20	25.14	1.69	6.50	24.51	0.87	7.54	9.47	1.47	3.41
90-100	12.11	26.76	1.69	6.43	22.56	0.90	8.08	8.14	1.34	3.22
All Classes	**11.66**	**22.32**	**0.90**	**3.45**	**7.91**	**0.65**	**5.27**	**5.12**	**0.70**	**1.70**

EAST GODAVARI

Table 3.1.1 : Per capita monthly expenditure, average size of household and Household Operational Land Holdings (acres)

Rural East Godavari <u>All Classes</u>

Fractile Classes	Monthly per capita average total expenditure (Rs 0.00)	Average size of house-hold	Household operatio-nal land holdings (in acres)
0 - 5	28.01	5.75	0.24
5 - 10	32.71	4.93	0.26
0 - 10	30.18	5.34	0.25
10- 20	36.66	4.80	0.21
20- 30	41.13	4.68	0.58
30- 40	45.93	4.25	0.48
40- 50	50.06	3.88	0.44
50- 60	55.41	4.02	0.84
60- 70	60.75	3.86	1.15
70- 80	68.68	3.47	0.79
80- 90	83.05	3.59	2.02
90- 95	113.46	3.25	1.86
95-100	211.41	4.11	6.20
90-100	168.14	3.68	4.03
All Classes	**60.91**	**4.16**	**1.08**

Table 3.1.2 : Per capita monthly expenditure, average size of household and Household Operational Land Holdings (acres)

Rural East Godavari <u>Cultivators</u>

Fractile Classes	Monthly per capita average total expenditure (Rs 0.00)	Average size of house-hold	Household operatio-nal land holdings (in acres)
0 - 5	33.33	6.17	1.61
5 - 10	41.22	5.83	2.70
0 - 10	37.17	6.00	2.15
10- 20	46.90	6.20	2.55
20- 30	53.69	6.10	3.63
30- 40	58.91	5.10	5.97
40- 50	66.93	5.00	3.12
50- 60	74.83	4.80	3.59
60- 70	87.48	4.10	3.61
70- 80	102.35	3.30	4.30
80- 90	138.70	4.60	5.05
90- 95	196.07	3.33	5.67
95-100	352.75	4.67	15.83
90-100	287.47	4.00	10.75
All Classes	**89.74**	**4.92**	**4.55**

Table 3.1.3 : Per capita monthly expenditure, average size of household and Household Operational Land Holdings (acres)

Rural East Godavari — Agricultural Labourers

Fractile Classes	Monthly per capita average total expenditure (Rs 0.00)	Average size of house-hold	Household operatio-nal land holdings (in acres)
0 - 5	26.72	5.82	0.08
5 - 10	30.81	4.94	0.26
0 - 10	28.60	5.38	0.17
10- 20	34.51	5.03	0.21
20- 30	38.02	4.24	0.09
30- 40	41.99	3.85	0.18
40- 50	45.94	3.79	0.08
50- 60	49.98	3.38	0.16
60- 70	55.21	3.33	0.12
70- 80	60.85	3.68	0.07
80- 90	68.24	2.71	0.13
90- 95	80.96	2.82	0.24
95-100	116.78	2.53	1.97
90-100	97.89	2.68	1.11
All Classes	**48.55**	**3.81**	**0.23**

Table 3.1.4 : Per capita monthly expenditure, average size of household and Hous Land Holdings (acres)

Rural East Godavari — Others

Fractile Classes	Monthly per capita average total expenditure (Rs 0.00)	Average size of house-hold	Household operatio-nal land holdings (in acres)
0 - 5	34.39	7.17	0.00
5 - 10	38.28	5.67	0.86
0 - 10	36.11	6.42	0.43
10- 20	40.95	5.33	0.27
20- 30	45.85	4.67	0.63
30- 40	49.13	4.42	0.10
40- 50	54.35	4.58	0.08
50- 60	58.49	3.58	0.50
60- 70	64.25	3.25	0.38
70- 80	71.78	4.50	0.74
80- 90	87.36	3.33	0.42
90- 95	110.19	4.17	1.00
95-100	167.59	5.00	0.83
90-100	141.50	4.58	0.92
All Classes	**62.94**	**4.47**	**0.45**

Table 3.1.5 : Per capita monthly expenditure, average size of household and Household Operational Land Holdings (acres)

Urban East Godavari <u>All Classes</u>

Fractile Classes	Monthly per capita average total expenditure (Rs 0.00)	Average size of household	Household operational land holdings (in acres)
0 - 5	32.69	6.75	0.00
5 - 10	37.97	5.13	0.09
0 - 10	34.97	5.94	0.05
10- 20	43.63	5.48	0.00
20- 30	49.07	4.77	0.08
30- 40	53.74	4.60	0.00
40- 50	57.99	3.77	0.21
50- 60	62.96	5.07	0.27
60- 70	71.57	4.90	0.40
70- 80	85.21	4.16	0.15
80- 90	109.17	3.90	0.58
90- 95	152.45	4.25	0.63
95-100	254.80	3.50	2.50
90-100	198.68	3.88	1.56
All Classes	**72.74**	**4.65**	**0.33**

Table 3.2.1 : Per capita monthly expenditure (Rs. 0.00) and quantity intake (Kgs) of major food items.

Rural East Godavari

All Classes

Fractile Classes	Cereals		Pulses		Milk and Milk Products	Edible Oil		Meat, Fish and Eggs.	Sugar	
	Q	V	Q	V	V	Q	V	V	Q	V
0-5	8.55	15.78	0.15	0.55	0.48	0.21	1.53	1.09	0.10	0.21
5-10	10.04	17.72	0.19	0.71	0.71	0.21	1.76	1.57	0.15	0.29
0-10	9.23	16.67	0.17	0.62	0.59	0.21	1.63	1.31	0.12	0.25
10-20	10.99	19.72	0.23	0.81	0.90	0.21	1.88	1.78	0.17	0.36
20-30	11.73	20.70	0.20	0.71	1.90	0.24	2.05	2.08	0.29	0.58
30-40	13.51	23.02	0.40	0.88	2.16	0.25	2.16	2.35	0.29	0.60
40-50	13.35	23.26	0.31	1.11	2.64	0.33	2.57	2.59	0.34	0.75
50-60	14.30	24.79	0.38	1.30	3.71	0.31	2.82	3.12	0.42	0.87
60-70	14.48	25.21	0.36	1.19	4.02	0.36	3.08	3.22	0.45	0.95
70-80	14.11	24.65	0.36	1.29	6.58	0.36	3.04	3.51	0.51	1.11
80-90	15.54	26.64	0.60	2.20	8.70	0.43	3.56	4.18	0.62	1.45
90-95	16.15	26.74	0.97	3.34	12.48	0.54	4.85	5.37	0.88	2.32
95-100	18.16	33.55	1.73	5.92	13.60	0.73	6.08	7.86	1.20	3.19
90-100	17.27	30.54	1.40	4.78	13.10	0.64	5.54	6.76	1.06	2.81
All Classes	**13.18**	**23.07**	**0.42**	**1.40**	**4.06**	**0.32**	**2.73**	**2.94**	**0.40**	**0.91**

Table 3.2.2 : Per capita monthly expenditure (Rs. 0.00) and quantity intake (Kgs) of major food items.

Rural East Godavari

Cultivators

Fractile Classes	Cereals		Pulses		Milk and Milk Products	Edible Oil		Meat, Fish and Eggs.	Sugar	
	Q	V	Q	V	V	Q	V	V	Q	V
0-5	7.70	16.42	0.22	0.73	2.68	0.17	1.62	2.02	0.24	0.48
5-10	10.71	21.00	0.19	0.71	2.83	0.20	1.92	2.39	0.30	0.56
0-10	9.17	18.65	0.21	0.72	2.75	0.18	1.77	2.20	0.27	0.52
10-20	11.97	20.10	0.24	0.76	4.73	0.28	2.39	2.79	0.36	0.77
20-30	14.18	26.74	0.45	1.65	3.22	0.29	2.70	3.14	0.39	0.90
30-40	14.62	25.86	0.52	1.37	5.30	0.34	3.08	2.86	0.52	1.10
40-50	13.22	23.29	0.31	1.15	6.45	0.34	3.14	4.10	0.52	1.14
50-60	16.12	28.20	0.74	2.54	12.05	0.44	3.79	2.68	0.64	2.50
60-70	14.76	25.46	0.98	3.43	12.32	0.50	3.99	3.39	0.78	1.98
70-80	16.21	28.81	1.35	4.58	17.02	0.59	5.21	5.69	0.93	2.53
80-90	19.15	33.12	0.97	3.43	13.47	0.54	4.50	8.02	0.77	2.04
90-95	25.70	46.72	2.52	8.50	11.80	1.38	9.98	4.52	1.30	2.77
95-100	16.14	31.52	2.96	9.97	18.75	0.68	6.52	10.91	1.87	5.02
90-100	20.12	37.85	2.78	9.36	15.85	0.97	7.97	8.25	1.63	4.08
All Classes	**14.52**	**26.16**	**0.78**	**2.63**	**8.41**	**0.42**	**3.64**	**4.09**	**0.64**	**1.52**

Table 3.2.3 : Per capita monthly expenditure (Rs. 0.00) and quantity intake (Kgs) of major food items.

Rural East Godavari

Agricultural Labourers Classes

Fractile Classes	Cereals		Pulses		Milk and Milk Products	Edible Oil		Meat, Fish and Eggs.	Sugar	
	Q	V	Q	V	V	Q	V	V	Q	V
0-5	8.33	14.83	0.12	0.44	0.41	0.15	1.34	1.06	0.10	0.21
5-10	9.56	17.59	0.16	0.60	0.05	0.29	1.78	1.58	0.12	0.21
0-10	8.90	16.10	0.14	0.51	0.24	0.21	1.54	1.30	0.11	0.21
10-20	10.67	19.14	0.21	0.79	0.78	0.20	1.86	1.48	0.13	0.26
20-30	11.74	20.85	0.21	0.71	0.67	0.20	1.84	1.82	0.15	0.33
30-40	12.87	21.67	0.20	0.67	2.14	0.26	2.21	2.04	0.29	0.58
40-50	13.90	23.60	0.16	0.61	1.32	0.25	2.10	2.60	0.27	0.53
50-60	14.22	25.18	0.23	0.85	0.84	0.33	2.39	2.05	0.27	0.55
60-70	14.64	24.40	0.32	1.13	3.76	0.31	2.79	3.22	0.39	0.76
70-80	15.41	27.33	0.27	0.96	2.98	0.32	2.68	3.05	0.35	0.75
80-90	16.20	27.90	0.31	1.12	3.59	0.35	3.01	3.46	0.43	1.00
90-95	16.02	27.69	0.45	1.92	6.89	0.41	3.43	5.04	0.52	1.09
95-100	18.70	31.67	0.58	1.95	3.77	0.46	3.91	4.83	0.58	1.20
90-100	17.29	29.57	0.51	1.93	5.41	0.43	3.66	4.94	0.55	1.14
All Classes	**13.05**	**22.74**	**0.24**	**0.87**	**1.88**	**0.27**	**2.29**	**2.40**	**0.27**	**0.55**

Table 3.2.4 : Per capita monthly expenditure (Rs. 0.00) and quantity intake (Kgs) of major food items.

Rural East Godavari

Fractile Classes	Cereals		Pulses		Others: Milk and Milk Products	Edible Oil		Meat, Fish and Eggs.	Sugar	
	Q	V	Q	V	V	Q	V	V	Q	V
0-5	10.42	18.74	0.33	1.20	1.37	0.23	2.07	1.08	0.24	0.52
5-10	11.18	18.97	0.15	0.56	2.00	0.18	1.48	1.81	0.28	0.60
0-10	10.75	18.84	0.25	0.91	1.65	0.20	1.81	1.40	0.26	0.55
10-20	11.47	19.58	0.25	0.90	1.12	0.25	2.05	2.19	0.33	0.66
20-30	11.59	20.48	1.06	1.48	3.03	0.25	2.29	2.11	0.38	0.76
30-40	12.21	20.22	0.38	1.41	3.24	0.33	2.75	2.71	0.44	0.90
40-50	12.72	21.89	0.39	1.36	5.01	0.31	2.66	3.16	0.45	1.03
50-60	13.95	24.06	0.47	1.58	3.50	0.39	3.33	2.75	0.49	1.06
60-70	12.77	21.76	0.44	1.58	7.01	0.40	3.46	4.26	0.54	1.16
70-80	11.37	19.32	0.37	1.36	8.05	0.41	3.33	3.17	0.73	1.36
80-90	14.55	24.39	0.44	1.57	6.55	0.43	3.63	6.59	0.64	1.51
90-95	11.68	18.97	0.72	2.43	14.66	0.50	4.64	2.82	0.98	2.99
95-100	13.20	23.87	1.13	4.06	14.30	0.58	5.33	7.31	1.12	3.48
90-100	12.51	21.64	0.95	3.32	14.46	0.55	5.02	5.27	1.05	3.26
All Classes	**12.20**	**20.93**	**0.49**	**1.51**	**5.10**	**0.34**	**2.93**	**3.16**	**0.51**	**1.19**

Table 3.2.5 : Per capita monthly expenditure (Rs. 0.00) and quantity intake (Kgs) of major food items.

Urban East Godavari

All Classes

Fractile Classes	Cereals		Pulses		Milk and Milk Products	Edible Oil		Meat, Fish and Eggs.	Sugar	
	Q	V	Q	V	V	Q	V	V	Q	V
0-5	9.20	15.33	0.22	0.75	1.16	0.20	1.67	1.91	0.30	0.65
5-10	10.37	17.60	0.13	0.46	1.21	0.22	1.78	2.58	0.24	0.54
0-10	9.71	16.31	0.18	0.63	1.18	0.21	1.72	2.20	0.27	0.60
10-20	11.02	19.38	0.23	0.87	1.83	0.27	2.27	2.28	0.34	0.82
20-30	12.24	22.37	0.25	0.91	2.94	0.28	2.36	3.22	0.41	0.85
30-40	11.92	21.64	0.31	1.16	3.19	0.34	2.84	2.48	0.44	0.99
40-50	11.91	22.32	0.39	1.37	3.15	0.34	2.92	2.96	0.41	0.99
50-60	12.01	21.60	0.42	1.50	5.02	0.38	3.18	3.65	0.54	1.28
60-70	12.88	23.49	0.44	1.56	6.80	0.40	3.26	3.59	0.66	1.54
70-80	12.63	23.37	0.61	2.03	8.89	0.51	4.37	3.86	0.70	1.74
80-90	12.00	22.76	0.88	3.09	12.30	0.61	5.07	5.66	1.00	2.46
90-95	13.10	25.58	1.58	5.81	13.57	0.67	6.15	7.06	1.32	3.59
95-100	12.52	23.66	1.73	6.11	21.73	1.12	9.69	7.38	1.38	3.35
90-100	12.83	24.71	1.65	5.94	17.26	0.87	7.75	7.20	1.35	3.48
All Classes	**11.81**	**21.50**	**0.50**	**1.78**	**5.79**	**0.40**	**3.41**	**3.57**	**0.58**	**1.40**

WEST GODAVARI

Table 4.1.1 : Per capita monthly expenditure, average size of household and Household Operational Land Holdings (acres)

Rural West Godavari — All Classes

Fractile Classes	Monthly per capita average total expenditure (Rs 0.00)	Average size of house-hold	Household operatio-nal land holdings (in acres)
0 - 5	30.14	5.95	0.09
5 - 10	35.99	5.71	0.71
0 - 10	33.01	5.83	0.40
10- 20	40.22	5.00	0.90
20- 30	46.41	4.59	0.95
30- 40	49.96	4.36	0.87
40- 50	53.05	4.40	0.99
50- 60	57.91	4.33	1.03
60- 70	64.35	4.10	3.14
70- 80	71.05	3.40	0.93
80- 90	85.59	3.00	1.78
90- 95	91.88	2.85	3.38
95-100	126.04	2.67	5.24
90-100	108.37	2.76	4.31
All Classes	**56.71**	**4.18**	**1.52**

Table 4.1.2 : Per capita monthly expenditure, average size of household and Household Operational Land Holdings (acres)

Rural West Godavari — Cultivators

Fractile Classes	Monthly per capita average total expenditure (Rs 0.00)	Average size of house-hold	Household operatio-nal land holdings (in acres)
0 - 5	37.41	6.00	3.62
5 - 10	41.99	5.00	3.67
0 - 10	39.49	5.50	3.65
10- 20	48.02	5.50	4.37
20- 30	51.56	5.37	3.66
30- 40	56.69	5.50	4.58
40- 50	63.17	5.77	14.33
50- 60	69.77	4.75	3.22
60- 70	74.15	4.88	3.67
70- 80	80.65	4.62	5.61
80- 90	92.33	4.50	7.96
90- 95	113.78	3.50	11.00
95-100	180.60	2.25	17.37
90-100	139.58	2.87	14.19
All Classes	**67.24**	**4.94**	**7.07**

Table 4.1.3 : Per capita monthly expenditure, average size of household and Household Operational Land Holdings (acres)

Rural West Godavari — Agricultural Labourers

Fractile Classes	Monthly per capita average total expenditure (Rs 0.00)	Average size of house-hold	Household operatio-nal land holdings (in acres)
0 - 5	28.62	5.91	0.07
5 - 10	33.88	5.27	0.00
0 - 10	31.10	5.59	0.04
10- 20	38.55	4.82	0.37
20- 30	41.95	4.95	0.38
30- 40	45.84	3.95	0.31
40- 50	50.08	3.81	0.17
50- 60	53.35	4.14	0.73
60- 70	59.02	3.32	0.13
70- 80	64.70	2.68	0.17
80- 90	72.46	2.04	0.11
90- 95	82.48	1.73	0.01
95-100	99.59	1.91	0.30
90-100	91.46	1.82	0.16
All Classes	**49.65**	**3.71**	**0.25**

Table 4.1.4 : Per capita monthly expenditure, average size of household and Household Operational Land Holdings (acres)

Rural West Godavari — Others

Fractile Classes	Monthly per capita average total expenditure (Rs 0.00)	Average size of house-hold	Household operatio-nal land holdings (in acres)
0 - 5	31.17	5.50	0.08
5 - 10	35.59	6.83	0.61
0 - 10	33.62	6.16	0.35
10- 20	42.01	5.25	0.50
20- 30	48.78	5.08	0.41
30- 40	51.71	4.91	0.36
40- 50	55.02	4.91	0.08
50- 60	59.87	4.16	0.00
60- 70	65.25	4.58	0.21
70- 80	71.48	4.00	0.41
80- 90	80.70	3.50	0.75
90- 95	97.48	2.66	0.83
95-100	130.58	2.50	0.00
90-100	113.49	2.58	0.02
All Classes	**57.80**	**4.52**	**0.35**

Table 4.1.5 : Per capita monthly expenditure, average size of household and Household Operational Land Holdings (acres)

Urban West Godavari

All Classes

Fractile Classes	Monthly per capita average total expenditure (Rs 0.00)	Average size of household	Household operational land holdings (in acres)
0 - 5	37.36	6.54	0.00
5 - 10	42.70	6.18	0.05
0 - 10	39.96	6.36	0.02
10- 20	48.00	6.04	0.43
20- 30	52.96	4.52	0.20
30- 40	58.20	4.05	0.60
40- 50	62.05	4.28	0.47
50- 60	68.64	3.80	0.50
60- 70	76.24	3.05	0.95
70- 80	85.62	3.61	0.04
80- 90	100.70	3.19	0.09
90- 95	122.24	3.18	1.82
95-100	208.54	2.55	0.73
90-100	160.58	2.86	0.90
All Classes	**68.80**	**4.19**	**0.42**

Table 4.2.1 : Per capita monthly expenditure (Rs. 0.00) and quantity intake (Kgs) of major food items.

Rural West Godavari

All Classes

Fractile Classes	Cereals		Pulses		Milk and Milk Products	Edible Oil		Meat, Fish and Eggs.	Sugar	
	Q	V	Q	V	V	Q	V	V	Q	V
0-5	9.76	15.86	0.24	1.06	1.40	0.18	1.53	1.84	0.13	0.29
5-10	11.45	18.79	0.27	1.22	1.27	0.20	1.67	2.27	0.14	0.31
0-10	10.59	17.30	0.25	1.14	1.34	0.19	1.60	2.05	0.13	0.30
10-20	12.06	20.22	0.32	1.46	1.95	0.23	1.95	2.81	0.25	0.59
20-30	12.49	21.90	0.39	1.55	2.62	0.27	2.35	2.47	0.24	0.53
30-40	12.42	22.86	0.40	1.74	3.43	0.29	2.43	3.14	0.32	0.71
40-50	13.43	22.85	0.37	1.64	3.69	0.28	2.43	3.53	0.34	0.77
50-60	13.64	23.72	0.52	2.21	4.90	0.33	2.71	3.58	0.42	1.04
60-70	14.77	25.93	0.57	2.40	5.36	0.39	3.27	3.44	0.52	1.25
70-80	15.90	29.15	0.51	2.16	6.27	0.41	3.55	3.97	0.54	1.30
80-90	15.97	29.02	0.58	2.41	7.22	0.42	3.70	4.71	0.56	1.37
90-95	16.60	30.96	0.72	2.91	8.04	0.51	4.35	4.32	0.67	1.76
95-100	16.35	30.20	1.06	4.04	14.48	0.70	6.23	4.67	1.20	3.25
90-100	16.48	30.59	0.88	3.46	11.15	0.60	5.26	4.49	0.93	2.48
All Classes	**13.49**	**23.51**	**0.45**	**1.90**	**4.25**	**0.32**	**2.73**	**3.26**	**0.38**	**0.92**

Table 4.2.2 : Per capita monthly expenditure (Rs. 0.00) and quantity intake (Kgs) of major food items.

Rural West Godavari — Cultivators

Fractile Classes	Cereals		Pulses		Milk and Milk Products	Edible Oil		Meat, Fish and Eggs.	Sugar	
	Q	V	Q	V	V	Q	V	V	Q	V
0-5	11.46	17.78	0.27	1.34	2.81	0.23	1.77	3.17	0.35	0.79
5-10	11.50	19.58	0.38	1.76	3.28	0.32	2.63	2.80	0.40	0.87
0-10	11.48	18.60	0.32	1.53	3.02	0.27	2.16	3.00	0.38	0.82
10-20	12.67	22.16	0.40	1.74	2.98	0.34	2.91	2.32	0.33	0.77
20-30	13.38	21.91	0.34	1.55	5.42	0.34	2.78	3.25	0.35	0.88
30-40	12.97	22.74	0.55	2.37	7.74	0.31	2.82	4.60	0.52	1.21
40-50	13.46	24.97	0.54	2.37	7.06	0.36	2.87	3.66	0.52	1.21
50-60	14.70	26.69	0.49	2.10	8.63	0.43	3.77	3.69	0.64	1.65
60-70	14.68	26.14	0.58	2.32	9.69	0.41	3.57	4.52	0.69	1.58
70-80	15.34	27.62	0.48	2.04	9.93	0.45	3.74	4.44	0.56	1.23
80-90	16.15	30.46	0.60	2.42	10.00	0.56	4.70	3.72	0.94	2.62
90-95	17.36	23.44	0.82	2.82	31.36	0.95	8.80	6.46	1.68	4.62
95-100	16.84	19.61	1.03	4.27	26.25	1.38	13.75	0.00	0.78	3.18
90-100	17.16	21.94	0.90	3.39	29.36	1.22	10.74	3.93	1.15	4.03
All Classes	**13.96**	**24.23**	**0.50**	**2.12**	**8.28**	**0.42**	**3.63**	**3.68**	**0.58**	**1.45**

Table 4.2.3 : Per capita monthly expenditure (Rs. 0.00) and quantity intake (Kgs) of major food items.

Rural West Godavari — Agricultural Labourers

Fractile Classes	Cereals		Pulses		Milk and Milk Products	Edible Oil		Meat, Fish and Eggs.	Sugar	
	Q	V	Q	V	V	Q	V	V	Q	V
0-5	9.93	16.02	0.23	1.03	1.36	0.18	1.55	1.90	0.15	0.34
5-10	11.32	18.84	0.36	1.31	0.89	0.20	1.60	2.36	0.11	0.24
0-10	10.58	19.84	0.29	1.16	1.14	0.15	1.57	2.12	0.13	0.29
10-20	12.18	20.33	0.30	1.35	1.65	0.21	1.76	3.16	0.17	0.39
20-30	12.51	21.52	0.31	1.38	2.09	0.24	1.83	2.75	0.19	0.41
30-40	14.09	24.53	0.36	1.56	2.18	0.24	2.15	3.01	0.21	0.44
40-50	14.18	24.12	0.38	1.71	2.84	0.24	2.04	2.99	0.30	0.71
50-60	14.47	23.84	0.40	1.79	2.37	0.28	2.35	3.40	0.28	0.70
60-70	15.65	27.35	0.37	1.72	2.81	0.31	2.61	3.75	0.35	0.79
70-80	17.40	27.32	0.52	2.23	4.53	0.37	3.09	4.09	0.36	0.76
80-90	19.24	35.03	0.45	2.11	2.74	0.42	3.57	4.53	0.29	0.64
90-95	20.35	37.07	0.44	2.03	2.89	0.38	3.21	5.82	0.29	0.61
95-100	21.53	39.67	0.58	2.35	3.17	0.46	3.87	6.01	0.27	0.55
90-100	20.97	38.43	0.51	2.20	3.03	0.42	3.56	5.92	0.28	0.58
All Classes	**14.15**	**24.48**	**0.37**	**1.61**	**2.32**	**0.26**	**2.24**	**3.27**	**0.24**	**0.53**

Table 4.2.4 : Per capita monthly expenditure (Rs. 0.00) and quantity intake (Kgs) of major food items.

Rural West Godavari

Fractile Classes	Cereals		Pulses		Others: Milk and Milk Products	Edible Oil		Meat, Fish and Eggs.	Sugar	
	Q	V	Q	V	V	Q	V	V	Q	V
0-5	9.39	15.09	0.26	1.04	2.06	0.20	1.34	1.58	0.12	0.26
5-10	10.49	16.37	0.24	1.01	1.15	0.19	1.84	1.20	0.76	1.70
0-10	9.99	15.80	0.25	1.02	1.56	0.19	1.62	1.37	0.47	1.06
10-20	12.34	21.47	0.29	1.28	2.60	0.27	2.22	2.17	0.36	0.91
20-30	12.23	21.32	0.32	1.29	3.82	0.30	3.83	2.84	0.40	0.86
30-40	13.27	23.55	0.43	1.85	4.17	0.33	2.75	3.12	0.37	0.85
40-50	11.88	20.65	0.51	2.15	4.61	0.36	3.05	4.26	0.38	0.97
50-60	13.35	23.01	0.46	1.89	3.64	0.30	2.54	3.75	0.39	1.04
60-70	13.37	24.27	0.66	2.71	6.63	0.48	3.86	2.14	0.76	1.86
70-80	14.23	26.14	0.55	2.21	6.68	0.39	3.30	4.19	0.57	1.36
80-90	14.69	27.99	0.75	2.90	6.93	0.47	4.13	4.33	0.71	1.70
90-95	13.87	24.03	0.78	3.00	9.09	0.58	4.79	4.66	0.97	2.26
95-100	12.99	23.81	0.83	3.30	13.96	0.60	5.33	4.92	1.04	2.85
90-100	13.44	23.92	0.81	3.15	11.52	0.59	5.06	4.79	1.00	2.55
All Classes	**12.67**	**22.30**	**0.47**	**1.92**	**4.70**	**0.35**	**3.07**	**3.11**	**0.51**	**1.23**

Table 4.2.5 : Per capita monthly expenditure (Rs. 0.00) and quantity intake (Kgs) of major food items.

Urban West Godavari — All Classes

Fractile Classes	Cereals		Pulses		Milk and Milk Products	Edible Oil		Meat, Fish and Eggs.	Sugar	
	Q	V	Q	V	V	Q	V	V	Q	V
0-5	10.48	17.71	0.22	1.00	1.69	0.22	1.77	2.39	0.21	0.47
5-10	12.14	20.67	0.32	1.49	1.92	0.25	2.09	2.82	0.20	0.48
0-10	11.28	19.14	0.27	1.24	1.80	0.24	1.93	2.60	0.21	0.47
10-20	11.50	20.24	0.41	1.75	3.35	0.29	2.37	2.70	0.37	0.88
20-30	12.31	22.07	0.40	1.72	3.39	0.29	2.39	3.44	0.37	0.89
30-40	12.59	22.27	0.49	2.08	4.44	0.32	2.63	3.08	0.42	1.04
40-50	13.45	24.04	0.50	2.10	5.32	0.41	3.21	3.66	0.60	1.35
50-60	13.97	24.80	0.52	2.24	5.54	0.39	3.03	4.28	0.46	1.06
60-70	13.22	24.93	0.69	2.80	7.92	0.52	4.32	5.57	0.75	1.81
70-80	13.98	26.43	0.95	3.75	8.07	0.51	4.38	4.10	0.77	1.90
80-90	13.03	24.00	0.94	3.66	11.82	0.52	4.41	5.09	0.92	2.21
90-95	13.01	25.23	0.93	3.49	11.40	0.60	5.53	6.71	0.93	2.13
95-100	14.63	28.25	1.38	5.34	15.89	0.73	6.93	8.03	1.06	2.44
90-100	13.78	26.56	1.12	4.32	15.89	0.73	6.93	8.03	1.06	2.40
All Classes	**12.72**	**22.85**	**0.53**	**2.35**	**5.88**	**0.39**	**3.26**	**3.92**	**0.53**	**1.26**

KRISHNA

Table 5.1.1 : Per capita monthly expenditure, average size of household and Household Operational Land Holdings (acres)

Rural Krishna — All Classes

Fractile Classes	Monthly per capita average total expenditure (Rs 0.00)	Average size of house-hold	Household operational land holdings (in acres)
0 - 5	30.26	5.10	0.53
5 - 10	37.10	4.86	1.21
0 - 10	33.60	4.98	0.87
10- 20	41.37	4.90	0.89
20- 30	47.01	4.46	1.03
30- 40	51.48	4.44	0.55
40- 50	56.32	3.54	1.29
50- 60	61.67	3.56	1.49
60- 70	67.99	3.93	1.42
70- 80	76.66	3.93	2.30
80- 90	91.35	4.90	9.54
90- 95	114.30	3.33	2.91
95-100	206.24	2.52	1.34
90-100	153.93	2.93	2.12
All Classes	**64.88**	**4.16**	**2.18**

Table 5.1.2 : Per capita monthly expenditure, average size of household and Household Operational Land Holdings (acres)

Rural Krishna — Cultivators

Fractile Classes	Monthly per capita average total expenditure (Rs 0.00)	Average size of house-hold	Household operational land holdings (in acres)
0 - 5	33.34	6.60	4.16
5 - 10	40.72	5.60	5.54
0 - 10	36.73	6.10	4.82
10- 20	46.50	4.44	2.89
20- 30	56.34	4.89	5.57
30- 40	61.60	4.25	4.21
40- 50	68.28	3.75	3.75
50- 60	73.77	4.75	6.60
60- 70	81.59	6.00	9.54
70- 80	90.88	5.56	6.49
80- 90	108.63	3.88	5.19
90- 95	134.58	3.20	7.49
95-100	190.74	2.20	1.63
90-100	157.46	2.70	4.56
All Classes	**73.47**	**4.63**	**5.30**

Table 5.1.3 : Per capita monthly expenditure, average size of household and Household Operational Land Holdings (acres)

Rural Krishna — Agricultural Labourers

Fractile Classes	Monthly per capita average total expenditure (Rs 0.00)	Average size of house-hold	Household operatio-nal land holdings (in acres)
0 - 5	29.44	5.00	0.20
5 - 10	35.24	5.09	0.56
0 - 10	32.37	5.05	0.35
10- 20	39.17	5.09	0.61
20- 30	43.53	4.00	0.24
30- 40	47.89	4.20	0.50
40- 50	51.89	4.33	0.48
50- 60	55.78	3.15	0.25
60- 70	60.72	2.85	0.46
70- 80	66.72	3.48	0.42
80- 90	78.13	3.33	0.70
90- 95	95.43	2.00	0.18
95-100	133.06	3.00	0.45
90-100	118.01	2.50	0.33
All Classes	**55.33**	**3.80**	**0.42**

Table 5.1.4 : Per capita monthly expenditure, average size of household and Household Operational Land Holdings (acres)

Rural Krishna — Others

Fractile Classes	Monthly per capita average total expenditure (Rs 0.00)	Average size of house-hold	Household operatio-nal land holdings (in acres)
0 - 5	33.79	4.33	0.52
5 - 10	40.86	5.33	0.00
0 - 10	37.69	4.83	0.24
10- 20	45.58	4.42	0.40
20- 30	49.58	4.83	0.72
30- 40	54.12	4.55	0.36
40- 50	59.72	3.58	0.68
50- 60	65.17	4.09	1.23
60- 70	69.83	4.64	0.23
70- 80	79.77	3.75	0.34
80- 90	91.22	3.83	0.23
90- 95	113.74	2.33	0.00
95-100	267.23	3.50	0.00
90-100	205.84	2.92	0.00
All Classes	**70.73**	**4.14**	**0.46**

Table 5.1.5 : Per capita monthly expenditure, average size of household and Household Operational Land Holdings (acres)

Urban Krishna — All Classes

Fractile Classes	Monthly per capita average total expenditure (Rs 0.00)	Average size of house-hold	Household operatio-nal land holdings (in acres)
0 - 5	35.06	5.10	0.05
5 - 10	44.06	5.95	0.53
0 - 10	39.90	5.52	0.29
10- 20	50.65	4.61	0.01
20- 30	60.39	4.76	0.17
30- 40	69.52	4.95	0.00
40- 50	80.71	4.85	0.27
50- 60	91.80	5.07	0.17
60- 70	104.68	4.49	0.24
70- 80	124.01	4.29	0.17
80- 90	151.36	4.76	1.85
90- 95	197.75	4.65	1.46
95-100	312.17	4.45	0.68
90-100	253.71	4.55	1.07
All Classes	**100.54**	**4.78**	**0.42**

Table 5.2.1 : Per capita monthly expenditure (Rs. 0.00) and quantity intake (Kgs) of major food items.

Rural Krishna

All Classes

Fractile Classes	Cereals		Pulses		Milk and Milk Products	Edible Oil		Meat, Fish and Eggs.	Sugar	
	Q	V	Q	V	V	Q	V	V	Q	V
0-5	11.26	16.48	0.21	0.72	1.28	0.18	1.48	1.74	0.07	0.20
5-10	13.65	20.00	0.15	0.53	1.79	0.22	1.85	1.51	0.16	0.47
0-10	12.43	18.20	0.18	0.63	1.53	0.20	1.66	1.63	0.12	0.33
10.20	14.01	19.59	0.26	0.84	2.15	0.22	2.02	1.91	0.09	0.24
20-30	15.29	23.33	0.43	1.48	2.48	0.34	2.39	2.65	0.17	0.51
30-40	16.50	24.33	0.32	1.22	2.14	0.29	2.72	2.98	0.18	0.40
40-50	17.14	24.00	0.37	1.44	3.77	0.42	4.17	5.12	0.17	0.43
50-60	17.86	24.33	0.32	1.27	4.18	0.34	2.88	4.39	0.27	0.70
60-70	18.65	27.58	0.64	1.99	5.94	0.47	4.15	4.05	0.29	0.80
70-80	17.48	25.32	0.45	1.74	8.05	0.41	3.48	4.89	0.29	0.75
80-90	14.49	20.48	0.54	1.79	10.28	0.43	3.49	4.86	0.34	0.95
90-95	23.36	32.80	0.81	2.48	10.14	0.54	5.83	5.69	0.60	1.68
95-100	21.01	32.99	1.14	4.15	13.62	0.66	5.47	11.77	0.82	2.10
90-100	22.35	32.88	0.95	3.20	11.64	0.59	5.67	8.31	0.70	1.86
All Classes	**16.22**	**23.43**	**0.43**	**1.48**	**4.97**	**0.36**	**3.30**	**3.94**	**0.24**	**0.65**

Table 5.2.2 : Per capita monthly expenditure (Rs. 0.00) and quantity intake (Kgs) of major food items.

Rural Krishna — Cultivators

Fractile Classes	Cereals		Pulses		Milk and Milk Products	Edible Oil		Meat, Fish and Eggs.	Sugar	
	Q	V	Q	V	V	Q	V	V	Q	V
0-5	11.36	18.09	0.19	0.61	1.68	0.17	1.58	1.68	0.20	0.58
5-10	13.75	18.05	0.25	0.88	4.02	0.28	2.27	2.30	0.13	0.30
0-10	12.46	18.07	0.22	0.73	2.75	0.22	1.90	1.97	0.16	0.45
10-20	15.30	22.82	0.56	1.52	3.75	0.32	2.88	1.53	0.20	0.55
20-30	17.26	20.45	0.40	1.52	6.78	0.58	5.01	4.17	0.27	0.75
30-40	17.41	23.50	0.36	1.37	6.62	0.40	3.28	3.47	0.33	0.75
40-50	18.08	24.84	0.39	1.25	3.25	0.33	2.75	2.39	0.24	0.60
50-60	20.75	26.23	0.89	2.67	10.31	0.43	3.60	5.19	0.42	1.29
60-70	17.50	24.25	0.31	1.12	14.11	0.47	3.98	5.76	0.32	0.77
70-80	15.22	19.59	0.75	2.23	20.93	0.41	3.46	3.91	0.50	1.33
80-90	21.35	28.90	0.84	2.65	14.03	0.69	6.25	5.78	0.92	2.39
90-95	24.50	29.90	1.41	3.50	20.72	0.63	4.81	4.31	0.88	2.62
95-100	25.73	35.82	1.80	6.13	12.14	1.07	9.34	6.37	1.95	4.86
90-100	25.00	32.31	1.57	4.57	17.22	0.81	6.66	5.30	1.31	3.54
All Classes	**17.35**	**23.45**	**0.58**	**1.81**	**9.81**	**0.45**	**3.78**	**3.84**	**0.42**	**1.11**

Table 5.2.3 : Per capita monthly expenditure (Rs. 0.00) and quantity intake (Kgs) of major food items.

Rural Krishna — Agricultural Labourers

Fractile Classes	Cereals		Pulses		Milk and Milk Products	Edible Oil		Meat, Fish and Eggs.	Sugar	
	Q	V	Q	V	V	Q	V	V	Q	V
0-5	11.50	16.54	0.18	0.61	1.05	0.18	1.52	1.58	0.07	0.22
5-10	13.10	19.09	0.14	0.66	0.07	0.22	1.71	2.18	0.07	0.16
0-10	12.31	17.83	0.16	0.64	0.87	0.20	1.62	1.88	0.07	0.19
10-20	14.32	20.56	0.14	0.49	1.78	0.20	2.01	1.84	0.07	0.17
20-30	15.17	21.88	0.24	0.78	1.70	0.25	2.19	2.45	0.09	0.36
30-40	16.41	25.74	0.29	1.50	1.51	0.43	2.36	2.98	0.13	0.32
40-50	17.17	24.91	0.27	1.08	1.93	0.30	3.08	4.98	0.21	0.46
50-60	17.70	25.56	0.38	1.43	2.31	0.32	2.73	3.53	0.13	0.30
60-70	19.40	26.64	0.33	1.23	3.11	0.30	2.85	5.57	0.21	0.56
70-80	20.00	30.05	0.55	1.59	4.08	0.39	3.50	6.45	0.17	0.44
80-90	16.12	23.97	0.35	1.42	4.46	0.33	2.79	3.56	0.25	0.66
90-95	26.43	39.36	0.34	1.09	5.75	0.35	6.74	7.67	0.10	0.24
95-100	19.26	29.05	0.73	2.43	6.35	0.38	18.34	14.61	0.27	0.76
90-100	22.13	33.18	0.57	1.89	6.11	0.37	13.70	11.84	0.20	0.55
All Classes	**16.53**	**24.24**	**0.30**	**1.12**	**2.52**	**0.30**	**3.27**	**4.06**	**0.14**	**0.38**

Table 5.2.4 : Per capita monthly expenditure (Rs. 0.00) and quantity intake (Kgs) of major food items.

Rural Krishn

Others

Fractile Classes	Cereals		Pulses		Milk and Milk Products	Edible Oil		Meat, Fish and Eggs.	Sugar	
	Q	V	Q	V	V	Q	V	V	Q	V
0-5	10.35	14.45	0.33	1.01	3.52	0.17	1.44	0.81	0.13	0.42
5-10	14.22	18.84	0.22	1.22	1.45	0.20	1.61	1.18	0.11	0.26
0-10	12.48	16.87	0.27	1.12	2.38	0.18	1.53	1.01	0.13	0.33
10-20	12.21	19.72	0.80	1.66	2.61	0.23	2.11	1.84	0.23	0.74
20-30	15.66	22.32	0.30	1.18	3.19	0.26	2.24	3.52	0.20	0.47
30-40	14.81	22.25	0.36	1.33	2.78	0.33	4.31	7.50	0.13	0.31
40-50	18.08	24.13	0.31	1.32	4.19	0.41	3.34	3.73	0.21	0.48
50-60	16.33	23.75	0.48	1.91	6.72	0.39	3.36	2.78	0.47	1.33
60-70	15.76	25.63	0.63	2.37	0.04	0.61	5.21	1.80	0.25	0.66
70-80	18.88	25.30	0.54	2.16	7.52	0.40	3.51	1.18	0.32	0.87
80-90	18.21	28.00	0.77	2.86	9.31	0.45	3.58	5.17	0.43	1.26
90-95	21.64	35.19	0.66	2.80	6.14	0.50	3.72	6.63	0.36	1.06
95-100	19.93	36.44	0.97	3.97	13.16	0.54	4.03	4.12	0.60	1.66
90-100	20.61	35.94	0.84	3.51	10.35	0.52	3.91	5.12	0.50	1.42
All Classes	**15.94**	**23.82**	**0.52**	**1.87**	**5.21**	**0.37**	**3.23**	**3.55**	**0.27**	**0.75**

Table 5.2.5 : Per capita monthly expenditure (Rs. 0.00) and quantity intake (Kgs) of major food items.

Urban Krishna

All Classes

Fractile Classes	Cereals		Pulses		Milk and Milk Products	Edible Oil		Meat, Fish and Eggs	Sugar	
	Q	V	Q	V	V	Q	V	V	Q	V
0-5	11.00	18.85	0.32	1.28	2.34	0.22	1.85	2.48	0.16	0.35
5-10	11.99	19.36	0.24	2.95	3.14	0.23	2.02	2.04	0.25	0.61
0-10	11.53	19.13	0.27	1.10	2.27	0.23	1.94	2.24	0.21	0.49
10-20	12.51	20.69	0.30	1.27	3.28	0.33	2.34	2.81	0.21	0.47
20-30	13.52	24.19	0.39	1.59	4.38	0.31	2.56	2.78	0.32	0.76
30-40	14.67	26.53	0.51	2.07	5.67	0.35	2.87	3.14	0.35	0.81
40-50	13.05	24.46	0.74	2.66	8.45	0.44	3.74	6.47	0.66	1.56
50-60	14.86	27.91	0.77	3.06	8.73	0.48	4.00	4.13	0.66	1.60
60-70	12.82	24.54	1.06	3.98	13.23	0.54	4.50	4.74	0.82	1.91
70-80	13.90	26.89	1.15	4.31	16.15	0.66	5.50	4.17	1.04	2.69
80-90	14.15	26.07	1.51	5.62	20.02	0.73	5.88	5.44	1.17	2.79
90-95	14.37	28.73	1.87	6.60	27.85	0.93	8.95	2.84	1.41	3.39
95-100	14.30	29.44	2.30	8.39	26.08	1.10	10.16	5.63	1.74	4.76
90-100	14.34	29.08	2.08	7.47	31.88	1.01	9.54	4.21	1.57	4.06
All Classes	**13.52**	**24.86**	**0.86**	**3.24**	**11.13**	**0.50**	**4.21**	**3.99**	**0.68**	**1.67**

GUNTUR

Table 6.1.1 : Per capita monthly expenditure, average size of household and Household Operational Land Holdings (acres)

Rural Guntur — All Classes

Fractile Classes	Monthly per capita average total expenditure (Rs0.00)	Average size of house-hold	Household operational land holdings (in acres)
0 - 5	33.20	5.25	0.32
5 - 10	38.57	4.79	0.62
0 - 10	35.76	5.02	0.45
10- 20	42.52	4.63	0.74
20- 30	47.29	4.64	0.70
30- 40	51.42	4.57	1.33
40- 50	55.59	4.15	1.37
50- 60	60.62	3.98	1.55
60- 70	66.35	4.00	2.48
70- 80	72.74	4.02	3.66
80- 90	82.09	3.56	3.70
90- 95	93.27	3.08	3.02
95-100	112.98	3.04	4.50
90-100	103.06	3.06	3.76
All Classes	**59.30**	**4.16**	**1.95**

Table 6.1.2 : Per capita monthly expenditure, average size of household and Household Operational Land Holdings (acres)

Rural Guntur — Cultivators

Fractile Classes	Monthly per capita average total expenditure (Rs 0.00)	Average size of house-hold	Household operational land holdings (in acres)
0 - 5	45.17	5.71	6.35
5 - 10	50.90	5.00	3.66
0 - 10	47.84	5.36	5.01
10- 20	55.00	5.92	5.65
20- 30	61.12	4.46	4.63
30- 40	65.82	5.38	6.94
40- 50	70.78	4.75	7.17
50- 60	73.53	5.08	5.69
60- 70	78.90	4.77	4.82
70- 80	83.67	4.31	8.34
80- 90	84.23	4.00	6.29
90- 95	103.83	3.86	7.14
95-100	123.76	3.14	5.56
90-100	112.78	3.50	6.35
All Classes	**72.13**	**4.75**	**6.08**

Table 6.1.3 : Per capita monthly expenditure, average size of household and Household Operational Land Holdings (acres)

Rural Guntur Fractile Classes	Agricultural Labourers Monthly per capita average total expenditure (Rs 0.00)	Average size of house-hold	Household operatio-nal land holdings (in acres)
0 - 5	33.35	5.27	0.36
5 - 10	37.15	4.45	0.07
0 - 10	35.09	4.86	0.22
10- 20	40.15	4.32	0.51
20- 30	42.94	5.18	0.45
30- 40	46.58	3.92	0.18
40- 50	50.24	4.09	0.42
50- 60	54.73	3.73	0.27
60- 70	59.03	3.77	0.20
70- 80	65.27	2.86	0.47
80- 90	72.60	2.73	0.62
90- 95	82.80	2.18	0.50
95-100	101.82	1.73	0.53
90-100	91.20	1.95	0.51
All Classes	**51.96**	**3.74**	**0.39**

Table 6.1.4 : Per capita monthly expenditure, average size of household and Household Operational Land Holdings (acres)

Rural Guntur Fractile Classes	Others Monthly per capita average total expenditure (Rs 0.00)	Average size of house-hold	Household operatio-nal land holdings (in acres)
0 - 5	29.95	5.83	0.00
5 - 10	36.73	5.00	0.50
0 - 10	33.08	5.42	0.25
10- 20	41.86	4.54	0.13
20- 30	46.51	5.25	0.75
30- 40	50.04	5.33	0.50
40- 50	52.82	4.00	0.25
50- 60	55.72	3.83	0.58
60- 70	60.78	4.00	0.15
70- 80	66.85	4.33	0.88
80- 90	78.57	3.54	0.67
90- 95	90.88	3.50	0.17
95-100	117.27	2.00	0.50
90-100	100.47	2.75	0.33
All Classes	**55.68**	**4.30**	**0.45**

Table 6.1.5 : Per capita monthly expenditure, average size of household and Household Operational Land Holdings (acres)

Urban Guntur Fractile Classes	All Classes		
	Monthly per capita average total expenditure (Rs 0.00)	Average size of house-hold	Household operational land holdings (in acres)
0 - 5	34.47	5.22	2.09
5 - 10	42.71	5.11	0.05
0 - 10	38.54	5.17	1.03
10- 20	47.30	5.30	0.11
20- 30	53.56	5.06	0.20
30- 40	58.93	4.75	0.81
40- 50	63.74	4.75	0.19
50- 60	68.48	4.11	0.04
60- 70	75.99	4.56	0.91
70- 80	86.92	4.25	2.39
80- 90	101.50	4.32	0.13
90- 95	127.06	4.00	12.12
95-100	183.26	3.11	0.34
90-100	151.65	3.56	6.48
All Classes	**71.57**	**4.58**	**1.24**

Table 6.2.1 : Per capita monthly expenditure (Rs. 0.00) and quantity intake (Kgs) of major food items.

Rural Guntur

All Classes

Fractile Classes	Cereals		Pulses		Milk and Milk Products	Edible Oil		Meat, Fish and Eggs	Sugar	
	Q	V	Q	V	V	Q	V	V	Q	V
0-5	9.64	17.63	0.26	1.45	3.07	0.18	1.45	1.40	0.02	0.05
5-10	12.30	21.04	0.28	1.25	3.06	0.22	1.78	1.80	0.04	0.16
0-10	10.91	19.26	0.27	1.36	3.07	0.20	1.61	1.59	0.03	0.10
10-20	13.20	22.96	0.37	2.03	3.55	0.25	2.10	2.02	0.07	0.18
20-30	13.33	22.83	0.38	1.63	4.91	0.24	2.11	3.21	0.09	0.30
30-40	14.23	25.05	0.38	1.61	6.24	0.26	2.20	2.41	0.11	0.24
40-50	15.13	25.74	0.39	1.64	6.17	0.29	2.54	3.23	0.13	0.33
50-60	15.91	28.30	0.39	1.63	6.66	0.32	2.76	4.23	0.11	0.28
60-70	14.98	27.75	0.48	2.01	8.91	0.35	3.00	2.46	0.20	0.57
70-80	17.15	30.03	0.52	2.22	13.07	0.40	3.71	3.68	0.27	0.70
80-90	17.03	31.89	0.57	2.41	12.39	0.46	3.62	2.91	0.36	1.18
90-95	18.50	36.03	0.62	2.58	14.19	0.45	3.99	3.37	0.36	7.87
95-100	19.36	35.68	0.84	3.48	19.34	0.54	5.73	3.53	0.67	2.23
90-100	18.93	35.85	0.73	3.03	16.75	0.50	4.86	3.45	0.51	5.07
All Classes	**14.80**	**26.37**	**0.43**	**1.91**	**7.82**	**0.32**	**2.73**	**2.86**	**0.17**	**0.75**

Table 6.2.2 : Per capita monthly expenditure (Rs. 0.00) and quantity intake (Kgs) of major food items.

Rural Guntur

Cultivators

Fractile Classes	Cereals		Pulses		Milk and Milk Products	Edible Oil		Meat, Fish and Eggs	Sugar	
	Q	V	Q	V	V	Q	V	V	Q	V
0-5	11.50	18.44	0.34	1.37	9.70	0.25	2.18	2.40	0.22	0.80
5-10	14.43	25.37	0.41	1.70	7.29	0.26	2.24	2.34	0.20	0.39
0-10	12.87	21.68	0.37	1.52	8.57	0.25	2.21	2.37	0.21	0.61
10-20	14.09	23.10	0.41	1.72	10.40	0.29	2.50	2.68	0.17	0.39
20-30	14.66	26.72	0.41	1.74	9.07	0.35	2.95	3.29	0.22	0.54
30-40	14.46	25.38	0.36	1.56	12.79	0.35	2.86	5.77	0.14	0.34
40-50	15.09	26.16	0.57	2.39	13.59	0.39	3.34	6.71	0.38	1.13
50-60	17.29	30.52	0.53	2.28	15.14	0.39	3.17	2.30	0.27	0.72
60-70	17.90	33.13	0.49	2.05	13.74	0.38	3.24	3.34	0.39	1.27
70-80	17.99	33.61	0.56	2.35	15.41	0.50	4.21	3.14	0.41	1.33
80-90	18.63	36.96	0.63	2.60	16.98	0.45	4.02	2.89	0.44	1.38
90-95	18.52	34.15	0.96	3.99	20.33	0.57	4.88	2.28	0.80	2.89
95-100	21.36	39.86	0.80	3.19	16.11	0.55	4.86	4.09	0.64	2.22
90-100	19.80	36.71	0.89	3.63	18.44	0.56	4.87	3.09	0.72	2.59
All Classes	**16.03**	**28.77**	**0.51**	**2.12**	**13.09**	**0.38**	**3.24**	**3.53**	**0.32**	**0.96**

Table 6.2.3 : Per capita monthly expenditure (Rs. 0.00) and quantity intake (Kgs) of major food items.

Rural Guntur

Agricultural Labourers

Fractile Classes	Cereals		Pulses		Milk and Milk Products	Edible Oil		Meat, Fish and Eggs	Sugar	
	Q	V	Q	V	V	Q	V	V	Q	V
0-5	9.66	18.74	0.27	1.08	1.29	0.13	1.28	1.17	0.00	0.00
5-10	10.71	19.78	0.29	2.11	3.88	0.30	2.41	1.85	0.03	0.07
0-10	10.14	19.22	0.28	1.55	2.48	0.21	1.80	1.48	0.01	0.03
10-20	12.63	21.79	0.33	2.41	2.74	0.23	1.94	1.43	0.03	0.10
20-30	13.99	23.70	0.31	1.37	3.69	0.24	2.03	2.01	0.03	0.07
30-40	14.48	25.22	0.38	1.59	2.85	0.21	2.08	2.50	0.07	0.17
40-50	14.14	24.82	0.38	1.70	5.24	0.24	2.01	1.91	0.06	0.17
50-60	17.38	29.11	0.37	1.56	4.10	0.28	2.43	3.64	0.05	0.13
60-70	17.47	29.77	0.36	1.48	6.62	0.30	2.71	3.42	0.04	0.09
70-80	15.40	28.79	0.48	2.03	5.41	0.33	2.82	2.23	0.00	0.32
80-90	19.33	33.82	0.45	1.95	8.43	0.45	4.34	2.77	0.12	0.30
90-95	15.21	30.08	0.51	2.22	8.94	0.38	3.11	2.08	0.21	0.66
95-100	19.47	34.89	0.63	2.73	14.33	0.53	8.61	4.89	0.41	1.29
90-100	17.09	32.21	0.56	2.45	11.32	0.44	5.54	3.33	0.30	0.94
All Classes	**14.73**	**25.90**	**0.37**	**1.75**	**4.72**	**0.28**	**2.51**	**2.36**	**0.06**	**0.18**

Table 6.2.4 : Per capita monthly expenditure (Rs. 0.00) and quantity intake (Kgs) of major food items.

Rural Guntur

Fractile Classes	Cereals		Pulses		Others: Milk and Milk Products	Edible Oil		Meat, Fish and Eggs	Sugar	
	Q	V	Q	V	V	Q	V	V	Q	V
0-5	8.57	14.03	0.23	1.03	2.11	0.14	1.06	2.11	0.03	0.06
5-10	11.67	21.50	0.28	1.30	5.60	0.20	1.17	1.62	0.03	0.08
0-10	10.00	17.48	0.25	1.15	3.72	0.17	1.11	1.88	0.03	0.07
10-20	12.71	22.92	0.46	2.09	2.83	0.24	1.83	2.13	0.08	0.19
20-30	12.70	21.32	0.41	1.72	5.51	0.27	2.31	3.72	0.17	0.63
30-40	13.66	24.47	0.36	1.52	4.00	0.27	2.35	4.03	0.07	0.18
40-50	13.23	25.35	0.42	1.71	5.02	0.28	2.42	2.34	0.17	0.38
50-60	12.39	21.07	0.40	1.70	5.76	0.30	2.48	3.77	0.18	0.49
60-70	14.27	25.80	0.35	1.54	4.79	0.31	2.54	2.31	0.10	0.30
70-80	15.29	29.06	0.59	2.34	7.33	0.39	3.41	2.36	0.38	0.95
80-90	15.76	28.70	0.68	2.96	12.60	0.45	3.71	1.76	0.36	0.94
90-95	17.14	32.14	0.57	2.49	14.57	0.43	3.67	4.76	0.33	0.99
95-100	16.92	32.61	0.85	3.81	11.85	0.50	4.19	3.67	0.37	1.20
90-100	17.06	32.31	0.67	2.97	13.58	0.45	3.86	4.36	0.35	1.07
All Classes	**13.45**	**24.27**	**0.44**	**1.90**	**6.02**	**0.30**	**2.49**	**2.83**	**0.17**	**0.48**

Table 6.2.5 : Per capita monthly expenditure (Rs. 0.00) and quantity intake (Kgs) of major food items.

Urban Guntur

All Classes

Fractile Classes	Cereals		Pulses		Milk and Milk Products	Edible Oil		Meat, Fish and Eggs	Sugar	
	Q	V	Q	V	V	Q	V	V	Q	V
0-5	10.32	18.56	0.23	1.01	2.72	0.16	1.26	1.53	0.02	0.04
5-10	11.79	21.73	0.24	1.10	3.76	0.20	1.60	1.72	0.10	0.23
0-10	11.05	20.13	0.24	1.05	3.24	0.18	1.43	1.62	0.06	0.14
10-20	12.30	23.14	0.41	1.57	3.89	0.24	2.05	1.91	0.15	0.38
20-30	12.48	23.38	0.36	1.47	6.15	0.27	2.32	1.73	0.20	0.46
30-40	12.77	24.79	0.49	2.05	6.31	0.31	2.61	2.14	0.27	0.65
40-50	13.62	26.27	0.48	2.01	8.50	0.32	2.78	2.40	0.29	0.65
50-60	13.42	35.93	0.52	2.19	8.83	0.36	3.02	1.85	0.32	0.72
60-70	14.78	29.69	0.53	2.22	10.87	0.38	3.31	2.75	0.45	1.07
70-80	14.24	28.49	0.69	2.91	14.78	0.46	3.72	1.78	0.52	1.20
80-90	13.99	28.66	0.74	3.03	18.54	0.52	4.38	2.12	0.72	1.71
90-95	14.42	29.27	0.95	3.89	28.43	0.62	5.59	3.54	0.84	2.12
95-100	14.39	30.34	1.08	4.27	31.89	0.81	7.10	2.37	1.34	3.50
90-100	14.41	29.74	1.01	4.06	29.95	0.70	6.25	3.03	1.06	2.72
All Classes	**13.22**	**25.76**	**0.53**	**2.17**	**10.35**	**0.36**	**3.06**	**2.11**	**0.38**	**0.90**

PRAKASAM

Table 7.1.1 : Per capita monthly expenditure, average size of household and Household Operational Land Holdings (acres)

Rural Prakasam Fractile Classes	All Classes		
	Monthly per capita average total expenditure (Rs 0.00)	Average size of household	Household operational land holdings (in acres)
0 - 5	26.08	4.29	1.54
5 - 10	32.54	4.88	0.53
0 - 10	29.52	4.59	1.03
10- 20	37.32	4.66	0.96
20- 30	42.01	4.62	1.00
30- 40	46.29	4.97	5.18
40- 50	50.18	4.37	3.94
50- 60	53.94	4.32	4.20
60- 70	58.09	3.65	2.22
70- 80	63.46	3.97	4.73
80- 90	70.42	4.23	5.87
90- 95	78.13	3.94	3.97
95-100	98.06	3.12	3.71
90-100	86.94	3.53	3.84
All Classes	**52.54**	**4.29**	**3.30**

Table 7.1.2 : Per capita monthly expenditure, average size of household and Household Operational Land Holdings (acres)

Rural Prakasam Fractile Classes	Cultivators		
	Monthly per capita average total expenditure (Rs 0.00)	Average size of household	Household operational land holdings (in acres)
0 - 5	39.61	5.00	4.25
5 - 10	44.22	5.63	7.46
0 - 10	42.05	5.31	5.86
10- 20	46.72	6.07	8.50
20- 30	49.80	4.80	5.97
30- 40	52.13	5.57	7.46
40- 50	55.14	5.07	7.07
50- 60	60.21	4.50	6.75
60- 70	63.85	4.50	6.93
70- 80	69.52	4.80	10.49
80- 90	75.62	3.53	4.67
90- 95	83.66	4.50	5.94
95-100	104.66	2.88	4.44
90-100	91.84	3.69	5.19
All Classes	**58.87**	**4.78**	**6.87**

Table 7.1.3 : Per capita monthly expenditure, average size of household and Household Operational Land Holdings (acres)

Rural Prakasam Fractile Classes	Agricultural Labourers: Monthly per capita average total expenditure (Rs 0.00)	Average size of household	Household operational land holdings (in acres)
0 - 5	24.62	4.13	3.26
5 - 10	28.99	4.23	0.00
0 - 10	26.84	4.19	1.63
10- 20	32.78	4.86	0.64
20- 30	35.92	4.79	0.29
30- 40	38.25	4.21	0.43
40- 50	41.01	4.40	0.57
50- 60	44.17	3.71	0.14
60- 70	49.26	2.86	0.07
70- 80	53.19	3.43	0.25
80- 90	58.33	2.86	0.50
90- 95	65.72	3.00	0.28
95-100	74.57	3.88	0.94
90-100	70.71	3.44	0.61
All Classes	**43.49**	**3.88**	**0.53**

Table 7.1.4 : Per capita monthly expenditure, average size of household and Household Operational Land Holdings (acres)

Rural Prakasam Fractile Classes	Others: Monthly per capita average total expenditure (Rs 0.00)	Average size of household	Household operational land holdings (in acres)
0 - 5	25.83	5.00	0.02
5 - 10	35.93	6.33	0.67
0 - 10	31.48	5.67	0.34
10- 20	42.97	5.80	0.00
20- 30	46.86	4.00	0.00
30- 40	53.79	3.75	0.13
40- 50	57.33	3.50	0.00
50- 60	59.17	3.00	1.00
60- 70	62.45	3.50	1.00
70- 80	66.02	3.40	2.40
80- 90	71.13	3.80	1.20
90- 95	76.58	4.33	1.00
95-100	111.85	2.67	0.00
90-100	90.02	3.50	0.50
All Classes	**55.50**	**4.04**	**0.66**

Table 7.1.5 : Per capita monthly expenditure, average size of household and Household Operational Land Holdings (acres)

Urban Prakasam Fractile Classes	All Classes		
	Monthly per capita average total expenditure (Rs 0.00)	Average size of household	Household operational land holdings (in acres)
0 - 5	33.78	4.80	0.00
5 - 10	40.77	4.00	0.40
0 - 10	36.96	4.40	0.20
10- 20	43.27	4.60	0.30
20- 30	47.17	5.00	0.28
30- 40	50.33	3.67	0.17
40- 50	53.82	3.60	1.20
50- 60	56.97	4.22	1.34
60- 70	60.33	3.33	0.56
70- 80	68.09	4.00	1.11
80- 90	75.61	3.60	2.67
90- 95	91.78	2.60	1.80
95-100	114.45	2.80	0.00
90-100	103.53	2.70	0.90
All Classes	**57.36**	**3.91**	**0.88**

Table 7.2.1 : Per capita monthly expenditure (Rs. 0.00) and quantity intake (Kgs) of major food items.

Rural Prakasam — All Classes

Fractile Classes	Cereals		Pulses		Milk and Milk Products	Edible Oil		Meat, Fish and Eggs	Sugar	
	Q	V	Q	V	V	Q	V	V	Q	V
0-5	10.81	15.66	0.15	0.62	0.88	0.15	1.31	0.46	0.05	0.12
5-10	12.41	19.44	0.19	0.79	1.19	0.19	1.59	1.09	0.08	0.21
0-10	11.66	17.67	0.17	0.71	1.05	0.17	1.46	0.81	0.07	0.17
10-20	14.04	22.58	0.26	1.66	2.05	0.21	1.70	1.67	0.15	0.35
20-30	12.70	23.11	0.25	1.00	2.45	0.21	1.76	1.64	0.18	0.45
30-40	13.38	24.17	0.34	1.42	4.71	0.25	2.15	1.28	0.24	0.65
40-50	12.99	24.33	0.39	1.43	4.83	0.29	2.42	1.76	0.27	0.69
50-60	15.10	28.48	0.37	1.54	4.39	0.28	2.30	1.76	0.21	0.50
60-70	14.58	26.51	0.45	1.80	6.33	0.31	2.75	2.13	0.36	0.92
70-80	15.56	31.39	0.54	2.12	6.42	0.35	3.08	2.60	0.30	0.71
80-90	16.05	31.79	0.59	2.41	8.31	0.40	3.46	2.41	0.40	1.10
90-95	15.90	30.60	0.51	2.07	7.13	0.42	3.71	2.62	0.41	1.02
95-100	19.00	33.64	0.82	3.24	11.42	0.58	4.90	4.91	0.61	1.41
90-100	17.31	31.95	0.64	2.59	9.09	0.49	4.24	3.45	0.50	1.20
All Classes	**14.22**	**25.90**	**0.39**	**3.57**	**4.77**	**0.29**	**2.46**	**1.90**	**0.26**	**0.65**

Table 7.2.2 : Per capita monthly expenditure (Rs. 0.00) and quantity intake (Kgs) of major food items.

Rural Prakasam

Cultivators

Fractile Classes	Cereals		Pulses		Milk and Milk Products	Edible Oil		Meat, Fish and Eggs	Sugar	
	Q	V	Q	V	V	Q	V	V	Q	V
0-5	13.54	23.14	0.36	1.36	4.64	0.27	2.46	0.42	0.27	0.75
5-10	13.11	23.13	0.36	1.50	5.71	0.21	1.79	1.27	0.25	0.59
0-10	13.31	23.14	0.36	1.43	5.21	0.24	2.11	0.87	0.25	0.67
10-20	13.02	23.75	0.38	1.57	5.34	0.26	2.25	1.21	0.29	0.79
20-30	13.26	22.43	0.43	1.70	5.71	0.34	2.94	1.90	0.35	0.92
30-40	13.05	28.41	0.40	1.44	4.49	0.25	2.11	1.37	0.20	0.49
40-50	14.06	27.68	0.44	1.79	7.79	0.32	2.70	1.53	0.39	0.91
50-60	15.08	31.22	0.52	2.07	6.89	0.33	2.74	1.41	0.29	0.74
60-70	15.48	31.86	0.56	2.13	7.37	0.37	3.34	1.90	0.30	0.72
70-80	15.83	32.74	0.57	2.33	7.76	0.37	3.28	1.77	0.38	0.90
80-90	16.32	32.38	0.56	2.28	8.31	0.49	4.14	3.08	0.52	1.30
90-95	16.53	32.60	0.58	2.34	9.51	0.46	4.09	2.76	0.46	1.08
95-100	20.83	36.65	1.08	4.10	12.76	0.72	5.90	4.10	0.67	1.54
90-100	18.20	34.18	0.77	3.03	10.78	0.56	4.80	3.29	0.54	1.26
All Classes	**14.55**	**28.27**	**0.48**	**1.92**	**6.71**	**0.34**	**2.93**	**1.74**	**0.34**	**0.85**

Table 7.2.3 : Per capita monthly expenditure (Rs. 0.00) and quantity intake (Kgs) of major food items.

Rural Prakasam — Agricultural Labourers

Fractile Classes	Cereals Q	Cereals V	Pulses Q	Pulses V	Milk and Milk Products V	Edible Oil Q	Edible Oil V	Meat, Fish and Eggs V	Sugar Q	Sugar V
0-5	11.33	15.85	0.16	0.62	0.52	0.14	1.13	0.30	0.06	0.15
5-10	11.62	18.03	0.15	0.64	1.00	0.16	1.40	0.47	0.01	0.02
0-10	11.48	16.96	0.15	0.65	0.76	0.15	1.27	0.39	0.03	0.09
10-20	12.21	19.48	0.18	0.77	1.28	0.19	1.59	1.33	0.10	0.25
20-30	14.25	22.81	0.22	0.91	0.93	0.18	1.55	1.64	0.08	0.20
30-40	14.36	22.69	0.23	0.99	1.48	0.21	1.47	1.75	0.14	0.35
40-50	13.56	24.18	0.23	1.02	2.55	0.20	1.63	1.50	0.17	0.40
50-60	13.18	23.22	0.25	1.04	2.62	0.19	1.60	2.27	0.11	0.27
60-70	15.00	24.70	0.27	1.09	3.54	0.21	1.77	1.85	0.14	0.30
70-80	16.44	28.06	0.31	1.28	2.05	0.26	1.96	2.19	0.13	0.32
80-90	17.25	27.81	0.40	1.66	5.09	0.26	2.21	2.96	0.32	0.88
90-95	16.67	25.98	0.54	2.33	5.08	0.32	2.70	4.79	0.35	0.77
95-100	15.35	24.27	0.58	2.38	8.16	0.36	2.99	3.52	0.60	1.47
90-100	15.93	25.02	0.56	2.36	6.82	0.34	2.86	4.08	0.49	1.17
All Classes	**14.12**	**23.05**	**0.27**	**1.14**	**2.51**	**0.22**	**1.75**	**1.90**	**0.16**	**0.40**

Table 7.2.4 : Per capita monthly expenditure (Rs. 0.00) and quantity intake (Kgs) of major food items.

Rural Prakasam

Fractile Classes	Cereals		Pulses		Others: Milk and Milk Products	Edible Oil		Meat, Fish and Eggs	Sugar	
	Q	V	Q	V	V	Q	V	V	Q	V
0-5	9.33	13.37	0.12	0.50	1.20	0.17	1.40	0.67	0.10	0.18
5-10	11.32	16.42	0.34	1.36	1.97	0.29	2.57	2.11	0.11	0.25
0-10	10.44	15.07	0.24	0.98	1.63	0.24	2.05	1.47	0.10	0.22
10-20	12.24	24.88	0.21	0.89	0.93	0.22	1.96	2.12	0.21	0.51
20-30	11.75	23.80	0.29	1.18	2.88	0.27	2.40	0.90	0.27	0.65
30-40	11.33	23.57	0.43	1.62	4.07	0.33	3.23	2.60	0.33	0.73
40-50	12.86	23.89	0.46	1.79	4.36	0.32	3.10	3.07	0.36	0.96
50-60	14.00	24.05	0.43	1.67	2.97	0.28	2.67	2.64	0.20	0.43
60-70	14.29	29.50	0.50	1.85	6.32	0.36	3.54	2.50	0.29	0.61
70-80	14.41	32.85	0.49	2.02	5.47	0.41	3.41	3.24	0.47	1.13
80-90	16.32	30.97	0.50	1.98	10.12	0.36	3.17	2.72	0.47	1.09
90-95	16.54	35.96	0.69	2.72	8.19	0.42	4.08	1.08	0.31	0.80
95-100	19.75	31.81	0.65	2.62	6.56	0.44	3.94	9.76	0.38	0.77
90-100	17.76	34.38	0.67	2.68	7.57	0.43	4.03	4.39	0.33	0.79
All Classes	**13.30**	**25.46**	**0.40**	**1.57**	**4.24**	**0.31**	**2.81**	**2.45**	**0.28**	**0.66**

Table 7.2.5 : Per capita monthly expenditure (Rs. 0.00) and quantity intake (Kgs) of major food items.

Urban Prakasam — All Classes

Fractile Classes	Cereals		Pulses		Milk and Milk Products	Edible Oil		Meat, Fish and Eggs	Sugar	
	Q	V	Q	V	V	Q	V	V	Q	V
0-5	9.79	18.00	0.13	0.52	0.92	0.15	1.24	1.83	0.02	0.05
5-10	11.50	23.00	0.22	0.93	1.57	0.20	1.67	1.65	0.05	0.13
0-10	10.57	20.27	0.17	0.70	1.22	0.17	1.44	1.75	0.03	0.09
10-20	12.43	24.38	0.27	1.07	2.75	0.20	1.63	1.75	0.14	0.33
20-30	12.56	23.66	0.24	1.01	4.73	0.22	1.80	1.90	0.13	0.30
30-40	13.94	28.27	0.35	1.38	3.09	0.21	1.70	2.47	0.11	0.26
40-50	14.44	29.62	0.36	1.48	3.79	0.26	2.56	2.53	0.18	0.43
50-60	13.82	27.63	0.38	1.47	4.50	0.34	2.70	3.39	0.27	0.62
60-70	15.50	30.32	0.37	1.54	4.83	0.31	2.42	3.43	0.23	0.54
70-80	14.22	27.83	0.62	2.40	6.54	0.39	3.15	3.69	0.33	0.73
80-90	16.25	36.24	0.63	2.50	6.78	0.44	3.65	3.23	0.49	0.86
90-95	15.23	31.69	0.40	1.63	8.62	0.33	2.79	3.46	0.38	0.89
95-100	17.43	31.99	0.73	2.99	10.18	0.64	5.19	6.27	0.64	1.50
90-100	16.37	31.84	0.57	2.33	9.43	0.49	4.04	4.92	0.52	1.21
All Classes	**13.78**	**27.50**	**0.38**	**1.53**	**4.53**	**0.29**	**2.37**	**2.78**	**0.23**	**0.50**

NELLORE

Table 8.1.1 : Per capita monthly expenditure, average size of household and Household Operational Land Holdings (acres)

Rural Nellore Fractile Classes	All Classes: Monthly per capita average total expenditure (Rs 0.00)	Average size of house-hold	Household operational land holdings (in acres)
0 - 5	34.81	4.50	3.54
5 - 10	37.87	5.25	0.83
0 - 10	36.46	4.88	2.19
10- 20	40.78	5.26	0.40
20- 30	45.21	4.78	0.43
30- 40	48.95	4.70	1.36
40- 50	51.63	4.25	1.25
50- 60	56.48	4.83	1.76
60- 70	59.87	3.61	1.86
70- 80	64.10	3.13	0.85
80- 90	74.04	2.35	0.70
90- 95	87.07	3.33	2.50
95-100	104.34	2.75	3.42
90-100	94.88	3.04	2.96
All Classes	**54.16**	**4.08**	**1.38**

Table 8.1.2 : Per capita monthly expenditure, average size of household and Household Operational Land Holdings (acres)

Rural Nellore Fractile Classes	Cultivators: Monthly per capita average total expenditure (Rs 0.00)	Average size of house-hold	Household operational land holdings (in acres)
0 - 5	37.58	5.25	2.38
5 - 10	42.37	3.75	1.55
0 - 10	39.58	4.50	1.96
10- 20	48.16	5.83	2.61
20- 30	49.57	5.50	2.79
30- 40	51.44	4.86	3.79
40- 50	55.38	5.17	4.75
50- 60	58.78	6.14	5.37
60- 70	62.34	3.86	3.21
70- 80	70.87	3.17	2.83
80- 90	84.66	3.50	4.67
90- 95	98.18	4.25	6.63
95-100	113.38	2.50	5.50
90-100	103.81	3.38	6.06
All Classes	**59.97**	**4.57**	**3.83**

Table 8.1.3 : Per capita monthly expenditure, average size of household and Household Operational Land Holdings (acres)

Rural Nellore Fractile Classes	Agricultural Labourers: Monthly per capita average total expenditure (Rs 0.00)	Average size of house-hold	Household operational land holdings (in acres)
0 - 5	34.95	4.29	0.06
5 - 10	37.91	5.14	0.54
0 - 10	36.24	4.71	0.30
10- 20	39.78	6.08	0.20
20- 30	42.45	4.58	0.21
30- 40	45.99	4.58	0.15
40- 50	48.53	3.67	0.07
50- 60	51.13	4.00	0.07
60- 70	57.01	4.00	0.17
70- 80	61.66	2.50	0.09
80- 90	68.32	1.92	0.10
90- 95	79.48	2.43	0.00
95-100	92.97	2.29	0.00
90-100	86.02	2.36	0.00
All Classes	**49.94**	**3.83**	**0.14**

Table 8.1.4 : Per capita monthly expenditure, average size of household and Household Operational Land Holdings (acres)

Rural Nellore Fractile Classes	Others: Monthly per capita average total expenditure (Rs 0.00)	Average size of house-hold	Household operational land holdings (in acres)
0 - 5	30.73	3.50	0.00
5 - 10	37.56	5.50	1.00
0 - 10	34.90	4.50	0.50
10- 20	43.26	6.75	0.00
20- 30	50.74	4.00	0.38
30- 40	53.80	4.75	0.07
40- 50	57.12	4.00	0.70
50- 60	60.18	3.25	0.32
60- 70	62.12	3.75	0.15
70- 80	63.14	4.25	0.10
80- 90	71.54	3.00	0.00
90- 95	89.06	2.50	0.00
95-100	99.58	2.00	0.00
90-100	93.74	2.25	0.00
All Classes	**55.76**	**4.05**	**0.22**

Table 8.1.5 : Per capita monthly expenditure, average size of household and Household Operational Land Holdings (acres)

Urban Nellore Fractile Classes	All Classes Monthly per capita average total expenditure (Rs 0.00)	Average size of household	Household operational land holdings (in acres)
0 - 5	43.20	5.57	0.00
5 - 10	46.56	5.86	0.00
0 - 10	44.92	5.71	0.00
10- 20	50.58	4.93	0.00
20- 30	56.26	4.08	0.19
30- 40	61.60	3.62	0.38
40- 50	68.99	4.29	1.86
50- 60	73.51	3.62	0.00
60- 70	80.85	3.92	2.27
70- 80	95.59	3.23	4.65
80- 90	122.94	3.86	1.57
90- 95	144.70	4.43	1.57
95-100	172.93	3.14	0.00
90-100	156.42	3.79	0.79
All Classes	**78.46**	**4.12**	**1.16**

Table 8.2.1 : Per capita monthly expenditure (Rs. 0.00) and quantity intake (Kgs) of major food items.

Rural Nellore

All Classes

Fractile Classes	Cereals		Pulses		Milk and Milk Products	Edible Oil		Meat, Fish and Eggs	Sugar	
	Q	V	Q	V	V	Q	V	V	Q	V
0-5	10.48	19.22	0.30	1.27	0.99	0.20	1.74	1.71	0.11	0.27
5-10	11.32	21.19	0.27	1.15	0.57	0.28	1.48	1.79	0.09	0.23
0-10	10.93	20.28	0.28	1.21	0.76	0.24	1.60	1.76	0.10	0.25
10-20	11.46	21.83	0.31	1.30	0.87	0.17	1.60	1.90	0.10	0.24
20-30	13.43	26.15	0.35	1.45	0.64	0.18	1.70	1.76	0.06	0.15
30-40	11.60	22.61	0.40	1.59	3.12	0.23	1.97	3.13	0.20	0.48
40-50	12.67	25.41	0.31	1.29	1.66	0.34	2.19	2.24	0.19	0.46
50-60	12.59	25.06	0.36	1.46	3.18	0.24	2.19	3.03	0.23	0.55
60-70	12.82	24.79	0.44	1.75	4.86	0.28	2.36	3.31	0.28	0.67
70-80	15.72	29.95	0.42	1.73	2.40	0.26	2.42	3.84	0.20	0.51
80-90	15.96	31.80	0.61	2.39	3.76	0.33	3.01	3.60	0.16	0.36
90-95	14.44	30.33	0.54	2.06	3.79	0.41	3.39	3.94	0.50	1.17
95-100	14.67	30.64	0.65	2.68	6.45	0.48	3.88	4.85	0.70	1.65
90-100	14.54	30.47	0.59	2.34	4.99	0.44	3.61	4.35	0.59	1.39
All Classes	**12.83**	**25.09**	**0.38**	**1.57**	**2.38**	**0.26**	**2.15**	**2.73**	**0.20**	**0.47**

Table 8.2.2 : Per capita monthly expenditure (Rs. 0.00) and quantity intake (Kgs) of major food items.

Rural Nellore

<u>Cultivators</u>

Fractile Classes	Cereals		Pulses		Milk and Milk Products	Edible Oil		Meat, Fish and Eggs	Sugar	
	Q	V	Q	V	V	Q	V	V	Q	V
0-5	9.71	19.12	0.33	1.28	0.76	0.19	1.48	2.62	0.19	0.44
5-10	10.00	19.33	0.37	1.35	2.53	0.27	3.13	2.33	0.20	0.47
0-10	9.83	19.21	0.35	1.31	1.50	0.22	1.75	2.50	0.19	0.45
10-20	11.37	22.68	0.37	1.38	3.83	0.24	2.18	2.56	0.20	0.45
20-30	10.09	20.12	0.39	1.47	3.85	0.22	1.87	2.58	0.31	0.78
30-40	11.62	23.47	0.36	1.32	2.75	0.26	2.44	2.38	0.22	0.52
40-50	13.26	26.44	0.40	1.46	2.48	0.24	2.26	4.63	0.31	0.71
50-60	11.63	23.20	0.41	1.61	7.48	0.27	2.27	3.10	0.30	0.76
60-70	13.22	26.43	0.51	1.96	4.91	0.29	2.78	3.83	0.46	1.08
70-80	14.47	28.87	0.58	2.29	7.24	0.31	3.03	4.76	0.18	0.38
80-90	14.57	30.29	0.57	2.25	5.07	0.44	3.61	4.23	0.48	1.13
90-95	13.53	28.12	0.65	2.71	5.56	0.53	4.06	5.58	0.76	1.79
95-100	15.80	32.05	0.85	3.53	11.95	0.60	4.80	5.10	1.30	3.06
90-100	14.37	29.57	0.72	3.01	7.93	0.56	4.33	5.40	0.96	2.26
All Classes	**12.15**	**24.38**	**0.45**	**1.73**	**4.57**	**0.29**	**2.54**	**3.44**	**0.35**	**0.82**

Table 8.2.3 : Per capita monthly expenditure (Rs. 0.00) and quantity intake (Kgs) of major food items.

Rural Nellore — Agricultural Labourers

Fractile Classes	Cereals		Pulses		Milk and Milk Products	Edible Oil		Meat, Fish and Eggs	Sugar	
	Q	V	Q	V	V	Q	V	V	Q	V
0-5	10.20	18.63	0.28	1.30	0.50	0.19	1.67	2.03	0.07	0.17
5-10	11.69	21.25	0.26	1.11	0.61	0.18	1.59	1.83	0.07	0.21
0-10	11.02	20.06	0.27	1.19	0.56	0.19	1.62	1.92	0.07	0.19
10-20	12.56	24.19	0.29	1.27	0.57	0.24	1.39	1.46	0.06	0.13
20-30	12.65	23.35	0.28	1.33	0.51	0.15	1.62	1.91	0.08	0.21
30-40	14.07	26.93	0.36	1.54	0.33	0.16	1.49	1.95	0.05	0.11
40-50	13.00	24.64	0.42	1.71	1.11	0.23	1.99	3.82	0.13	0.31
50-60	13.75	27.50	0.26	1.14	0.77	0.43	1.98	1.82	0.16	0.42
60-70	12.87	25.89	0.33	1.39	0.92	0.22	2.00	2.62	0.15	0.35
70-80	16.00	30.10	0.27	1.10	0.13	0.24	2.13	2.63	0.13	0.35
80-90	18.68	35.60	0.41	1.70	0.60	0.27	2.55	2.98	0.05	0.14
90-95	15.41	31.94	0.44	1.69	0.00	0.31	2.57	3.00	0.12	0.29
95-100	14.69	32.31	0.47	1.59	0.00	0.33	2.72	3.83	0.25	0.63
90-100	15.06	32.12	0.45	1.65	0.00	0.32	2.64	3.40	0.18	0.45
All Classes	**13.42**	**25.88**	**0.32**	**1.37**	**0.57**	**0.24**	**1.83**	**2.28**	**0.10**	**0.25**

Table 8.2.4 : Per capita monthly expenditure (Rs. 0.00) and quantity intake (Kgs) of major food items.

Rural Nellore

Fractile Classes	Cereals		Pulses		Others						
					Milk and Milk Products	Edible Oil		Meat, Fish and Eggs	Sugar	
	Q	V	Q	V	V	Q	V	V	Q	V
0-5	10.00	20.00	0.36	1.70	0.86	0.14	1.21	2.07	0.07	0.14
5-10	8.64	17.27	0.41	1.45	2.95	0.27	2.55	0.82	0.27	0.62
0-10	9.17	18.33	0.39	1.55	2.14	0.22	2.03	1.31	0.19	0.43
10-20	10.56	21.11	0.28	1.11	1.35	0.19	1.85	1.46	0.07	0.19
20-30	11.37	22.72	0.44	2.00	3.16	0.30	2.38	3.75	0.19	0.41
30-40	12.11	24.21	0.39	1.72	4.18	0.28	2.26	1.29	0.13	0.31
40-50	12.50	24.25	0.33	1.26	6.31	0.28	2.40	1.44	0.31	0.72
50-60	13.38	25.12	0.60	2.44	2.62	0.24	2.27	1.85	0.15	0.33
60-70	12.20	21.15	0.53	2.56	3.40	0.32	2.53	6.23	0.20	0.47
70-80	15.06	29.48	0.44	1.79	2.53	0.28	2.32	5.35	0.29	0.74
80-90	16.50	32.12	0.75	2.91	5.45	0.34	3.29	2.71	0.25	0.54
90-95	14.30	28.46	0.70	2.74	13.00	0.35	3.50	2.80	0.70	1.51
95-100	15.25	29.12	0.63	2.88	7.25	0.38	3.75	3.61	0.00	0.00
90-100	14.72	28.76	0.67	2.80	10.44	0.36	3.61	3.16	0.39	0.84
All Classes	**12.38**	**24.08**	**0.45**	**1.87**	**3.66**	**0.27**	**2.38**	**2.72**	**0.20**	**0.46**

Table 8.2.5 : Per capita monthly expenditure (Rs. 0.00) and quantity intake (Kgs) of major food items.

Urban Nellore

All Classes

Fractile Classes	Cereals		Pulses		Milk and Milk Products	Edible Oil		Meat, Fish and Eggs	Sugar	
	Q	V	Q	V	V	Q	V	V	Q	V
0-5	11.28	23.08	0.26	1.06	0.46	0.17	1.40	2.44	0.08	0.19
5-10	11.24	22.56	0.39	1.48	2.15	0.21	2.06	2.17	0.16	0.36
0-10	11.26	22.81	0.32	1.27	1.33	0.19	1.74	2.30	0.12	0.28
10-20	11.14	22.46	0.39	1.46	3.12	0.23	2.26	1.54	0.32	0.72
20-30	12.77	24.14	0.40	1.38	2.06	0.25	2.18	2.53	0.25	0.57
30-40	12.28	24.79	0.96	1.78	2.29	0.30	2.70	3.56	0.26	0.58
40-50	11.95	24.51	0.67	2.70	4.49	0.39	3.25	2.21	0.62	1.35
50-60	13.00	26.23	0.79	2.94	4.66	0.39	3.25	2.63	0.61	1.19
60-70	11.88	24.55	0.61	2.98	6.96	0.44	3.61	2.72	0.62	1.36
70-80	13.62	27.92	0.90	3.58	7.95	0.51	4.53	3.49	0.65	1.45
80-90	12.98	26.64	0.88	4.27	13.88	0.59	4.58	3.10	0.99	2.19
90-95	12.08	24.55	0.57	8.21	28.92	0.37	3.16	3.31	0.65	1.38
95-100	12.68	26.43	0.91	3.80	10.32	0.59	5.07	9.36	0.89	1.97
90-100	12.33	25.33	0.71	6.38	21.20	0.46	3.95	5.82	0.75	1.63
All Classes	**12.20**	**24.69**	**0.63**	**2.75**	**6.46**	**0.36**	**3.09**	**2.89**	**0.49**	**1.08**

KURNOOL

Table 9.1.1 : Per capita monthly expenditure, average size of household and Household Operational Land Holdings (acres)

Rural Kurnool Fractile Classes	All Classes Monthly per capita average total expenditure (Rs 0.00)	Average size of household	Household operational land holdings (in acres)
0 - 5	25.85	7.42	2.76
5 - 10	29.57	5.32	2.08
0 - 10	27.40	6.37	2.42
10- 20	32.84	6.30	4.59
20- 30	36.27	5.41	2.89
30- 40	39.39	5.22	4.07
40- 50	43.57	6.06	4.15
50- 60	46.84	5.19	6.27
60- 70	41.03	4.86	5.86
70- 80	57.80	4.62	6.31
80- 90	71.18	5.16	11.87
90- 95	86.11	4.16	9.87
95-100	145.40	5.00	12.64
90-100	118.48	4.56	11.26
All Classes	**50.59**	**5.38**	**5.98**

Table 9.1.2 : Per capita monthly expenditure, average size of household and Household Operational Land Holdings (acres`

Rural Kurnool Fractile Classes	Cultivators Monthly per capita average total expenditure (Rs 0.00)	Average size of household	Household operational land holdings (in acres)
0 - 5	23.97	8.71	11.11
5 - 10	33.37	5.86	10.43
0 - 10	31.34	7.29	10.77
10- 20	36.75	6.23	8.62
20- 30	40.63	6.23	11.81
30- 40	44.68	6.75	10.02
40- 50	47.85	5.31	13.60
50- 60	51.09	6.67	13.92
60- 70	56.73	4.67	11.58
70- 80	66.17	6.54	16.69
80- 90	77.18	5.46	24.92
90- 95	87.26	5.00	14.39
95-100	144.73	5.00	24.43
90-100	115.99	5.00	19.41
All Classes	**55.24**	**6.12**	**14.20**

Table 9.1.3 : Per capita monthly expenditure, average size of household and Household Operational Land Holdings (acres)

Rural Kurnool Fractile Classes	Agricultural Labourers: Monthly per capita average total expenditure (Rs 0.00)	Average size of house-hold	Household operational land holdings (in acres)
0 - 5	23.88	6.25	1.63
5 - 10	27.46	8.50	1.94
0 - 10	25.94	7.38	1.78
10- 20	29.51	5.25	1.41
20- 30	32.87	5.88	1.42
30- 40	35.58	5.67	0.75
40- 50	37.76	4.44	1.13
50- 60	39.84	4.33	1.33
60- 70	43.16	4.93	0.57
70- 80	47.34	4.06	1.10
80- 90	53.38	3.50	0.73
90- 95	61.29	2.63	1.13
95-100	77.71	3.50	2.57
90-100	70.67	3.06	1.84
All Classes	**38.89**	**4.85**	**1.21**

Table 9.1.4: Per capita monthly expenditure, average size of household and Household Operational Land Holdings (acres)

Rural Kurnool Fractile Classes	Others: Monthly per capita average total expenditure (Rs 0.00)	Average size of house-hold	Household operational land holdings (in acres)
0 - 5	28.50	5.25	1.63
5 - 10	31.76	6.00	1.50
0 - 10	30.26	5.63	1.56
10- 20	35.90	6.22	1.88
20- 30	42.65	7.33	3.03
30- 40	45.61	5.75	1.33
40- 50	49.88	4.88	0.44
50- 60	55.41	4.25	0.75
60- 70	60.29	6.25	3.79
70- 80	71.52	4.33	0.84
80- 90	95.06	3.00	1.03
90- 95	120.44	7.50	15.44
95-100	203.87	5.00	0.75
90-100	153.81	6.25	8.09
All Classes	**62.33**	**5.38**	**2.25**

Table 9.1.5 : Per capita monthly expenditure, average size of household and Household Operational Land Holdings (acres)

Urban Kurnool

All Classes

Fractile Classes	Monthly per capita average total expenditure (Rs 0.00)	Average size of household	Household operational land holdings (in acres)
0 - 5	31.78	6.09	1.16
5 - 10	36.98	6.45	0.36
0 - 10	34.46	6.27	0.76
10- 20	42.73	5.61	0.04
20- 30	47.79	6.35	0.39
30- 40	52.88	5.13	0.21
40- 50	58.29	4.91	0.50
50- 60	63.26	4.73	2.82
60- 70	70.20	5.09	0.48
70- 80	85.06	5.04	2.04
80- 90	112.52	4.39	8.02
90- 95	149.14	4.00	5.91
95-100	226.08	4.45	18.18
90-100	189.68	4.23	12.05
All Classes	**71.32**	**5.18**	**2.71**

Table 9.2.1 : Per capita monthly expenditure (Rs. 0.00) and quantity intake (Kgs) of major food items.

Rural Kurnool — All Classes

Fractile Classes	Cereals		Pulses		Milk and Milk Products	Edible Oil		Meat, Fish and Eggs	Sugar	
	Q	V	Q	V	V	Q	V	V	Q	V
0-5	12.65	15.20	0.25	1.12	0.04	0.11	0.87	1.29	0.07	0.15
5-10	12.38	15.19	0.30	1.41	0.16	0.12	0.99	1.35	0.07	0.16
0-10	12.53	15.20	0.27	1.24	0.09	0.11	0.92	1.31	0.07	0.15
10-20	12.18	16.18	0.40	1.84	0.11	0.16	1.18	1.60	0.09	0.22
20-30	13.48	18.77	0.41	1.71	0.15	0.13	1.13	1.54	0.17	0.36
30-40	13.08	18.90	0.47	2.10	0.63	0.15	1.28	1.70	0.22	0.47
40-50	13.32	22.23	0.46	2.00	1.30	0.17	2.25	2.31	0.32	0.65
50-60	14.98	23.29	0.54	2.27	1.19	0.19	1.91	1.93	0.32	0.64
60-70	14.75	23.68	0.52	2.30	2.15	0.20	1.74	2.00	0.43	0.93
70-80	17.60	26.94	0.64	2.87	3.41	0.25	2.07	1.45	0.56	1.29
80-90	17.64	28.75	0.79	3.58	4.41	0.30	2.78	2.34	0.66	1.55
90-95	18.76	32.94	0.95	4.37	9.53	0.47	4.23	2.99	0.96	2.52
95-100	17.62	31.66	1.29	5.77	9.15	0.57	4.85	2.37	1.02	2.52
90-100	18.14	32.24	1.14	5.13	9.32	0.52	4.57	2.65	0.99	2.52
All Classes	**14.68**	**22.13**	**0.55**	**2.42**	**2.08**	**0.21**	**1.92**	**1.86**	**0.36**	**0.82**

Table 9.2.2 : Per capita monthly expenditure (Rs. 0.00) and quantity intake (Kgs) of major food items.

Rural Kurnool — Cultivators

Fractile Classes	Cereals		Pulses		Milk and Milk Products	Edible Oil		Meat, Fish and Eggs	Sugar	
	Q	V	Q	V	V	Q	V	V	Q	V
0-5	12.33	14.67	0.38	1.74	0.25	0.18	1.49	1.25	0.05	0.13
5-10	13.56	14.56	0.41	1.92	0.10	0.16	1.24	1.71	0.09	0.20
0-10	12.82	14.63	0.39	1.81	0.19	0.17	1.39	1.43	0.06	0.15
10-20	13.42	18.20	0.52	2.24	0.10	0.16	1.30	1.96	0.20	0.43
20-30	13.30	19.72	0.44	2.14	1.91	0.18	1.45	1.14	0.39	0.73
30-40	15.80	23.33	0.41	1.90	1.04	0.20	1.67	1.81	0.20	0.38
40-50	14.75	21.56	0.54	2.51	1.77	0.24	1.98	2.00	0.44	0.90
50-60	14.90	22.78	0.54	2.38	3.06	0.20	1.66	1.75	0.51	1.21
60-70	15.79	22.42	0.71	3.15	3.93	0.23	2.00	1.71	0.54	1.11
70-80	17.94	28.64	0.79	3.39	4.45	0.24	2.22	1.49	0.65	1.32
80-90	16.68	28.11	0.89	4.54	6.62	0.42	3.66	2.54	0.80	1.88
90-95	22.66	40.50	1.03	4.74	8.69	0.46	4.59	2.91	0.89	1.96
95-100	22.91	37.77	1.60	6.90	7.09	0.70	5.97	4.43	1.16	2.73
90-100	22.79	39.13	1.31	5.82	7.89	0.58	5.28	3.67	1.02	2.34
All Classes	**15.66**	**23.44**	**0.64**	**2.90**	**2.91**	**0.25**	**2.19**	**1.91**	**0.46**	**0.99**

Table 9.2.3 : Per capita monthly expenditure (Rs. 0.00) and quantity intake (Kgs) of major food items.

Rural Kurnool

Agricultural Labourers

Fractile Classes	Cereals		Pulses		Milk and Milk Products	Edible Oil		Meat, Fish and Eggs	Sugar	
	Q	V	Q	V	V	Q	V	V	Q	V
0-5	11.94	14.26	0.18	0.82	0.00	0.08	0.66	0.86	0.04	0.09
5-10	12.74	15.51	0.26	1.17	0.09	0.10	0.86	1.48	0.12	0.24
0-10	12.40	14.98	0.23	1.02	0.05	0.09	0.78	1.22	0.08	0.18
10-20	12.12	15.19	0.30	1.41	0.19	0.11	0.89	1.33	0.09	0.20
20-30	11.99	17.20	0.36	1.62	0.00	0.17	1.05	1.59	0.10	0.25
30-40	13.73	19.38	0.32	1.46	0.15	0.12	1.04	1.68	0.18	0.38
40-50	13.01	18.37	0.46	1.74	0.08	0.12	1.05	1.46	0.13	0.29
50-60	13.65	21.75	0.37	1.68	0.23	0.11	1.00	1.48	0.12	0.25
60-70	14.59	23.05	0.39	1.76	0.61	0.12	1.09	1.70	0.19	0.39
70-80	15.22	24.11	0.48	2.11	1.05	0.13	1.99	2.29	0.28	0.59
80-90	16.71	29.36	0.32	1.42	0.43	0.15	1.49	2.19	0.27	0.43
90-95	20.33	33.26	0.42	1.91	0.67	0.16	1.49	2.71	0.38	0.71
95-100	17.71	27.66	0.68	2.93	2.20	0.27	2.57	4.36	0.63	1.83
90-100	18.84	30.06	0.57	2.49	1.54	0.23	2.11	3.65	0.52	1.35
All Classes	**13.82**	**20.26**	**0.36**	**1.60**	**0.35**	**0.13**	**1.17**	**1.74**	**0.17**	**0.38**

Table 9.2.4 : Per capita monthly expenditure (Rs. 0.00) and quantity intake (Kgs) of major food items.

Rural Kurnool

Fractile Classes	Cereals		Pulses		Others: Milk and Milk Products	Edible Oil		Meat, Fish and Eggs	Sugar	
	Q	V	Q	V	V	Q	V	V	Q	V
0-5	12.00	16.83	0.43	2.07	0.00	0.16	1.49	2.14	0.00	0.00
5-10	11.67	16.54	0.38	1.73	0.00	0.08	0.69	1.86	0.04	0.08
0-10	11.82	16.68	0.40	1.89	0.00	0.12	1.06	2.00	0.02	0.04
10-20	12.77	17.06	0.51	2.13	0.38	0.18	1.48	1.32	0.16	0.32
20-30	13.48	19.75	0.61	2.53	1.29	0.18	4.05	1.15	0.48	1.09
30-40	13.09	21.79	0.65	2.20	1.11	0.18	1.66	6.20	0.32	0.66
40-50	13.46	22.15	0.67	2.94	2.05	0.31	2.65	1.67	0.35	0.77
50-60	16.74	24.22	0.75	3.60	2.49	0.32	2.74	1.66	0.50	1.10
60-70	18.18	29.50	0.72	3.18	4.33	0.30	2.47	1.22	0.74	2.04
70-80	17.59	28.95	0.65	2.67	5.30	0.32	2.76	2.41	0.62	1.58
80-90	14.15	25.48	0.97	4.46	10.83	0.55	4.68	1.78	1.19	3.67
90-95	15.50	30.00	1.23	5.70	10.18	0.43	3.87	1.82	0.87	2.57
95-100	13.11	26.27	1.00	4.32	13.35	0.50	4.00	1.50	1.10	2.34
90-100	14.54	28.51	1.14	5.15	11.45	0.46	3.92	1.09	0.96	2.48
All Classes	**14.57**	**25.05**	**0.69**	**2.99**	**3.56**	**0.27**	**2.71**	**2.00**	**0.50**	**1.28**

Table 9.2.5 : Per capita monthly expenditure (Rs. 0.00) and quantity intake (Kgs) of major food items.

Urban Kurnool — All Classes

Fractile Classes	Cereals		Pulses		Milk and Milk Products	Edible Oil		Meat, Fish and Eggs	Sugar	
	Q	V	Q	V	V	Q	V	V	Q	V
0-5	10.01	13.13	0.40	1.55	0.25	0.21	1.93	1.56	0.16	0.43
5-10	11.55	18.13	0.40	1.89	0.00	0.14	1.10	1.64	0.14	0.30
0-10	10.80	15.70	0.40	1.73	0.12	0.17	1.51	1.60	0.15	0.36
10-20	12.35	21.06	0.47	2.02	1.64	0.17	1.58	2.02	0.26	0.56
20-30	13.05	22.08	0.50	2.16	1.62	6.20	1.69	2.14	0.38	0.89
30-40	12.60	21.97	0.60	2.66	2.62	0.27	2.26	2.50	0.42	1.00
40-50	12.42	22.14	0.65	2.90	2.93	0.31	2.62	2.86	0.46	1.05
50-60	13.07	22.54	0.59	2.54	3.43	0.46	4.39	4.76	0.47	1.09
60-70	13.38	23.64	0.96	4.07	3.93	0.45	3.89	3.91	0.64	1.64
70-80	13.84	25.54	0.92	4.39	9.94	0.53	4.09	2.82	0.85	1.91
80-90	14.81	27.33	1.15	5.30	11.77	0.75	6.18	3.87	1.12	2.59
90-95	13.32	24.25	1.16	5.21	15.65	0.82	6.92	6.70	1.27	2.92
95-100	16.14	29.97	1.67	8.17	25.60	1.31	10.71	6.16	1.67	3.93
90-100	14.81	27.27	1.43	6.77	20.89	1.08	8.92	6.42	1.48	3.45
All Classes	**13.01**	**22.61**	**0.73**	**3.30**	**5.29**	**0.41**	**3.46**	**3.13**	**0.58**	**1.36**

ANANTAPUR

Table 10.1.1: Per capita monthly expenditure, average size of household and Household Operational Land Holdings (acres)

Rural Anantapur <u>All Classes</u>

Fractile Classes	Monthly per capita average total expenditure (Rs 0.00)	Average size of house-hold	Household operatio-nal land holdings (in acres)
0 - 5	24.54	5.17	0.59
5 - 10	28.43	5.70	1.17
0 - 10	26.57	5.44	0.88
10- 20	31.00	5.77	3.26
20- 30	33.72	4.76	3.10
30- 40	38.46	4.67	2.82
40- 50	39.87	4.91	5.54
50- 60	43.72	4.35	5.77
60- 70	48.84	4.70	11.36
70- 80	53.72	5.14	12.13
80- 90	61.50	4.34	9.14
90- 95	73.11	5.47	8.12
95-100	123.18	5.23	19.17
90-100	103.19	4.35	13.92
All Classes	**46.60**	**4.84**	**6.75**

Table 10.1.2: Per capita monthly expenditure, average size of household and Household Operational Land Holdings (acres)

Rural Anantapur <u>Cultivators</u>

Fractile Classes	Monthly per capita average total expenditure (Rs 0.00)	Average size of house-hold	Household operatio-nal land holdings (in acres)
0 - 10	30.80	6.88	8.67
10- 20	36.63	6.12	7.37
20- 30	39.99	5.60	9.68
30- 40	43.22	5.33	8.98
40- 50	46.61	4.86	13.12
50- 60	49.49	5.60	16.13
60- 70	52.41	5.60	21.13
70- 80	58.39	5.73	20.64
80- 90	68.43	4.43	12.33
90- 95	82.11	3.00	14.97
95-100	114.01	7.38	30.99
90-100	104.78	5.10	22.98
All Classes	**51.97**	**5.54**	**14.08**

Table 10.1.3: Per capita monthly expenditure, average size of household and Household Operational Land Holdings (acres)

Rural Anantapur — Agricultural Labourers

Fractile Classes	Monthly per capita average total expenditure (Rs 0.00)	Average size of house-hold	Household operational land holdings (in acres)
0 - 5	21.67	4.57	0.01
5 - 10	26.45	5.00	0.63
0 - 10	24.17	4.78	0.32
10- 20	28.13	5.84	0.34
20- 30	30.44	4.77	0.17
30- 40	31.63	5.92	0.70
40- 50	33.61	3.69	0.38
50- 60	35.64	4.15	0.74
60- 70	37.39	3.61	0.28
70- 80	40.45	3.38	0.24
80- 90	47.65	2.84	0.41
90- 95	57.17	3.71	0.72
95-100	67.79	1.71	2.00
90-100	60.51	2.71	1.36
All Classes	**35.02**	**4.17**	**0.50**

Table 10.1.4: Per capita monthly expenditure, average size of household and Household Operational Land Holdings (acres)

Rural Anantapur — Others

Fractile Classes	Monthly per capita average total expenditure (Rs 0.00)	Average size of house-hold	Household operational land holdings (in acres)
0 - 5	27.21	7.00	1.00
5 - 10	30.60	4.66	0.67
0 - 10	28.56	5.83	0.84
10- 20	33.48	4.83	1.60
20- 30	37.21	3.83	0.11
30- 40	39.59	5.80	1.81
40- 50	42.49	4.33	2.17
50- 60	50.03	3.80	1.30
60- 70	53.33	6.00	3.21
70- 80	56.75	3.66	0.60
80- 90	64.21	4.16	1.10
90- 95	73.52	3.00	0.01
95-100	201.75	4.33	0.71
90-100	155.81	3.66	0.36
All Classes	**53.50**	**4.56**	**1.30**

Table 10.1.5 :Per capita monthly expenditure, average size of household and Household Operational Land Holdings (acres)

Urban Anantapur <u>All Classes</u>

Fractile Classes	Monthly per capita average total expenditure (Rs 0.00)	Average size of household	Household operational land holdings (in acres)
0 - 5	29.50	6.00	1.73
5 - 10	34.91	6.44	1.78
0 - 10	32.39	6.22	1.75
10- 20	41.64	6.50	1.44
20- 30	48.11	6.61	3.92
30- 40	52.87	5.05	1.30
40- 50	58.45	6.08	0.36
50- 60	64.24	6.58	0.19
60- 70	70.16	4.58	1.42
70- 80	78.15	4.61	2.45
80- 90	101.37	7.16	1.19
90- 95	129.41	3.33	0.27
95-100	184.27	3.55	0.00
90-100	157.72	3.44	0.14
All Classes	**66.60**	**5.76**	**1.42**

Table 10.2.1: Per capita monthly expenditure (Rs. 0.00) and quantity intake (Kgs) of major food items.

Rural Anantapur

All Classes

Fractile Classes	Cereals		Pulses		Milk and Milk Products	Edible Oil		Meat, Fish and Eggs	Sugar	
	Q	V	Q	V	V	Q	V	V	Q	V
0-5	12.27	14.46	0.13	0.49	0.16	0.09	0.45	0.89	0.14	0.22
5-10	13.52	16.30	0.17	0.63	0.47	0.08	0.68	1.07	0.30	0.45
0-10	12.92	15.42	0.15	0.56	0.33	0.07	0.58	0.98	0.23	0.35
10-20	13.24	16.88	0.33	1.07	0.65	0.11	0.80	1.43	0.39	0.59
20-30	13.44	17.38	0.30	1.18	0.86	0.10	0.82	1.51	0.43	0.66
30-40	13.58	19.04	0.39	1.58	1.01	0.11	0.97	1.77	0.62	0.69
40-50	13.96	20.00	0.43	1.74	1.91	0.15	1.25	1.67	0.65	1.10
50-60	14.37	21.26	0.49	2.03	2.25	0.21	1.82	1.85	0.69	1.13
60-70	14.74	21.71	0.78	3.18	2.85	0.20	2.15	1.83	0.88	1.51
70-80	14.70	23.29	0.63	2.53	3.01	0.28	2.35	2.62	0.84	1.49
80-90	14.55	25.11	0.89	3.55	4.34	0.35	2.90	3.17	0.96	1.88
90-95	15.35	25.90	0.96	3.83	6.83	0.41	3.53	3.88	0.97	2.16
95-100	17.85	30.04	0.99	3.53	6.03	0.40	3.68	3.56	1.32	2.84
90-100	16.85	28.39	0.98	3.65	6.35	0.41	3.62	3.69	1.18	2.57
All Classes	**14.84**	**20.60**	**0.52**	**2.04**	**2.23**	**0.20**	**1.66**	**2.00**	**0.67**	**1.15**

Table 10.2.2: Per capita monthly expenditure (Rs. 0.00) and quantity intake (Kgs) of major food items.

Rural Anantapur

<u>Cultivators</u>

Fractile Classes	Cereals		Pulses		Milk and Milk Products	Edible Oil		Meat, Fish and Eggs	Sugar	
	Q	V	Q	V	V	Q	V	V	Q	V
0-5	13.89	16.41	0.13	0.55	0.43	0.07	0.65	1.82	0.30	0.46
5-10	12.93	16.60	0.35	1.20	1.30	0.10	0.81	1.52	0.54	0.70
0-10	13.41	16.50	0.24	0.88	0.87	0.09	0.73	1.67	0.42	0.58
10-20	13.14	17.30	0.35	1.40	1.09	0.09	0.84	1.91	0.74	0.77
20-30	13.74	19.40	0.43	1.68	2.02	0.16	1.37	1.78	0.75	1.20
30-40	13.87	20.15	0.50	2.13	2.01	0.21	1.80	1.90	0.69	1.07
40-50	13.71	20.11	0.65	2.92	3.75	0.28	2.40	1.76	0.98	1.70
50-60	15.38	22.99	0.84	3.40	2.73	0.29	2.34	2.27	1.01	1.71
60-70	15.12	24.49	0.56	2.46	3.57	0.28	2.34	2.86	0.91	1.57
70-80	14.33	21.88	0.65	3.07	4.00	0.37	3.04	3.24	1.20	2.12
80-90	15.34	27.35	0.96	3.49	5.30	0.36	3.09	3.41	0.82	1.84
90-95	17.12	25.24	1.00	4.22	9.85	0.50	4.27	4.25	1.17	2.16
95-100	18.32	31.32	1.06	3.64	5.58	0.42	4.02	3.64	1.37	3.16
90-100	17.97	29.56	1.04	3.01	6.66	0.44	4.08	3.80	1.32	2.90
All Classes	**14.54**	**20.96**	**0.60**	**2.44**	**3.04**	**0.25**	**2.12**	**2.41**	**0.87**	**1.55**

Table 10.2.3: Per capita monthly expenditure (Rs. 0.00) and quantity intake (Kgs) of major food items.

Rural Anantapur — Agricultural Labourers

Fractile Classes	Cereals		Pulses		Milk and Milk Products	Edible Oil		Meat, Fish and Eggs	Sugar	
	Q	V	Q	V	V	Q	V	V	Q	V
0-5	13.31	17.09	0.19	0.56	0.23	0.09	0.72	1.19	0.30	0.56
5-10	12.60	15.30	0.14	0.61	0.14	0.06	0.49	0.94	0.17	0.26
0-10	12.94	16.15	0.16	0.59	0.18	0.07	0.61	1.07	0.24	0.41
10-20	13.47	16.34	0.12	0.41	0.51	0.06	0.54	1.15	0.26	0.38
20-30	13.64	17.50	0.21	0.84	0.43	0.12	0.73	1.21	0.32	0.50
30-40	13.72	17.31	0.37	1.33	0.67	0.11	0.86	1.07	0.33	0.53
40-50	13.68	17.57	0.33	1.52	0.68	0.13	1.08	1.39	0.43	0.65
50-60	14.11	18.88	0.31	1.20	0.84	0.09	0.78	1.59	0.42	0.62
60-70	15.00	21.45	0.47	1.74	0.90	0.10	0.84	1.36	0.29	0.43
70-80	15.06	20.68	0.47	2.01	0.92	0.12	1.00	1.60	0.52	0.87
80-90	16.43	22.58	0.56	2.04	1.42	0.11	0.92	0.91	0.39	0.57
90-95	14.71	23.90	0.86	3.16	2.45	0.16	1.43	3.73	0.73	1.35
95-100	17.10	32.08	0.90	3.77	2.62	0.21	1.69	3.35	0.42	0.87
90-100	15.46	26.00	0.87	3.35	2.50	0.18	1.51	3.61	0.63	1.20
All Classes	**12.97**	**18.95**	**0.35**	**1.38**	**0.80**	**0.11**	**0.84**	**1.41**	**0.36**	**0.58**

Table 10.2.4: Per capita monthly expenditure (Rs. 0.00) and quantity intake (Kgs) of major food items.

Rural Anantapur — Others

Fractile Classes	Cereals		Pulses		Milk and Milk Products	Edible Oil		Meat, Fish and Eggs	Sugar	
	Q	V	Q	V	V	Q	V	V	Q	V
0-5	11.15	15.38	0.14	0.64	0.86	0.18	1.54	1.29	0.25	0.63
5-10	12.43	14.54	0.29	1.30	0.75	0.14	1.11	1.25	0.61	0.89
0-10	11.16	15.04	0.20	0.90	0.80	0.16	1.30	1.27	0.45	0.78
10-20	11.65	15.92	0.37	1.48	1.00	0.12	0.97	1.80	0.53	0.91
20-30	12.15	18.76	0.33	1.48	0.75	0.11	0.87	1.93	0.52	0.80
30-40	13.18	20.09	0.32	1.39	3.88	0.13	1.12	1.70	0.64	1.16
40-50	13.30	21.67	0.48	2.26	1.99	0.20	1.59	1.72	0.55	1.04
50-60	13.27	20.86	0.61	1.78	2.24	0.19	1.77	2.26	0.62	1.12
60-70	13.88	23.33	0.74	2.80	2.38	0.29	2.33	1.28	0.52	1.05
70-80	14.68	23.90	0.98	4.03	2.60	0.29	2.42	2.98	0.87	1.51
80-90	12.50	24.34	0.85	3.67	4.37	0.47	3.91	1.30	0.83	1.70
90-95	16.56	28.18	0.44	2.11	3.29	0.33	2.72	7.57	1.14	2.07
95-100	12.03	24.25	1.40	5.29	8.79	0.54	4.43	2.49	1.29	3.07
90-100	13.88	25.86	1.01	3.99	6.95	0.47	3.86	4.18	1.24	3.07
All Classes	**12.93**	**20.63**	**0.56**	**2.28**	**2.56**	**0.24**	**1.94**	**1.94**	**0.66**	**1.26**

Table 10.2.5: Per capita monthly expenditure (Rs. 0.00) and quantity intake (Kgs) of major food items

Urban Anantapur — All Classes

Fractile Classes	Cereals		Pulses		Milk and Milk Products	Edible Oil		Meat, Fish and Eggs	Sugar	
	Q	V	Q	V	V	Q	V	V	Q	V
0-5	12.60	16.23	0.24	0.79	0.48	0.12	1.12	0.98	0.18	0.29
5-10	13.23	18.75	0.35	1.55	0.65	0.08	0.67	1.38	0.41	0.71
0-10	12.92	17.53	0.30	1.18	0.57	0.10	0.88	1.19	0.30	0.51
10-20	12.43	19.41	0.47	2.10	0.88	0.16	1.27	1.98	0.48	0.87
20-30	12.92	21.78	0.43	1.85	1.74	0.27	1.93	2.20	0.48	0.93
30-40	12.84	22.38	0.64	2.40	1.78	0.27	2.20	2.42	0.57	1.17
40-50	12.17	22.39	0.65	3.58	2.03	0.31	2.16	2.30	0.59	1.18
50-60	12.22	23.42	0.66	3.02	3.49	0.31	2.59	3.55	0.73	1.43
60-70	12.45	23.17	0.72	3.21	4.17	0.31	2.57	3.58	0.82	1.55
70-80	13.26	26.12	0.82	3.45	6.40	0.38	3.14	2.36	0.86	2.02
80-90	12.08	24.26	1.46	5.90	12.09	0.58	5.04	3.01	1.10	2.58
90-95	14.18	30.17	1.20	5.05	11.65	0.66	5.99	0.95	1.20	2.59
95-100	14.18	28.04	1.55	6.49	14.94	0.65	6.18	0.54	1.36	3.08
90-100	14.18	29.07	1.38	5.79	13.24	0.66	6.08	0.75	1.28	2.82
All Classes	**12.65**	**23.45**	**0.73**	**3.17**	**4.30**	**0.32**	**2.64**	**2.38**	**0.69**	**1.44**

CUDDAPAH

Table 11.1.1: Per capita monthly expenditure, average size of household and Household Operational Land Holdings (acres)

Rural Cuddapah <u>All Classes</u>

Fractile Classes	Monthly per capita average total expenditure (Rs 0.00)	Average size of house-hold	Household operatio-nal land holdings (in acres)
0 - 5	26.16	6.14	1.44
5 - 10	33.00	5.36	1.68
0 - 10	29.34	5.75	1.56
10- 20	36.37	5.69	3.27
20- 30	41.15	5.96	4.51
30- 40	46.36	5.12	2.68
40- 50	50.76	4.67	3.04
50- 60	56.75	5.19	5.45
60- 70	62.81	3.96	3.39
70- 80	71.65	3.81	2.38
80- 90	83.79	3.88	5.95
90- 95	114.23	3.07	12.30
95-100	173.97	4.29	5.50
90-100	149.03	3.68	8.90
All Classes	**58.69**	**4.77**	**4.13**

Table 11.1.2: Per capita monthly expenditure, average size of household and Household Operational Land Holdings (acres)

Rural Cuddapah <u>Cultivators</u>

Fractile Classes	Monthly per capita average total expenditure (Rs 0.00)	Average size of house-hold	Household operatio-nal land holdings (in acres)
0 - 5	29.00	7.66	4.60
5 - 10	35.34	7.60	4.56
0 - 10	37.17	7.60	4.58
10- 20	39.14	6.60	4.92
20- 30	43.09	7.00	7.75
30- 40	46.99	6.40	5.17
40- 50	52.75	5.18	6.72
50- 60	58.25	5.73	8.11
60- 70	63.97	5.09	6.68
70- 80	73.95	4.40	6.10
80- 90	82.71	5.10	12.28
90- 95	109.37	4.20	33.60
95-100	158.50	6.20	14.20
90-100	138.66	5.20	23.90
All Classes	**60.09**	**5.82**	**8.58**

Table 11.1.3: Per capita monthly expenditure, average size of household and Household Operational Land Holdings (acres)

Rural Cuddapah — Agricultural Labourers

Fractile Classes	Monthly per capita average total expenditure (Rs 0.00)	Average size of house-hold	Household operational land holdings (in acres)
0 - 5	22.64	5.40	0.50
5 - 10	29.09	5.00	0.33
0 - 10	25.75	5.20	0.41
10- 20	33.12	5.50	1.65
20- 30	37.11	5.30	2.76
30- 40	42.49	5.10	2.13
40- 50	47.52	5.10	1.82
50- 60	50.90	3.10	1.50
60- 70	55.54	4.90	2.85
70- 80	63.49	3.20	1.00
80- 90	72.74	2.90	0.85
90- 95	93.02	1.80	0.21
95-100	138.94	3.40	0.50
90-100	123.04	2.60	0.35
All Classes	**49.76**	**4.33**	**1.53**

Table 11.1.4: Per capita monthly expenditure, average size of household and Household Operational Land Holdings (acres)

Rural Cuddapah — Others

Fractile Classes	Monthly per capita average total expenditure (Rs 0.00)	Average size of house-hold	Household operational land holdings (in acres)
0 - 5	28.87	5.33	0.00
5 - 10	34.58	5.33	2.84
0 - 10	31.78	5.33	1.42
10- 20	38.34	4.50	1.17
20- 30	45.30	3.17	0.21
30- 40	51.08	4.00	1.83
40- 50	56.61	4.57	1.19
50- 60	64.12	2.86	0.86
60- 70	74.66	3.71	0.43
70- 80	86.37	3.00	0.07
80- 90	112.78	3.50	1.38
90- 95	164.99	2.67	1.94
95-100	251.76	3.33	0.67
90-100	213.20	3.00	1.30
All Classes	**71.45**	**3.76**	**0.98**

Table 11.1.5: Per capita monthly expenditure, average size of household and Household Operational Land Holdings (acres)

Urban Cuddapah <u>All Classes</u>

Fractile Classes	Monthly per capita average total expenditure (Rs 0.00)	Average size of household	Household operational land holdings (in acres)
0 - 5	29.27	5.56	0.00
5 - 10	36.24	5.89	0.11
0 - 10	32.86	5.72	0.06
10- 20	42.15	5.61	0.64
20- 30	49.35	5.47	0.24
30- 40	54.39	4.65	3.25
40- 50	62.34	4.56	0.64
50- 60	68.19	5.12	0.97
60- 70	73.77	4.88	1.26
70- 80	84.25	5.65	2.15
80- 90	105.17	4.44	2.33
90- 95	145.85	3.89	2.72
95-100	225.59	2.89	2.00
90-100	179.84	3.39	2.36
All Classes	**70.74**	**4.94**	**1.38**

Table 11.2.1: Per capita monthly expenditure (Rs. 0.00) and quantity intake (Kgs) of major food items.

Rural Cuddapah — All Classes

Fractile Classes	Cereals		Pulses		Milk and Milk Products	Edible Oil		Meat, Fish and Eggs	Sugar	
	Q	V	Q	V	V	Q	V	V	Q	V
0-5	12.90	17.56	0.18	0.73	0.98	0.05	0.38	0.72	0.08	0.17
5-10	14.16	19.24	0.22	0.90	1.03	0.11	0.97	0.99	0.14	0.24
0-10	13.48	18.34	0.20	0.81	1.00	0.08	0.65	0.84	0.11	0.20
10-20	12.35	18.39	0.33	1.32	1.57	0.14	1.22	5.83	0.29	0.51
20-30	14.45	21.93	0.37	1.55	1.10	0.14	1.26	1.23	0.23	0.44
30-40	14.03	22.16	0.45	1.76	1.60	0.13	1.11	2.19	0.23	0.45
40-50	15.38	26.73	0.54	2.22	1.64	0.16	1.43	2.14	0.24	0.45
50-60	15.26	26.15	0.73	2.95	4.09	0.18	1.53	2.03	0.47	0.80
60-70	17.02	28.07	0.58	2.25	4.37	0.19	1.63	3.61	0.56	1.11
70-80	14.61	26.75	0.53	2.16	3.39	0.26	2.16	4.70	0.48	1.13
80-90	18.12	29.79	0.78	3.09	5.29	0.33	2.79	5.28	0.67	1.43
90-95	17.45	29.61	1.06	4.26	7.65	0.43	3.68	2.46	1.29	2.51
95-100	22.77	40.17	1.76	6.25	7.69	0.50	4.32	5.72	1.52	3.06
90-100	20.55	35.76	1.47	5.42	7.68	0.47	4.05	4.36	1.42	2.83
All Classes	**15.23**	**24.65**	**0.56**	**2.21**	**2.89**	**0.19**	**1.66**	**3.04**	**0.43**	**0.84**

Table 11.2.2: Per capita monthly expenditure (Rs. 0.00) and quantity intake (Kgs) of major food items.

Rural Cuddapah — Cultivators

Fractile Classes	Cereals		Pulses		Milk and Milk Products	Edible Oil		Meat, Fish and Eggs	Sugar	
	Q	V	Q	V	V	Q	V	V	Q	V
0-5	15.26	19.05	0.30	1.24	2.37	0.07	0.54	0.97	0.08	0.16
5-10	11.01	17.34	0.38	1.49	1.13	0.12	1.06	1.92	0.39	0.70
0-10	13.14	18.20	0.34	1.36	1.75	0.09	0.80	1.45	0.24	0.43
10-20	12.42	20.45	0.27	1.15	2.66	0.16	1.42	1.12	0.31	0.69
20-30	15.27	23.02	0.52	1.99	1.16	0.14	1.27	1.41	0.28	0.42
30-40	14.59	23.52	0.46	1.84	2.26	0.17	1.51	2.16	0.33	0.69
40-50	16.06	25.68	0.74	2.68	3.64	0.15	1.34	2.46	0.45	0.80
50-60	15.35	27.24	0.81	3.35	4.96	0.20	1.59	2.62	0.52	0.89
60-70	17.82	27.87	0.75	2.80	4.09	0.19	1.63	3.33	0.77	1.33
70-80	16.18	29.18	0.59	2.49	4.04	0.28	2.40	5.04	0.59	1.52
80-90	20.04	32.43	0.78	3.27	5.85	0.29	2.39	4.47	0.73	1.34
90-95	19.86	33.09	1.14	3.97	9.10	0.39	3.42	4.93	0.86	1.94
95-100	22.26	37.81	2.10	7.31	8.94	0.55	4.21	4.26	1.13	2.29
90-100	21.29	35.90	1.71	5.96	9.00	0.49	3.89	4.53	1.02	2.15
All Classes	**15.93**	**25.70**	**0.67**	**2.58**	**3.72**	**0.20**	**1.73**	**2.67**	**0.49**	**0.96**

Table 11.2.3: Per capita monthly expenditure (Rs. 0.00) and quantity intake (Kgs) of major food items.

Rural Cuddapan — Agricultural Labourers

Fractile Classes	Cereals		Pulses		Milk and Milk Products	Edible Oil		Meat, Fish and Eggs	Sugar	
	Q	V	Q	V	V	Q	V	V	Q	V
0-5	9.63	14.89	0.07	0.31	0.00	0.03	0.30	0.73	0.09	0.19
5-10	13.16	17.76	0.14	0.55	0.00	0.03	0.26	0.80	0.04	0.09
0-10	11.33	16.27	0.11	0.42	0.00	0.03	0.28	0.76	0.07	0.14
10-20	15.31	20.69	0.24	0.97	0.96	0.10	0.89	0.89	0.15	0.26
20-30	13.28	18.83	0.45	1.85	0.32	0.14	1.14	1.87	0.19	0.29
30-40	12.33	19.72	0.24	1.01	0.75	0.11	0.95	1.53	0.22	0.44
40-50	14.45	23.78	0.39	1.64	0.93	0.10	0.94	1.93	0.23	0.39
50-60	17.13	26.06	0.61	2.70	1.52	0.24	2.14	1.56	0.13	0.23
60-70	13.87	25.52	0.55	2.21	3.17	0.15	1.31	2.14	0.51	0.87
70-80	16.59	29.11	0.25	0.99	3.61	0.18	1.44	3.78	0.33	0.69
80-90	15.24	27.47	0.38	1.64	3.32	0.26	2.01	5.36	0.38	0.68
90-95	19.00	32.02	0.69	3.00	4.22	0.52	4.67	6.17	0.71	1.39
95-100	30.18	51.69	1.62	5.93	2.76	0.49	5.00	3.76	2.28	3.49
90-100	26.31	44.88	1.30	4.91	3.27	0.50	4.88	4.60	1.74	2.77
All Classes	**14.84**	**23.67**	**0.40**	**1.65**	**1.52**	**0.15**	**1.35**	**2.18**	**0.33**	**0.56**

Table 11.2.4: Per capita monthly expenditure (Rs. 0.00) and quantity intake (Kgs) of major food items.

Rural Cuddapah

Fractile Classes	Cereals		Pulses		Others: Milk and Milk Products	Edible Oil		Meat, Fish and Eggs	Sugar	
	Q	V	Q	V	V	Q	V	V	Q	V
0-5	10.00	15.31	0.13	0.52	1.13	0.14	1.31	0.63	0.16	0.31
5-10	17.19	19.06	0.28	1.14	1.38	0.15	1.32	1.63	0.16	0.26
0-10	13.59	17.19	0.20	0.83	1.25	0.14	1.32	1.13	0.16	0.29
10-20	12.22	18.78	0.27	1.09	1.11	0.14	1.21	1.06	0.24	0.41
20-30	13.05	20.84	0.27	1.12	1.74	0.12	0.99	2.74	0.10	0.14
30-40	15.50	29.00	0.41	1.92	0.67	0.16	1.45	2.33	0.06	0.19
40-50	15.97	27.94	0.70	2.99	2.50	0.17	1.47	1.79	0.09	0.20
50-60	12.50	21.62	0.45	1.77	3.90	0.15	1.43	4.01	0.47	1.08
60-70	13.81	24.35	0.79	3.07	2.21	0.33	2.65	4.00	0.40	1.06
70-80	13.94	24.08	0.64	2.67	7.53	0.37	3.25	8.22	0.56	1.47
80-90	17.43	28.75	1.02	3.94	5.41	0.38	3.40	0.38	1.64	3.15
90-95	10.06	20.44	1.06	3.84	9.81	0.72	6.31	7.88	1.50	4.46
95-100	15.40	32.95	1.40	5.42	11.75	0.30	2.65	9.80	1.15	3.50
90-100	13.03	27.39	1.25	4.72	10.89	0.49	4.28	8.94	1.31	3.93
All Classes	**14.16**	**23.79**	**0.57**	**2.32**	**3.29**	**0.23**	**2.02**	**5.08**	**0.45**	**1.04**

Table 11.2.5: Per capita monthly expenditure (Rs. 0.00) and quantity intake (Kgs) of major food items.

Urban Cuddapah — All Classes

Fractile Classes	Cereals		Pulses		Milk and Milk Products	Edible Oil		Meat, Fish and Eggs	Sugar	
	Q	V	Q	V	V	Q	V	V	Q	V
0-5	7.86	15.04	0.22	0.88	0.59	0.07	0.57	1.26	0.12	0.28
5-10	10.98	21.13	0.23	0.90	1.14	0.12	1.12	1.41	0.21	0.44
0-10	9.47	18.17	0.22	0.89	0.87	0.10	0.86	1.34	0.17	0.36
10-20	11.22	20.67	0.25	1.08	1.58	0.19	1.52	2.47	0.24	0.52
20-30	11.82	22.83	0.33	1.38	2.43	0.18	1.43	2.92	0.24	0.51
30-40	12.76	24.77	0.31	1.12	2.22	0.22	1.84	3.41	0.35	0.70
40-50	13.31	27.56	0.50	2.05	4.35	0.30	2.56	3.74	0.47	1.05
50-60	12.24	24.05	0.38	1.56	5.17	0.30	2.65	5.05	0.52	1.11
60-70	12.99	24.00	0.50	2.04	6.91	0.37	3.07	2.83	0.63	1.52
70-80	12.79	24.31	0.79	3.08	6.48	0.42	3.49	4.94	0.58	1.25
80-90	13.21	27.67	0.73	2.73	11.06	0.50	4.26	4.16	0.92	2.27
90-95	15.43	32.54	1.19	4.33	11.37	0.59	5.29	5.93	0.90	2.03
95-100	13.17	26.36	0.98	3.88	17.12	0.70	5.95	7.63	1.31	2.89
90-100	14.47	29.90	1.10	4.14	13.82	0.64	5.57	6.65	1.07	2.40
All Classes	**12.27**	**23.99**	**0.49**	**1.92**	**5.07**	**0.31**	**2.58**	**3.61**	**0.49**	**1.10**

CHITTOOR

Table 12.1.1: Per capita monthly expenditure, average size of household and Household Operational Land Holdings (acres)

Rural Chittoor — All Classes

Fractile Classes	Monthly per capita average total expenditure (Rs 0.00)	Average size of house-hold	Household operatio-nal land holdings (in acres)
0 - 5	28.24	5.65	0.95
5 - 10	33.16	5.25	0.76
0 - 10	30.60	5.45	0.86
10- 20	37.20	5.41	1.65
20- 30	41.36	5.05	1.52
30- 40	44.77	4.42	1.64
40- 50	48.44	5.56	2.68
50- 60	52.16	5.66	2.48
60- 70	56.72	5.05	3.01
70- 80	63.76	3.87	2.36
80- 90	76.06	4.23	2.89
90- 95	95.11	5.10	5.25
95-100	149.10	3.40	2.83
90-100	116.71	4.25	4.04
All Classes	**55.00**	**4.89**	**2.31**

Table 12.1.2: Per capita monthly expenditure, average size of household and Household Operational Land Holdings (acres)

Rural Chittoor — Cultivators

Fractile Classes	Monthly per capita average total expenditure (Rs 0.00)	Average size of house-hold	Household operatio-nal land holdings (in acres)
0 - 5	30.93	6.14	4.52
5 - 10	38.42	6.14	5.20
0 - 10	34.60	6.14	4.86
10- 20	42.63	5.86	3.04
20- 30	47.40	6.40	4.89
30- 40	51.11	7.46	3.66
40- 50	53.82	6.00	4.39
50- 60	57.14	6.06	5.42
60- 70	62.65	4.80	4.52
70- 80	71.96	5.46	3.95
80- 90	85.85	4.80	7.14
90 = 95	105.20	3.86	5.62
95-100	168.26	4.57	6.28
90-100	139.44	4.21	5.95
All Classes	**61.33**	**5.72**	**5.73**

Table 12.1.3: Per capita monthly expenditure, average size of household and Household Operational Land Holdings (acres)

Rural Chittoor Fractile Classes	Agricultural Labourers: Monthly per capita average total expenditure (Rs 0.00)	Average size of house-hold	Household operatio-nal land holdings (in acres)
0 - 5	25.49	5.89	0.60
5 - 10	31.15	6.33	1.30
0 - 10	28.42	6.11	0.95
10- 20	34.19	4.72	0.56
20- 30	37.55	5.59	0.60
30- 40	40.49	4.23	0.78
40- 50	43.42	3.55	0.68
50- 60	46.88	4.64	1.27
60- 70	50.15	4.64	1.26
70- 80	54.80	3.00	0.89
80- 90	63.95	3.17	0.85
90- 95	77.96	3.78	1.65
95-100	96.41	3.11	0.83
90-100	86.30	3.44	1.24
All Classes	**46.09**	**4.31**	**0.91**

Table 12.1.4: Per capita monthly expenditure, average size of household and Household Operational Land Holdings (acres)

Rural Chittoor Fractile Classes	Others: Monthly per capita average total expenditure (Rs 0.00)	Average size of house-hold	Household operatio-nal land holdings (in acres)
0 - 5	31.46	6.00	0.33
5 - 10	34.97	6.00	0.00
0 - 10	33.21	6.00	0.17
10- 20	38.63	5.43	0.81
20- 30	42.67	5.43	0.91
30- 40	44.89	3.43	0.46
40- 50	49.07	5.71	0.58
50- 60	54.52	5.50	0.64
60- 70	59.72	4.28	0.18
70- 80	72.49	3.71	0.75
80- 90	94.22	4.14	0.28
90- 95	123.58	4.00	0.00
95-100	168.67	2.33	1.33
90-100	140.20	3.17	0.67
All Classes	**58.13**	**4.67**	**0.55**

Table 12.1.5: Per capita monthly expenditure, average size of household and Household Operational Land Holdings (acres)

Urban Chittoor <u>All Classes</u>

Fractile Classes	Monthly per capita average total expenditure (Rs 0.00)	Average size of household	Household operational land holdings (in acres)
0 - 5	33.76	5.44	0.00
5 - 10	40.49	5.44	0.18
0 - 10	37.13	5.44	0.09
10- 20	46.59	5.88	0.38
20- 30	53.17	5.06	0.35
30- 40	60.62	5.23	0.77
40- 50	67.01	5.65	0.30
50- 60	72.14	4.94	1.29
60- 70	75.67	5.65	0.41
70- 80	83.43	4.41	0.18
80- 90	97.92	4.47	1.15
90- 95	124.29	4.22	1.39
95-100	169.00	3.11	0.02
90-100	143.26	3.67	0.70
All Classes	**70.64**	**5.03**	**0.56**

Table 12.2.1: Per capita monthly expenditure (Rs. 0.00) and quantity intake (Kgs) of major food items.

Rural Chittoor

All Classes

Fractile Classes	Cereals		Pulses		Milk and Milk Products	Edible Oil		Meat, Fish and Eggs	Sugar	
	Q	V	Q	V	V	Q	V	V	Q	V
0-5	12.38	19.18	0.18	0.71	0.20	0.08	0.65	0.48	0.07	0.08
5-10	12.20	19.30	0.20	0.76	0.00	0.11	0.92	1.24	0.11	0.15
0-10	12.28	19.24	0.19	0.73	0.10	0.09	0.78	0.85	0.09	0.10
10-20	12.09	20.75	0.64	0.89	0.19	0.12	1.03	1.29	0.17	0.22
20-30	13.77	22.90	0.29	1.04	0.44	0.23	1.38	1.69	0.14	0.30
30-40	15.10	25.72	0.41	1.53	0.75	0.18	1.41	1.65	0.16	0.33
40-50	15.44	26.99	0.42	1.66	0.97	0.21	1.70	1.89	0.22	0.50
50-60	15.74	27.10	0.44	1.70	0.90	0.22	1.87	1.78	0.21	0.38
60-70	16.54	29.10	0.55	1.88	1.97	0.23	1.90	2.38	0.36	0.83
0-80	16.48	30.82	0.44	1.80	3.08	0.27	2.04	1.88	0.37	0.77
80-90	17.45	32.09	0.64	2.42	2.34	0.29	2.36	2.52	0.29	0.71
90-95	18.82	33.12	0.87	2.53	3.21	0.40	3.31	4.42	0.63	1.64
95-100	16.10	30.35	0.94	3.72	6.78	0.38	3.66	3.64	0.91	2.42
90-100	17.74	32.08	0.89	3.55	1.95	0.39	3.45	4.11	0.74	1.95
All Classes	**15.11**	**26.29**	**0.48**	**1.66**	**1.41**	**0.22**	**1.74**	**1.95**	**0.27**	**0.58**

Table 12.2.2: Per capita monthly expenditure (Rs. 0.00) and quantity intake (Kgs) of major food items.

Rural Chittoor

<u>Cultivators</u>

Fractile Classes	Cereals		Pulses		Milk and Milk Products	Edible Oil		Meat, Fish and Eggs	Sugar	
	Q	V	Q	V	V	Q	V	V	Q	V
0-5	12.26	19.44	0.20	0.95	0.86	0.14	1.08	0.99	0.36	0.38
5-10	12.21	18.13	0.36	1.57	0.84	0.21	1.85	2.33	0.20	0.52
0-10	12.24	18.79	0.28	1.26	0.85	0.18	1.47	1.66	0.28	0.45
10-20	13.03	22.97	0.41	1.58	0.88	0.19	1.39	1.86	0.10	0.29
20-30	14.36	26.04	0.43	1.90	1.64	0.21	1.59	2.44	0.30	0.67
30-40	14.99	26.23	0.43	1.68	1.16	0.21	1.68	1.47	0.29	0.58
40-50	16.48	28.38	0.45	1.80	2.32	0.27	2.24	2.12	0.30	0.68
50-60	16.05	28.08	0.61	2.02	2.43	0.26	2.11	2.48	0.50	1.08
60-70	16.05	30.50	0.39	1.60	3.23	0.29	2.70	2.11	0.44	0.89
70-80	17.16	33.04	0.46	1.87	3.11	0.29	2.36	2.24	0.38	0.93
80-90	20.29	36.51	0.84	3.20	3.52	0.41	3.46	3.18	0.56	1.38
90-95	16.30	30.42	1.09	4.73	5.33	0.40	3.09	2.85	0.69	1.92
95-100	17.81	34.64	0.95	2.69	10.00	0.39	4.47	4.66	1.19	2.88
90-100	17.12	32.71	1.01	3.63	7.86	0.40	3.84	3.83	0.96	2.44
All Classes	**15.60**	**26.79**	**0.51**	**1.98**	**2.45**	**0.26**	**2.18**	**2.26**	**0.39**	**0.86**

Table 12.2.3: Per capita monthly expenditure (Rs. 0.00) and quantity intake (Kgs) of major food items.

Rural Chittoor — Agricultural Labourers

Fractile Classes	Cereals		Pulses		Milk and Milk Products	Edible Oil		Meat, Fish and Eggs	Sugar	
	Q	V	Q	V	V	Q	V	V	Q	V
0-5	11.71	18.42	0.12	0.50	0.06	0.05	0.42	0.32	0.05	0.06
5-10	12.07	20.20	0.24	0.92	0.00	0.11	1.08	0.81	0.07	0.08
0-10	11.90	19.34	0.18	0.72	0.03	0.08	0.76	0.57	0.06	0.07
10-20	12.54	19.82	0.12	0.52	0.12	0.09	0.83	0.98	0.13	0.16
20-30	13.11	22.10	0.20	0.67	-	0.10	0.93	0.99	0.16	0.17
30-40	14.28	23.27	0.21	0.80	-	0.11	1.09	1.64	0.10	0.12
40-50	15.93	26.93	0.32	1.19	0.02	0.12	1.22	1.26	0.10	0.11
50-60	16.10	26.00	0.45	1.50	0.16	0.16	1.51	1.41	0.15	0.23
60-70	15.79	28.70	0.43	1.66	0.38	0.15	1.56	1.48	0.12	0.22
70-80	17.51	30.38	0.41	1.47	-	0.14	1.53	1.67	0.23	0.27
80-90	16.44	32.22	0.59	2.45	0.61	0.20	1.53	1.58	0.18	0.38
90-95	20.03	34.42	0.44	1.58	0.18	0.21	1.71	1.98	0.21	0.31
95-100	16.98	25.43	0.70	2.03	0.18	0.30	2.30	0.00	0.49	0.74
90-100	18.65	30.36	0.56	1.78	0.18	0.25	1.98	1.09	0.34	0.50
All Classes	**14.82**	**25.07**	**0.32**	**1.19**	**0.20**	**0.18**	**1.23**	**1.21**	**0.15**	**0.20**

Table 12.2.4: Per capita monthly expenditure (Rs. 0.00) and quantity intake (Kgs) of major food items.

Rural Chittoor

Fractile Classes	Cereals		Pulses		Others: Milk and Milk Products	Edible Oil		Meat, Fish and Eggs	Sugar	
	Q	V	Q	V	V	Q	V	V	Q	V
0-5	11.44	18.39	0.32	1.24	-	0.07	0.53	1.44	0.11	0.17
5-10	14.72	21.86	0.39	1.22	-	0.12	1.11	0.61	0.06	0.38
0-10	13.08	20.13	0.36	1.23	-	0.09	0.82	1.03	0.08	0.28
10-20	12.06	21.11	0.30	1.21	0.79	0.18	1.47	1.84	0.24	0.53
20-30	12.87	22.75	0.33	1.33	0.20	0.21	1.81	1.71	0.16	0.27
30-40	14.27	24.39	0.44	1.14	0.42	0.13	0.95	1.79	0.18	0.25
40-50	16.30	26.67	0.33	1.34	1.25	0.25	2.09	2.86	0.32	0.69
50-60	18.79	30.85	0.52	1.74	0.45	0.18	1.66	1.82	0.15	0.46
60-70	14.03	27.22	0.61	2.02	1.00	0.28	2.41	3.06	0.27	0.77
70-80	19.23	27.70	0.79	3.84	1.68	0.25	1.71	4.28	0.27	0.73
80-90	12.89	25.45	1.11	4.55	3.08	0.45	3.36	1.43	0.55	1.71
90-95	12.17	23.75	0.96	3.39	5.00	0.19	1.81	2.17	0.58	3.33
95-100	13.00	26.82	1.00	4.04	9.86	0.79	6.07	4.51	1.14	4.14
90-100	12.48	24.57	0.98	3.63	6.79	0.41	3.38	3.03	0.79	3.63
All Classes	**14.58**	**24.93**	**0.54**	**2.05**	**1.46**	**0.23**	**1.90**	**2.21**	**0.27**	**0.79**

Table 12.2.5: Per capita monthly expenditure (Rs. 0.00) and quantity intake (Kgs) of major food items.

Urban Chittoor — All Classes

Fractile Classes	Cereals		Pulses		Milk and Milk Products	Edible Oil		Meat, Fish and Eggs	Sugar	
	Q	V	Q	V	V	Q	V	V	Q	V
0-5	12.47	19.44	0.26	0.98	0.37	0.12	1.11	0.88	0.30	0.65
5-10	12.28	20.98	0.32	1.28	0.91	0.16	1.28	1.73	0.14	0.23
0-10	12.38	20.21	0.29	1.13	0.64	0.14	1.19	1.31	0.22	0.44
10-20	11.21	21.77	0.37	1.70	1.69	0.19	1.38	1.43	0.32	0.65
20-30	12.90	24.61	0.47	2.03	1.92	0.24	2.07	2.67	0.41	0.86
30-40	14.19	26.74	0.67	2.81	3.31	0.31	2.52	3.19	0.43	1.00
40-50	13.38	27.60	0.62	2.59	4.07	0.30	2.52	2.91	0.53	1.18
50-60	12.66	24.66	0.73	2.94	4.46	0.31	2.56	3.72	0.55	1.47
60-70	13.09	26.12	0.92	3.65	4.34	0.34	2.96	3.32	0.55	1.38
70-80	11.81	23.61	0.82	3.37	8.02	0.52	3.37	3.05	2.05	2.25
80-90	13.25	27.96	1.36	6.10	9.45	0.58	4.51	4.57	0.90	2.67
90-95	13.50	28.44	1.27	5.42	10.89	0.78	6.68	5.28	0.91	2.48
95-100	15.41	33.17	1.57	6.49	12.18	1.00	8.66	8.17	1.36	3.42
90-100	14.31	30.45	1.40	5.87	11.43	0.87	7.52	6.51	1.10	2.88
All Classes	**12.87**	**25.16**	**0.73**	**3.52**	**4.56**	**0.36**	**2.88**	**3.12**	**0.66**	**1.39**

HYDERABAD

Levels of Living in a State Setting

Table 13.1.1: Per capita monthly expenditure, average size of household and Household Operational Land Holdings (acres)

Rural Hyderabad — All Classes

Fractile Classes	Monthly per capita average total expenditure (Rs 0.00)	Average size of household	Household operational land holdings (in acres)
0 - 5	25.16	4.70	0.09
5 - 10	30.76	5.60	2.24
0 - 10	28.21	5.15	1.18
10- 20	33.02	4.21	0.93
20- 30	37.37	5.00	9.60
30- 40	41.22	4.00	3.40
40- 50	44.64	5.00	8.20
50- 60	48.69	4.11	6.73
60- 70	52.34	4.53	4.53
70- 80	59.63	3.05	2.63
80- 90	69.42	3.63	8.32
90- 95	84.20	2.70	8.02
95-100	123.20	2.90	17.17
90-100	104.80	2.80	12.60
All Classes	**48.94**	**4.15**	**5.64**

Table 13.1.2: Per capita monthly expenditure, average size of household and Household Operational Land Holdings (acres)

Rural Hyderabad — Cultivators

Fractile Classes	Monthly per capita average total expenditure (Rs 0.00)	Average size of household	Household operational land holdings (in acres)
0 - 5	32.98	7.00	42.49
5 - 10	38.82	5.75	7.59
0 - 10	35.61	6.38	25.05
10- 20	42.31	5.25	7.61
20- 30	44.92	5.13	16.30
30- 40	47.77	4.00	5.96
40- 50	50.25	5.29	8.51
50- 60	52.12	5.00	6.90
60- 70	58.62	3.63	6.71
70- 80	68.98	4.63	12.30
80- 90	82.59	3.25	16.38
90- 95	113.13	3.00	11.19
95-100	139.34	3.50	29.75
90-100	137.24	3.25	20.48
All Classes	**57.11**	**4.57**	**12.57**

Table 13.1.3: Per capita monthly expenditure, average size of household and Household Operational Land Holdings (acres)

Rural Hyderabad — Agricultural Labourers

Fractile Classes	Monthly per capita average total expenditure (Rs 0.00)	Average size of house-hold	Household operational land holdings (in acres)
0 - 5	23.20	4.25	0.00
5 - 10	26.52	5.00	0.25
0 - 10	24.99	4.63	0.14
10- 20	30.21	5.29	0.05
20- 30	31.95	4.00	0.16
30- 40	33.23	4.00	0.28
40- 50	34.35	3.86	0.00
50- 60	37.48	3.57	0.29
60- 70	42.47	3.57	0.00
70- 80	46.79	2.86	0.00
80- 90	54.51	2.43	0.70
90- 95	67.06	2.25	0.00
95-100	83.33	1.00	0.00
90-100	72.07	1.63	0.00
All Classes	**37.33**	**3.57**	**0.14**

Table 13.1.4 : Per capita monthly expenditure, average size of household and Household Operational Land Holdings (acres)

Rural Hyderabad — Others

Fractile Classes	Monthly per capita average total expenditure (Rs 0.00)	Average size of house-hold	Household operational land holdings (in acres)
0 - 5	27.60	6.00	7.98
5 - 10	35.68	6.00	0.00
0 - 10	31.64	6.00	4.00
10- 20	38.12	4.75	2.61
20- 30	39.84	6.25	1.88
30- 40	43.23	4.00	1.64
40- 50	48.57	5.60	2.41
50- 60	53.34	2.75	0.25
60- 70	58.48	4.25	0.51
70- 80	61.12	3.00	0.75
80- 90	64.95	4.00	3.76
90- 95	85.84	4.00	2.52
95-100	89.25	1.00	0.00
90-100	86.53	2.50	1.25
All Classes	**49.16**	**4.34**	**1.91**

Table 13.1.5 : Per capita monthly expenditure, average size of household and Household Operational Land Holdings (acres)

Urban Hyderabad All Classes

Fractile Classes	Monthly per capita average total expenditure (Rs 0.00)	Average size of household	Household operational land holdings (in acres)
0 - 5	39.85	5.95	0.18
5 - 10	48.44	5.84	0.00
0 - 10	44.10	5.89	0.06
10- 20	53.98	5.55	0.00
20- 30	60.20	5.49	0.00
30- 40	64.82	4.97	0.00
40- 50	70.14	4.70	0.00
50- 60	76.61	4.70	0.00
60- 70	83.69	4.50	0.00
70- 80	94.54	4.39	0.04
80- 90	112.15	4.26	0.13
90- 95	139.49	3.89	0.16
95-100	227.96	3.79	8.38
90-100	183.12	3.84	4.26
All Classes	**80.27**	**4.80**	**0.43**

Table 13.2.1: Per capita monthly expenditure (Rs. 0.00) and quantity intake (Kgs) of major food items.

Rural Hyderabad

All Classes

Fractile Classes	Cereals		Pulses		Milk and Milk Products	Edible Oil		Meat, Fish and Eggs	Sugar	
	Q	V	Q	V	V	Q	V	V	Q	V
0-5	9.15	12.98	0.42	1.38	0.00	0.18	1.47	0.37	0.00	0.00
5-10	10.66	14.50	0.42	1.56	0.27	0.30	2.59	0.95	0.04	0.08
0-10	9.97	13.81	0.42	1.48	0.15	0.25	2.08	0.68	0.02	0.04
10-20	11.18	15.69	0.52	1.92	0.29	0.30	2.65	0.74	0.04	0.08
20-30	11.83	16.48	0.51	1.88	0.46	0.32	2.76	1.71	0.12	0.25
30-40	13.88	18.57	0.59	2.26	0.24	0.38	3.10	1.85	0.05	0.15
40-50	12.95	17.79	0.63	2.24	0.89	0.40	3.38	2.17	0.14	0.32
50-60	14.51	21.61	0.57	2.14	0.80	0.35	3.08	2.13	0.22	0.49
60-70	13.62	20.52	0.74	2.56	1.51	0.46	4.10	2.68	0.12	0.50
70-80	13.00	20.09	0.86	3.25	2.06	0.46	3.89	2.05	0.26	0.65
80-90	14.26	21.27	0.75	2.77	3.13	0.47	4.18	3.45	0.45	1.00
90-95	14.79	22.87	1.06	3.81	5.54	0.58	5.63	3.15	0.52	1.37
95-100	13.97	22.43	1.06	4.05	8.79	0.69	5.79	6.41	0.76	2.03
90-100	14.63	22.64	1.06	3.93	7.22	0.64	5.71	4.84	0.64	1.71
All Classes	**12.85**	**18.48**	**0.64**	**2.34**	**1.41**	**0.39**	**3.36**	**2.09**	**0.18**	**0.45**

Table 13.2.2: Per capita monthly expenditure (Rs. 0.00) and quantity intake (Kgs) of major food items.

Rural Hyderabad — Cultivators

Fractile Classes	Cereals		Pulses		Milk and Milk Products	Edible Oil		Meat, Fish and Eggs	Sugar	
	Q	V	Q	V	V	Q	V	V	Q	V
0-5	9.64	13.48	0.61	2.49	0.96	0.38	3.63	1.62	0.14	0.31
5-10	12.39	17.74	0.50	1.93	0.26	0.39	3.26	1.81	0.09	0.91
0-10	10.88	15.40	0.56	2.24	0.65	0.39	3.46	1.71	0.12	0.26
10-20	15.00	19.67	0.54	2.17	0.30	0.33	2.77	1.94	0.05	0.11
20-30	13.17	18.95	0.67	2.37	1.15	0.42	3.60	2.39	0.22	0.50
30-40	13.13	19.08	0.55	2.15	0.97	0.37	3.22	1.64	0.25	0.56
40-50	15.81	24.14	0.69	2.52	0.85	0.37	3.32	2.62	0.24	0.56
50-60	13.37	19.79	0.74	2.65	2.32	0.51	4.56	2.47	0.22	0.81
60-70	15.41	23.09	0.87	3.16	1.29	0.55	4.76	2.78	0.21	0.46
70-80	13.51	20.27	0.76	2.92	3.07	0.51	4.61	3.18	0.59	1.29
80-90	13.85	21.37	1.06	4.00	9.27	0.66	6.14	4.96	0.67	1.26
90-95	16.25	27.00	0.96	3.32	6.96	0.67	5.52	7.75	0.67	1.62
95-100	11.43	17.46	1.11	4.52	9.39	0.68	5.82	5.84	0.86	2.46
90-100	13.65	21.87	1.04	3.97	8.27	0.77	5.68	6.72	0.77	2.07
All Classes	**13.65**	**20.02**	**0.72**	**2.71**	**2.37**	**0.46**	**4.06**	**2.82**	**0.30**	**0.75**

Table 13.2.3: Per capita monthly expenditure (Rs. 0.00) and quantity intake (Kgs) of major food items.

Rural Hyderabad

Agricultural Labourers

Fractile Classes	Cereals		Pulses		Milk and Milk Products	Edible Oil		Meat, Fish and Eggs	Sugar	
	Q	V	Q	V	V	Q	V	V	Q	V
0-5	9.12	13.53	0.13	1.38	0.00	0.12	1.24	0.00	0.00	0.00
5-10	9.25	13.62	0.38	1.25	0.00	0.17	1.25	0.25	0.00	0.00
0-10	9.19	13.58	0.40	1.31	0.00	0.15	1.24	0.14	0.00	0.00
10-20	10.73	14.43	0.12	1.48	0.00	0.28	2.35	0.69	0.00	0.00
20-30	10.25	14.44	0.45	1.58	0.32	0.26	2.27	0.68	0.04	0.08
30-40	12.54	17.57	0.48	1.66	0.18	0.28	2.39	0.55	0.00	0.00
40-50	10.56	14.39	0.45	1.64	0.00	0.28	2.42	1.20	0.00	0.00
50-60	13.20	17.62	0.51	1.89	0.10	0.29	2.42	1.07	0.04	0.09
60-70	12.20	15.34	0.52	1.76	0.00	0.31	2.60	1.14	0.00	0.00
70-80	14.00	20.97	0.47	1.63	0.00	0.31	2.61	2.00	0.00	0.00
80-90	13.11	18.19	0.53	1.85	0.00	0.24	2.15	1.62	0.00	0.04
90-95	18.33	26.22	0.61	2.14	0.00	0.44	3.94	2.50	0.00	0.00
95-100	20.00	30.62	0.81	2.63	0.00	0.44	3.81	3.00	0.00	0.00
90-100	18.85	27.58	0.67	2.29	0.00	0.44	3.90	2.65	0.00	0.00
All Classes	**11.86**	**16.47**	**0.47**	**1.65**	**0.06**	**0.27**	**2.31**	**0.99**	**0.01**	**0.02**

Table 13.2.4: Per capita monthly expenditure (Rs. 0.00) and quantity intake (Kgs) of major food items.

Rural Hyderabad

Fractile Classes	Cereals		Pulses		Others: Milk and Milk Products	Edible Oil		Meat, Fish and Eggs	Sugar	
	Q	V	Q	V	V	Q	V	V	Q	V
0-5	8.33	11.17	0.46	1.84	1.25	0.33	3.25	1.33	0.17	0.36
5-10	11.67	15.42	0.67	2.46	0.00	0.42	3.33	1.25	0.00	0.00
0-10	10.00	13.29	0.56	2.15	0.63	0.38	3.29	1.29	0.08	0.18
10-20	11.84	16.84	0.55	1.83	1.16	0.29	2.55	2.61	0.32	0.70
20-30	13.80	18.76	0.61	2.31	0.00	0.33	2.88	1.92	0.08	0.12
30-40	12.50	16.62	0.72	2.56	0.94	0.47	3.75	3.22	0.13	0.30
40-50	13.21	19.71	0.66	2.23	1.88	0.50	4.29	2.68	0.07	0.43
50-60	14.09	20.82	0.80	2.95	0.61	0.52	4.39	2.84	0.14	0.29
60-70	10.00	14.97	0.76	2.80	1.76	0.38	2.85	1.47	0.12	0.29
70-80	15.42	22.92	0.92	3.83	3.50	0.28	3.33	2.42	0.50	1.33
80-90	13.56	20.72	0.84	2.91	2.25	0.41	3.78	2.91	0.31	0.69
90-95	14.00	24.75	1.00	3.36	3.13	0.44	3.88	0.50	0.38	0.94
95-100	17.25	28.75	1.50	5.63	3.00	0.50	4.25	1.23	0.75	1.80
90-100	16.15	23.15	1.10	3.81	3.10	0.45	3.95	0.65	0.45	1.11
All Classes	**12.55**	**18.24**	**1.71**	**2.57**	**1.41**	**0.40**	**3.46**	**2.21**	**0.91**	**0.47**

Table 13.2.5: Per capita monthly expenditure (Rs. 0.00) and quantity intake (Kgs) of major food items.

Urban Hyderabad — All Classes

Fractile Classes	Cereals		Pulses		Milk and Milk Products	Edible Oil		Meat, Fish and Eggs	Sugar	
	Q	V	Q	V	V	Q	V	V	Q	V
0-5	9.94	17.26	0.32	1.10	0.39	0.35	3.01	2.48	0.27	0.57
5-10	11.06	18.58	0.41	1.47	1.47	0.42	3.65	2.64	0.41	0.88
0-10	10.50	17.91	0.37	1.28	0.93	0.39	3.33	2.56	0.34	0.72
10-20	11.31	19.68	0.49	1.75	1.91	0.43	3.71	3.28	0.45	0.97
20-30	11.80	20.38	0.52	1.89	2.59	0.49	4.06	3.42	0.53	1.13
30-40	12.00	21.22	0.54	1.94	2.65	0.54	4.43	4.08	0.51	1.13
40-50	11.98	21.51	0.67	2.51	3.61	0.55	4.62	4.32	0.58	1.30
50-60	12.81	23.17	0.59	2.20	4.16	0.59	5.69	5.00	0.69	1.52
60-70	12.97	23.91	0.70	2.68	5.29	0.61	5.07	4.71	0.70	1.53
70-80	13.05	24.19	0.70	2.61	6.49	0.69	5.90	5.91	0.86	1.89
80-90	12.53	23.09	0.77	2.89	7.91	0.72	6.32	5.86	0.02	2.00
90-95	13.16	26.27	0.88	3.41	12.55	0.80	6.97	6.81	1.17	2.55
95-100	12.85	26.21	1.05	3.91	18.99	0.89	8.28	8.54	1.37	3.01
90-100	13.01	26.24	0.96	3.66	15.73	0.84	7.62	7.66	1.27	2.78
All Classes	**12.10**	**21.84**	**0.61**	**2.26**	**4.69**	**0.57**	**4.92**	**4.50**	**0.65**	**1.43**

NIZAMABAD

Table 14.1.1: Per capita monthly expenditure, average size of household and Household Operational Land Holdings (acres)

Rural Nizamabad — All Classes

Fractile Classes	Monthly per capita average total expenditure (Rs 0.00)	Average size of house-hold	Household operational land holdings (in acres)
0 - 5	28.15	5.20	3.15
5 - 10	32.49	4.30	2.79
0 - 10	30.12	4.75	2.97
10- 20	38.32	4.70	2.36
20- 30	43.97	4.70	1.74
30- 40	47.95	4.80	3.09
40- 50	51.94	5.63	1.46
50- 60	56.71	4.73	2.78
60- 70	60.90	5.10	3.00
70- 80	66.55	4.95	2.95
80- 90	78.24	3.25	3.22
90- 95	96.32	4.50	6.45
95-100	125.72	5.30	3.30
90-100	112.22	4.90	4.87
All Classes	**58.13**	**4.74**	**2.85**

Table 14.1.2: Per capita monthly expenditure, average size of household and Household Operational Land Holdings (acres)

Rural Nizamabad — Cultivators

Fractile Classes	Monthly per capita average total expenditure (Rs 0.00)	Average size of house-hold	Household operational land holdings (in acres)
0 - 5	29.95	5.20	6.30
5 - 10	33.62	4.80	3.60
0 - 10	31.70	5.00	4.95
10- 20	40.01	5.10	5.04
20- 30	46.20	5.20	3.81
30- 40	49.27	4.67	3.88
40- 50	55.89	5.80	4.09
50- 60	58.11	5.00	5.13
60- 70	61.73	5.20	5.56
70- 80	71.23	4.00	5.03
80- 90	83.17	4.10	6.00
90- 95	94.07	5.00	6.90
95-100	119.06	5.60	9.44
90-100	107.28	5.30	8.17
All Classes	**59.84**	**4.95**	**5.18**

Table 14.1.3: Per capita monthly expenditure, average size of household and Household Operational Land Holdings (acres)

Rural Nizamabad <u>Agricultural Labourers</u>

Fractile Classes	Monthly per capita average total expenditure (Rs 0.00)	Average size of house-hold	Household operatio-nal land holdings (in acres)
0 - 5	25.54	5.00	1.33
5 - 10	30.77	5.33	1.63
0 - 10	28.24	5.17	1.48
10- 20	34.19	4.16	1.00
20- 30	38.91	5.00	1.38
30- 40	40.94	3.83	0.63
40- 50	44.42	4.80	0.30
50- 60	48.36	4.66	1.44
60- 70	50.35	5.00	0.25
70- 80	55.09	4.60	0.34
80- 90	60.38	5.00	0.51
90- 95	68.64	4.00	0.83
95-100	86.81	2.00	0.26
90-100	74.69	3.00	0.55
All Classes	**46.54**	**4.50**	**0.81**

Table 14.1.4: Per capita monthly expenditure, average size of household and Household Operational Land Holdings (acres)

Rural Nizamabad <u>Others</u>

Fractile Classes	Monthly per capita average total expenditure (Rs 0.00)	Average size of house-hold	Household operatio-nal land holdings (in acres)
0 - 5	31.45	5.00	0.50
5 - 10	41.82	2.00	0.00
0 - 10	34.42	3.50	0.25
10- 20	45.82	4.50	0.00
20- 30	51.64	4.75	0.50
30- 40	53.75	5.75	0.00
40- 50	59.72	5.40	0.40
50- 60	64.20	5.50	0.75
60- 70	67.88	5.50	0.62
70- 80	74.99	2.60	0.35
80- 90	115.07	4.50	0.00
90- 95	127.15	3.00	0.00
95-100	139.84	5.50	0.00
90-100	135.36	4.25	0.00
All Classes	**69.38**	**4.59**	**0.29**

Table 14.1.5: Per capita monthly expenditure, average size of household and Household Operational Land Holdings (acres)

Urban Nizamabad <u>All Classes</u>

Fractile Classes	Monthly per capita average total expenditure (Rs 0.00)	Average size of household	Household operational land holdings (in acres)
0 - 5	28.17	4.80	2.90
5 - 10	33.70	5.60	1.92
0 - 10	31.19	5.20	2.41
10- 20	41.66	5.80	2.43
20- 30	46.37	5.44	1.22
30- 40	50.88	4.60	0.59
40- 50	54.49	6.00	1.75
50- 60	59.48	6.60	0.73
60- 70	66.75	5.20	0.83
70- 80	73.34	4.67	1.25
80- 90	82.32	3.90	0.15
90- 95	90.13	4.00	2.20
95-100	129.65	3.60	5.40
90-100	108.85	3.80	3.80
All Classes	**59.24**	**5.11**	**1.41**

Table 14.2.1: Per capita monthly expenditure (Rs. 0.00) and quantity intake (Kgs) of major food items.

Rural Nizamabad — All Classes

Fractile Classes	Cereals		Pulses		Milk and Milk Products	Edible Oil		Meat, Fish and Eggs	Sugar	
	Q	V	Q	V	V	Q	V	V	Q	V
0-5	10.19	14.03	0.38	1.59	0.29	0.21	1.65	0.94	0.08	0.13
5-10	11.21	15.63	0.44	1.86	0.58	0.23	1.86	1.90	0.08	0.19
0-10	10.65	14.75	0.41	1.72	0.42	0.22	1.75	1.37	0.08	0.16
10-20	11.43	16.52	0.48	1.92	1.04	0.29	2.32	2.74	0.15	0.29
20-30	11.26	16.73	0.61	2.40	2.02	0.32	2.26	3.34	0.27	0.61
30-40	12.33	18.48	0.70	2.58	2.70	0.34	2.68	4.22	0.31	0.70
40-50	12.10	19.39	0.62	2.60	2.60	0.33	2.82	3.89	0.29	0.62
50-60	12.88	19.56	0.72	2.82	3.64	0.36	3.02	4.73	0.37	0.82
60-70	12.84	20.57	0.70	2.61	3.67	0.33	2.92	4.58	0.41	0.86
70-80	13.67	21.84	0.79	3.04	3.98	0.37	3.15	5.38	0.44	0.95
80-90	15.41	23.82	0.82	3.27	5.63	0.43	3.86	6.97	0.44	0.97
90-95	14.04	22.09	0.99	3.81	4.14	0.57	5.06	7.84	0.58	1.28
95-100	11.58	20.40	0.61	2.23	5.17	0.37	3.30	6.53	0.45	1.00
90-100	12.71	21.18	0.79	2.95	6.99	0.46	4.11	7.13	0.51	1.13
All Classes	**12.43**	**19.16**	**0.66**	**2.57**	**3.20**	**0.34**	**2.90**	**4.36**	**0.32**	**0.70**

Table 14.2.2: Per capita monthly expenditure (Rs. 0.00) and quantity intake (Kgs) of major food items.

Rural Nizamabad

Cultivators

Fractile Classes	Cereals		Pulses		Milk and Milk Products	Edible Oil		Meat, Fish and Eggs	Sugar	
	Q	V	Q	V	V	Q	V	V	Q	V
0-5	9.81	11.03	0.46	1.94	0.58	0.23	1.85	0.88	0.08	0.14
5-10	11.04	15.49	0.43	1.77	1.20	0.27	2.08	2.06	0.00	0.00
0-10	10.40	13.17	0.44	1.86	0.90	0.25	1.97	1.49	0.04	0.07
10-20	11.98	17.21	0.53	2.08	1.52	0.28	2.27	2.76	0.14	0.30
20-30	11.71	17.19	0.69	2.79	2.63	0.33	2.62	4.52	0.34	0.75
30-40	11.90	18.78	0.68	2.33	2.83	0.29	2.64	3.96	0.39	0.91
40-50	11.68	17.98	0.69	2.69	2.99	0.36	2.98	4.67	0.28	0.63
50-60	13.75	21.13	0.74	2.85	3.98	0.30	2.58	4.37	0.40	0.81
60-70	12.71	20.66	0.69	2.79	4.04	0.36	3.09	4.50	0.37	0.78
70-80	15.55	25.43	0.86	3.50	4.64	0.31	2.61	5.73	0.50	1.20
80-90	16.28	25.03	0.89	3.43	7.85	0.48	4.37	7.43	0.46	1.02
90-95	12.84	20.33	0.99	3.87	9.80	0.60	5.60	7.80	0.68	1.43
95-100	11.75	20.03	0.67	2.57	5.86	0.46	3.98	6.36	0.32	0.75
90-100	12.26	20.17	0.82	3.18	8.48	0.53	5.06	7.32	0.49	1.20
All Classes	**12.65**	**19.37**	**0.69**	**2.72**	**3.85**	**0.35**	**2.96**	**4.56**	**0.33**	**0.66**

Table 14.2.3: Per capita monthly expenditure (Rs. 0.00) and quantity intake (Kgs) of major food items.

Rural Nizamabad — Agricultural Labourers

Fractile Classes	Cereals		Pulses		Milk and Milk Products	Edible Oil		Meat, Fish and Eggs	Sugar	
	Q	V	Q	V	V	Q	V	V	Q	V
0-5	9.00	12.05	0.33	1.38	0.33	0.18	1.73	1.07	0.10	0.16
5-10	11.25	14.81	0.44	1.83	0.31	0.22	1.75	0.63	0.22	0.51
0-10	10.16	13.47	0.39	1.61	0.32	0.20	1.74	0.84	0.16	0.34
10-20	12.02	16.58	0.46	1.91	0.80	0.26	2.08	2.44	0.12	0.24
20-30	11.30	16.78	0.45	1.80	1.10	0.28	2.33	2.50	0.17	0.34
30-40	11.57	17.65	0.63	2.46	0.43	0.33	2.61	3.57	0.18	0.37
40-50	10.71	16.64	0.46	1.72	1.63	0.21	1.92	2.43	0.25	0.49
50-60	13.96	20.62	0.57	2.32	2.14	0.34	2.79	3.39	0.18	0.47
60-70	12.37	19.74	0.56	2.23	2.43	0.30	2.60	3.61	0.37	0.75
70-80	14.78	22.20	0.60	2.28	3.00	0.30	2.75	3.28	0.43	0.85
80-90	14.50	22.47	0.69	2.48	2.52	0.28	2.60	4.52	0.37	0.59
90-95	14.67	21.88	0.54	2.04	2.46	0.25	2.08	3.67	0.29	0.72
95-100	13.25	20.85	1.00	4.12	3.76	0.35	4.67	9.17	0.33	0.76
90-100	14.19	21.54	0.70	2.73	2.89	0.33	2.94	5.50	0.31	0.73
All Classes	**12.48**	**18.64**	**0.52**	**2.12**	**1.69**	**0.28**	**2.41**	**3.20**	**0.25**	**0.51**

Table 14.2.4: Per capita monthly expenditure (Rs. 0.00) and quantity intake (Kgs) of major food items.

Rural Nizamabad

Fractile Classes	Cereals		Pulses		Others: Milk and Products	Edible Oil		Meat, Fish Eggs	Sugar	
	Q	V	Q	V	V	Q	V	V	Q	V
0-5	11.00	16.05	0.40	1.55	0.00	0.25	2.00	2.[illegible]	0.00	0.00
5-10	7.75	13.55	0.69	2.56	2.75	0.38	3.00	4.50	0.25	0.80
0-10	10.07	14.73	0.48	1.83	0.79	0.29	2.28	3.00	0.07	0.23
10-20	11.39	16.34	0.70	2.75	3.06	0.42	3.33	1.67	0.44	0.85
20-30	11.27	17.62	0.71	3.80	3.68	0.53	3.65	4.16	0.32	0.75
30-40	11.22	18.28	0.65	2.67	1.83	0.37	3.04	6.59	0.15	0.34
40-50	11.67	19.37	0.78	3.01	4.89	0.43	3.89	3.56	0.44	1.10
50-60	11.59	17.17	0.89	3.40	4.18	0.48	3.95	7.64	0.55	1.18
60-70	14.01	22.84	0.84	2.92	3.86	0.41	3.64	6.64	0.48	1.00
70-80	15.14	24.18	0.66	2.58	3.85	0.44	4.00	6.08	0.54	1.25
80-90	11.12	19.69	0.79	2.57	6.06	0.25	2.33	8.39	0.56	1.36
90-95	12.17	22.10	0.83	3.20	8.00	0.58	5.17	6.00	0.83	1.76
95-100	10.81	19.23	0.57	1.93	2.73	0.36	3.00	5.00	0.27	1.04
90-100	11.29	20.75	0.67	2.37	4.59	0.44	3.76	5.35	0.47	1.29
All Classes	**11.84**	**19.07**	**0.73**	**2.84**	**3.75**	**0.41**	**3.16**	**5.35**	**0.40**	**0.94**

Table 14.2.5: Per capita monthly expenditure (Rs. 0.00) and quantity intake (Kgs) of major food items.

Urban Nizamabad — All Classes

Fractile Classes	Cereals		Pulses		Milk and Milk Products	Edible Oil		Meat, Fish and Eggs	Sugar	
	Q	V	Q	V	V	Q	V	V	Q	V
0-5	11.04	16.37	0.44	1.71	0.00	0.19	1.54	0.42	0.13	0.19
5-10	11.60	17.34	0.52	1.88	0.38	0.25	2.04	1.66	0.18	0.32
0-10	11.34	16.89	0.49	1.80	0.20	0.22	1.81	1.09	0.15	0.26
10-20	10.40	16.85	0.47	1.76	2.22	0.25	2.09	3.12	0.24	0.75
20-30	10.86	18.62	0.48	1.80	2.80	0.30	2.49	3.61	0.55	0.86
30-40	9.85	17.09	0.44	1.66	2.60	0.30	2.61	4.45	0.37	0.74
40-50	10.54	18.72	0.57	2.20	3.13	0.39	3.26	4.41	0.41	0.83
50-60	10.21	17.86	0.66	2.56	3.91	0.41	3.36	4.70	0.39	0.92
60-70	9.44	16.66	0.58	2.18	4.19	0.41	3.53	5.40	0.53	1.15
70-80	11.79	20.35	0.79	2.67	4.67	0.44	3.82	4.95	0.43	0.95
80-90	11.57	20.23	0.84	3.22	4.46	0.50	4.29	6.38	0.54	1.16
90-95	10.70	18.76	0.99	3.88	7.25	0.63	5.50	8.50	0.63	1.36
95-100	15.11	26.70	0.95	3.90	6.56	0.63	5.61	9.69	0.78	1.83
90-100	12.79	22.53	0.97	3.89	6.92	0.63	5.55	9.07	0.70	1.58
All Classes	**10.79**	**18.40**	**0.66**	**2.31**	**3.37**	**0.38**	**3.18**	**4.53**	**0.42**	**0.89**

MEDAK

Table 15.1.1: Per capita monthly expenditure, average size of household and Household Operational Land Holdings (acres)

Rural Medak All Classes

Fractile Classes	Monthly per capita average total expenditure (Rs 0.00)	Average size of house-hold	Household operatio-nal land holdings (in acres)
0 - 5	27.00	4.93	0.50
5 - 10	27.44	5.57	2.90
0 - 10	27.23	5.25	1.70
10- 20	31.76	4.55	1.80
20- 30	35.07	5.11	3.55
30- 40	38.41	4.37	2.24
40- 50	42.07	4.00	2.01
50- 60	45.46	4.46	2.41
60- 70	47.74	4.00	3.12
70- 80	59.75	4.63	6.05
80- 90	64.54	4.15	5.12
90- 95	73.35	2.57	4.40
95-100	87.39	2.69	8.04
90-100	80.47	2.63	6.15
All Classes	**45.22**	**4.32**	**3.42**

Table 15.1.2: Per capita monthly expenditure, average size of household and Household Operational Land Holdings (acres)

Rural Medak Cultivators

Fractile Classes	Monthly per capita average total expenditure (Rs 0.00)	Average size of house-hold	Household operatio-nal land holdings (in acres)
0 - 5	26.29	6.66	6.00
5 - 10	31.34	6.16	6.50
0 - 10	28.72	6.41	6.25
10- 20	34.99	6.50	6.96
20- 30	38.58	4.92	4.60
30- 40	42.92	4.63	4.23
40- 50	45.74	4.36	4.48
50- 60	46.00	4.54	6.18
60- 70	53.67	4.45	6.36
70- 80	58.56	5.66	11.71
80- 90	66.15	5.16	11.38
90- 95	76.76	2.83	8.94
95-100	97.49	2.80	11.39
90-100	86.12	2.81	10.03
All Classes	**47.61**	**4.98**	**7.26**

Table 15.1.3: Per capita monthly expenditure, average size of household and Household Operational Land Holdings (acres)

Rural Medak — Agricultural Labourers

Fractile Classes	Monthly per capita average total expenditure (Rs 0.00)	Average size of house-hold	Household operational land holdings (in acres)
0 - 5	23.51	6.00	0.25
5 - 10	24.63	4.25	0.00
0 - 10	23.90	5.12	0.12
10- 20	28.12	3.87	0.12
20- 30	31.70	3.87	0.12
30- 40	33.42	4.00	0.53
40- 50	36.20	3.85	0.36
50- 60	39.12	3.28	0.21
60- 70	43.36	4.25	0.35
70- 80	47.37	3.37	0.00
80- 90	56.39	2.87	0.12
90- 95	66.80	2.00	1.41
95-100	73.98	1.50	0.15
90-100	69.88	1.75	0.78
All Classes	**38.21**	**3.63**	**0.27**

Table 15.1.4: Per capita monthly expenditure, average size of household and Household Operational Land Holdings (acres)

Rural Medak — Others

Fractile Classes	Monthly per capita average total expenditure (Rs 0.00)	Average size of house-hold	Household operational land holdings (in acres)
0 - 5	24.26	3.75	0.87
5 - 10	25.05	6.75	0.55
0 - 10	31.20	5.25	0.71
10- 20	32.36	4.25	0.79
20- 30	36.22	4.25	1.91
30- 40	40.12	4.12	1.02
40- 50	42.98	4.00	0.39
50- 60	45.49	4.57	0.07
60- 70	49.89	3.14	0.48
70- 80	55.96	4.86	0.43
80- 90	68.58	2.71	0.45
90- 95	74.56	3.00	0.00
95-100	82.28	2.75	2.50
90-100	78.25	2.88	1.25
All Classes	**45.60**	**4.01**	**0.77**

Table 15.1.5: Per capita monthly expenditure, average size of household and Household Operational Land Holdings (acres)

Urban Medak — All Classes

Fractile Classes	Monthly per capita average total expenditure (Rs 0.00)	Average size of household	Household operational land holdings (in acres)
0 - 5	29.55	8.50	2.34
5 - 10	31.88	5.00	0.50
0 - 10	30.41	6.75	1.42
10- 20	34.90	6.56	0.00
20- 30	39.75	4.44	1.11
30- 40	45.51	6.25	1.89
40- 50	50.84	5.44	1.09
50- 60	55.31	5.22	0.52
60- 70	59.77	6.00	0.24
70- 80	68.64	3.89	3.15
80- 90	86.45	5.00	9.90
90- 95	117.10	4.00	3.00
95-100	189.17	2.00	0.00
90-100	141.12	3.00	1.50
All Classes	**55.89**	**5.25**	**2.10**

Table 15.2.1: Per Capita monthly expenditure (Rs. 0.00) and quantity intake (Kgs) of major food items.

Rural Medak

All Classes

Fractile Classes	Cereals		Pulses		Milk and Milk Products	Edible Oil		Meat, Fish and Eggs	Sugar	
	Q	V	Q	V	V	Q	V	V	Q	V
0-5	10.65	13.00	0.41	1.40	0.33	0.25	2.20	0.51	0.09	0.19
5-10	10.96	13.47	0.41	1.51	0.22	0.24	1.91	0.26	0.07	0.16
0-10	10.82	13.25	0.41	1.46	0.27	0.25	2.04	0.38	0.08	0.17
10-20	11.82	15.11	0.56	2.06	0.15	0.52	2.47	0.32	0.08	0.19
20-30	12.17	16.13	0.44	2.01	0.36	0.31	2.62	0.49	0.07	0.15
30-40	12.53	17.07	0.58	2.13	0.19	0.39	2.81	0.27	0.09	0.19
40-50	13.30	19.04	0.59	2.05	0.46	0.39	3.38	0.80	0.14	0.33
50-60	13.60	20.42	0.54	1.93	0.77	0.35	3.25	0.63	0.23	0.56
60-70	13.56	20.04	0.66	2.28	0.53	0.38	3.16	1.30	0.14	0.31
70-80	14.84	21.87	0.78	2.70	1.68	0.47	4.03	0.66	0.30	0.66
80-90	15.89	23.13	0.89	2.81	2.17	0.56	5.07	0.99	0.32	0.70
90-95	15.42	23.89	1.04	3.84	2.64	0.57	5.25	2.29	0.43	1.08
95-100	15.34	22.65	0.90	3.49	3.10	0.66	5.80	2.30	0.47	1.26
90-100	15.38	23.28	0.97	3.67	2.87	0.61	5.52	2.30	0.45	1.17
All Classes	**13.22**	**18.54**	**0.62**	**2.23**	**0.85**	**0.41**	**3.30**	**0.73**	**0.18**	**0.40**

Table 15.2.2: Per capita monthly expenditure (Rs. 0.00) and quantity intake (Kgs) of major food items.

Rural Medak

Cultivators

Fractile Classes	Cereals		Pulses		Milk and Milk Products	Edible Oil		Meat, Fish and Eggs	Sugar	
	Q	V	Q	V	V	Q	V	V	Q	V
0-5	10.25	12.56	0.46	1.71	0.42	0.24	2.09	0.38	0.09	0.20
5-10	11.65	14.15	0.55	2.27	0.35	1.05	2.68	0.54	0.09	0.22
0-10	10.92	13.32	0.51	1.98	0.39	0.63	2.37	0.46	0.09	0.21
10-20	11.33	15.11	0.45	2.37	0.62	0.31	2.64	0.54	0.10	0.21
20-30	13.56	18.23	0.56	1.99	-	0.34	2.80	0.29	0.04	0.11
30-40	13.05	19.20	0.69	2.36	0.98	0.42	3.68	0.74	0.20	0.47
40-50	13.92	20.75	0.49	1.78	0.88	0.39	3.50	1.00	0.26	0.42
50-60	13.10	19.06	0.72	2.35	0.87	0.39	3.43	1.69	0.18	0.40
60-70	14.29	20.57	0.81	2.98	1.02	0.46	3.90	1.04	0.24	0.52
70-80	14.49	21.33	0.85	2.84	1.99	0.51	4.28	0.55	0.32	0.71
80-90	16.55	23.62	1.10	3.25	3.13	0.63	5.81	1.10	0.42	1.07
90-95	15.29	21.82	0.94	3.58	3.38	0.71	6.12	3.23	0.71	1.85
95-100	13.93	19.43	0.89	3.23	2.04	0.57	4.79	2.53	0.50	1.10
90-100	14.68	20.74	0.92	3.42	2.77	0.65	5.52	2.91	0.61	1.51
All Classes	**13.40**	**18.80**	**0.69**	**2.49**	**1.19**	**0.47**	**3.65**	**0.89**	**0.22**	**0.52**

Table 15.2.3: Per capita monthly expenditure (Rs. 0.00) and quantity intake (Kgs) of major food items

Rural Medak

Agricultural Labourers

Fractile Classes	Cereals		Pulses		Milk and Milk Products	Edible Oil		Meat, Fish and Eggs	Sugar	
	Q	V	Q	V	V	Q	V	V	Q	V
0-5	9.50	10.79	0.27	0.91	-	0.19	1.73	0.29	0.00	0.00
5-10	10.88	12.88	0.41	1.22	-	0.19	1.68	-	0.00	0.00
0-10	10.07	11.66	0.33	1.04	-	0.19	1.71	0.17	0.00	0.00
10-20	11.30	14.32	0.48	1.67	-	0.23	1.65	-	0.06	0.14
20-30	11.94	15.14	0.47	1.56	-	0.29	2.51	0.29	0.00	0.00
30-40	12.66	16.28	0.45	1.53	-	0.31	2.57	0.45	0.03	0.07
40-50	13.52	17.57	0.49	1.61	-	0.30	2.69	0.15	0.00	0.00
50-60	13.78	19.52	0.48	1.82	-	0.35	2.93	0.09	0.00	0.00
60-70	14.56	20.99	0.46	1.69	-	0.32	2.91	-	0.04	0.07
70-80	12.76	19.83	0.44	1.70	0.28	0.31	2.74	0.85	0.00	0.00
80-90	13.39	21.41	0.57	2.13	0.76	0.39	3.72	0.50	0.17	0.39
90-95	16.87	24.75	0.69	2.62	-	0.50	4.72	1.25	0.25	0.41
95-100	15.83	25.83	1.04	3.42	-	0.58	5.58	1.25	0.17	0.38
90-100	16.43	25.21	0.84	2.96	-	0.54	5.09	1.25	0.21	0.40
All Classes	**12.72**	**17.42**	**0.47**	**1.66**	**0.09**	**0.30**	**2.65**	**0.31**	**0.04**	**0.08**

Table 15.2.4: Per capita monthly expenditure (Rs. 0.00) and quantity intake (Kgs) of major food items.

Rural Medak

Fractile Classes	Cereals		Pulses	Others						
				Milk and Milk Products	Edible Oil		Meat, Fish and Eggs	Sugar		
	Q	V	Q	V	V	Q	V	V	Q	V
0-5	10.33	14.01	0.46	1.59	0.00	0.23	2.11	0.40	0.17	0.35
5-10	12.48	15.85	0.38	1.51	0.85	0.35	2.93	1.00	0.11	0.24
0.10	11.71	15.20	0.41	1.54	0.55	0.31	2.64	0.79	0.13	0.28
10-20	11.97	15.71	0.69	2.44	0.18	0.33	2.25	0.29	0.15	0.39
20-30	11.24	15.29	0.52	2.06	0.09	0.51	2.69	-	0.15	0.32
30-40	12.48	16.35	0.62	2.29	0.58	0.36	3.12	1.10	0.14	0.30
40-50	11.79	17.97	0.60	2.04	1.25	0.33	2.95	1.40	0.29	0.66
50-60	13.28	20.58	0.63	2.11	0.31	0.34	3.27	0.20	0.30	0.68
60-70	15.64	22.92	0.64	2.25	0.20	0.43	3.20	0.36	0.05	0.10
70-80	16.47	23.69	0.67	2.30	2.06	0.36	3.10	0.90	0.34	0.78
80-90	15.53	24.50	0.79	3.01	2.53	0.57	4.92	2.24	0.21	0.65
90-95	15.00	23.75	0.99	3.57	1.26	0.50	4.83	1.33	0.29	0.51
95-100	17.00	26.97	0.83	3.63	3.86	0.73	6.91	2.07	0.32	1.01
90-100	15.96	25.29	0.91	3.60	2.50	0.61	5.83	1.68	0.30	0.88
All Classes	**13.34**	**19.10**	**0.63**	**2.28**	**0.92**	**0.40**	**3.23**	**0.81**	**0.20**	**0.49**

Table 15.2.5: Per capita monthly expenditure (Rs. 0.00) and quantity intake (Kgs) of major food items.

Urban Medak — All Classes

Fractile Classes	Cereals		Pulses		Milk and Milk Products	Edible Oil		Meat, Fish and Eggs	Sugar	
	Q	V	Q	V	V	Q	V	V	Q	V
0-5	10.44	16.08	0.43	1.49	1.01	0.35	3.22	0.41	0.15	0.36
5-10	8.80	13.37	0.38	1.19	0.00	0.35	3.30	0.13	0.15	0.32
0-10	9.83	15.08	0.41	1.38	0.64	0.35	3.25	0.31	0.15	0.35
10-20	10.46	15.64	0.39	1.29	0.78	0.30	2.67	0.37	0.27	0.57
20-30	9.55	14.87	0.49	1.79	1.20	0.38	3.35	1.09	0.28	0.64
30-40	11.01	17.73	0.51	1.87	0.78	0.33	2.81	1.73	0.14	0.33
40-50	12.68	20.48	0.62	2.19	1.23	0.43	3.80	1.78	0.33	0.73
50-60	12.06	19.95	0.60	2.34	1.53	0.50	4.51	1.86	0.45	0.99
60-70	11.74	20.43	0.60	2.42	1.56	0.49	4.21	1.64	0.30	0.67
70-80	13.13	23.04	0.86	3.27	2.67	0.76	6.74	1.59	0.59	1.39
80-90	12.44	19.10	0.97	3.76	6.90	0.62	6.24	6.28	0.74	1.73
90-95	20.00	33.32	0.88	3.53	8.72	0.63	5.67	2.06	0.88	1.98
95-100	14.38	27.80	1.88	7.81	21.87	0.84	6.84	1.81	1.75	4.03
90-100	18.12	31.48	1.21	4.96	13.11	0.70	6.06	1.98	1.17	2.66
All Classes	**11.72**	**19.00**	**0.62**	**2.33**	**2.40**	**0.46**	**4.15**	**1.79**	**0.39**	**0.88**

MAHBUBNAGAR

Table 16.1.1: Per capita monthly expenditure, average size of household and Household Operational Land Holdings (acres)

Rural Mahbubnagar — All Classes

Fractile Classes	Monthly per capita average total expenditure (Rs 0.00)	Average size of house-hold	Household operational land holdings (in acres)
0 - 5	24.27	5.58	2.45
5 - 10	29.89	6.21	2.98
0 - 10	27.23	5.89	2.71
10- 20	33.62	6.58	3.95
20- 30	38.61	5.00	3.55
30- 40	41.91	5.57	5.68
40- 50	45.04	5.16	7.01
50- 60	48.42	5.11	5.21
60- 70	51.90	5.11	3.88
70- 80	57.06	4.89	5.29
80- 90	67.69	4.42	6.72
90- 95	87.46	4.16	12.97
95-100	127.80	4.74	11.84
90-100	108.94	4.45	12.41
All Classes	**50.16**	**5.36**	**5.81**

Table 16.1.2: Per capita monthly expenditure, average size of household and Household Operational Land Holdings (acres)

Rural Mahbubnagar — Cultivators

Fractile Classes	Monthly per capita average total expenditure (Rs 0.00)	Average size of house-hold	Household operational land holdings (in acres)
0 - 5	26.66	6.29	6.44
5 - 10	32.62	6.86	5.56
0 - 10	29.77	6.57	6.03
10- 20	37.88	7.20	10.73
20- 30	42.16	5.73	10.26
30- 40	44.66	5.20	10.92
40- 50	46.89	5.43	8.63
50- 60	49.92	6.67	9.67
60- 70	54.90	5.60	9.80
70- 80	61.88	4.87	9.93
80- 90	79.20	5.27	21.48
90- 95	98.09	5.14	10.69
95-100	140.86	6.00	23.16
90-100	121.12	5.57	16.93
All Classes	**55.42**	**5.81**	**11.48**

Table 16.1.3: Per capita monthly expenditure, average size of household and Household Operational Land Holdings (acres)

Rural Mahbubnagar <u>Agricultural Labourers</u>

Fractile Classes	Monthly per capita average total expenditure (Rs 0.00)	Average size of house-hold	Household operatio-nal land holdings (in acres)
0 - 5	22.25	5.14	1.23
5 - 10	27.84	6.43	3.54
0 - 10	25.36	5.79	2.37
10- 20	30.64	6.07	2.06
20- 30	34.41	5.36	1.66
30- 40	38.52	4.36	2.57
40- 50	41.12	5.13	2.36
50- 60	45.00	4.43	2.26
60- 70	49.62	3.93	1.18
70- 80	53.86	4.86	0.87
80- 90	59.59	4.14	2.03
90- 95	70.63	2.86	7.14
95-100	112.31	2.86	0.69
90-100	91.47	2.86	0.91
All Classes	**43.89**	**4.70**	**1.83**

Table 16.1.4: Per capita monthly expenditure, average size of household and Household Operational Land Holdings (acres)

Rural Mahbubnagar <u>Others</u>

Fractile Classes	Monthly per capita average total expenditure (Rs 0.00)	Average size of house-hold	Household operatio-nal land holdings (in acres)
0 - 5	26.50	6.00	0.18
5 - 10	30.57	5.00	1.20
0 - 10	28.35	5.50	0.72
10- 20	34.37	6.67	1.20
20- 30	38.34	4.33	1.65
30- 40	41.98	5.75	2.01
40- 50	45.38	5.88	1.65
50- 60	49.16	5.78	3.41
60- 70	53.08	4.22	1.86
70- 80	56.69	4.62	2.91
80- 90	66.02	4.44	2.09
90- 95	83.72	3.80	1.41
95-100	121.97	3.60	5.18
90-100	102.33	3.70	3.29
All Classes	**49.40**	**5.07**	**2.08**

Table 16.1.5: Per capita monthly expenditure, average size of household and Household Operational Land Holdings (acres)

Urban Mahbubnagar All Classes

Fractile Classes	Monthly per capita average total expenditure (Rs 0.00)	Average size of household	Household operational land holdings (in acres)
0 - 5	30.57	8.00	1.52
5 - 10	39.52	4.60	0.60
0 - 10	34.25	6.30	1.01
10- 20	42.17	4.50	0.72
20- 30	45.29	7.50	3.08
30- 40	49.98	7.13	1.57
40- 50	55.23	4.88	2.83
50- 60	60.49	4.88	0.88
60- 70	67.59	4.88	0.98
70- 80	74.35	5.25	10.13
80- 90	84.84	5.88	2.82
90- 95	110.79	3.60	0.00
95-100	154.97	4.60	0.00
90-100	135.57	4.10	0.00
All Classes	**62.53**	**5.51**	**2.37**

Table 16.2.1: Per capita monthly expenditure (Rs. 0.00) and quantity intake (Kgs) of major food items.

Rural Mahbubnagar — All Classes

Fractile Classes	Cereals		Pulses		Milk and Milk Products	Edible Oil		Meat, Fish and Eggs	Sugar	
	Q	V	Q	V	V	Q	V	V	Q	V
0-5	10.97	19.99	0.17	0.69	0.17	0.10	0.82	0.55	0.04	0.06
5-10	11.86	16.54	0.26	1.05	0.19	0.11	1.10	0.71	0.06	0.14
0-10	11.44	18.17	0.21	0.88	0.18	0.10	0.91	0.63	0.05	0.10
10-20	12.29	17.36	0.23	0.92	0.35	0.13	1.13	0.96	0.12	0.23
20-30	13.35	19.83	0.37	1.50	0.30	0.20	1.43	0.80	0.17	0.39
30-40	14.45	21.69	0.33	1.39	0.36	0.16	1.43	1.18	0.16	0.41
40-50	14.84	22.51	0.37	1.60	0.87	0.15	1.36	1.18	0.25	0.57
50-60	14.93	23.06	0.46	1.85	0.62	0.21	1.78	1.71	0.26	0.60
60-70	16.97	25.60	0.46	1.91	0.65	0.20	1.75	1.40	0.25	0.55
70-80	17.34	26.67	0.59	2.31	0.80	0.22	2.02	1.87	0.18	0.43
80-90	17.04	26.34	0.54	2.30	2.38	0.27	2.38	2.87	0.34	0.88
90-95	19.22	26.64	0.47	1.71	2.41	0.28	2.43	4.80	0.26	0.66
95-100	18.27	27.64	1.36	5.51	4.87	0.42	3.60	2.07	0.82	2.07
90-100	18.71	27.17	0.95	3.77	3.72	0.35	3.05	3.35	0.56	1.41
All Classes	**14.91**	**22.49**	**0.43**	**1.77**	**0.94**	**0.19**	**1.67**	**1.52**	**0.22**	**0.53**

Table 16.2.2: Per capita monthly expenditure (Rs. 0.00) and quantity intake (Kgs) of major food items.

Rural Mahbubnagar — Cultivators

Fractile Classes	Cereals		Pulses		Milk and Milk Products	Edible Oil		Meat, Fish and Eggs	Sugar	
	Q	V	Q	V	V	Q	V	V	Q	V
0-5	12.66	14.41	0.24	0.94	0.00	0.13	1.18	0.86	0.04	0.08
5-10	11.69	16.87	0.35	1.22	0.32	0.14	1.30	0.77	0.11	0.22
0-10	12.15	15.70	0.30	1.09	0.17	0.13	1.24	0.82	0.08	0.15
10-20	13.38	19.43	0.35	1.47	0.68	0.18	1.48	0.87	0.23	0.50
20-30	14.76	21.90	0.35	1.41	0.51	0.15	1.33	1.28	0.22	0.55
30-40	14.32	21.48	0.41	1.80	1.15	0.17	1.53	1.43	0.33	0.71
40-50	14.19	22.51	0.42	1.66	0.57	0.17	1.43	1.27	0.23	0.48
50-60	16.62	25.84	0.44	1.88	0.97	0.22	1.86	1.44	0.30	0.56
60-70	16.70	24.24	0.55	2.08	1.08	0.22	1.91	1.30	0.21	0.49
70-80	19.02	29.33	0.62	2.52	1.88	0.30	2.67	1.78	0.40	1.00
80-90	17.54	25.93	0.61	2.57	2.90	0.28	2.33	3.25	0.31	0.81
90-95	15.28	21.14	0.40	1.59	3.82	0.27	2.31	4.98	0.41	0.91
95-100	18.48	27.77	1.98	7.80	5.05	0.47	4.05	3.14	0.95	2.75
90-100	17.00	24.71	1.25	4.93	4.48	0.38	3.24	3.99	0.70	1.90
All Classes	**15.45**	**22.89**	**0.52**	**2.09**	**1.37**	**0.22**	**1.87**	**1.69**	**0.29**	**0.69**

Table 16.2.3: Per capita monthly expenditure (Rs. 0.00) and quantity intake (Kgs) of major food items.

Rural Mahbubnagar — Agricultural Labourers

Fractile Classes	Cereals		Pulses		Milk and Milk Products	Edible Oil		Meat, Fish and Eggs	Sugar	
	Q	V	Q	V	V	Q	V	V	Q	V
0-5	10.42	11.90	0.13	0.54	0.42	0.11	0.87	0.47	0.05	0.06
5-10	13.17	16.21	0.18	0.68	0.34	0.07	0.57	0.27	0.07	0.14
0-10	11.94	14.29	0.16	0.62	0.38	0.08	0.70	0.36	0.06	0.10
10-20	12.40	17.15	0.16	0.70	0.09	0.10	0.94	0.55	0.03	0.06
20-30	13.03	18.44	0.23	0.92	0.10	0.11	0.91	0.95	0.11	0.22
30-40	13.80	20.26	0.34	1.45	0.18	0.16	1.42	1.06	0.09	0.17
40-50	14.32	21.41	0.25	1.05	0.00	0.11	0.96	0.73	0.09	0.17
50-60	15.16	22.59	0.36	1.54	0.29	0.16	1.50	1.54	0.12	0.25
60-70	16.58	24.85	0.51	2.16	0.35	0.21	1.98	1.49	0.19	0.40
70-80	17.73	24.95	0.54	2.21	0.00	0.15	1.46	2.25	0.07	0.13
80-90	17.34	30.47	0.79	3.10	0.47	0.20	1.83	2.61	0.21	0.42
90-95	15.77	22.85	0.21	0.89	0.75	0.13	1.22	3.05	0.05	0.10
95-100	26.45	37.38	0.91	4.25	1.50	0.42	3.75	5.13	0.67	1.02
90-100	21.11	30.12	0.56	2.57	1.13	0.28	2.48	4.09	0.36	0.56
All Classes	**14.88**	**21.63**	**0.36**	**1.50**	**0.25**	**0.15**	**1.32**	**1.38**	**0.12**	**0.22**

Table 16.2.4: Per capita monthly expenditure (Rs. 0.00) and quantity intake (Kgs) of major food items.

Rural Mahbubnagar

Fractile Classes	Cereals		Pulses		Others: Milk and Milk Products	Edible Oil		Meat, Fish and Eggs	Sugar	
	Q	V	Q	V	V	Q	V	V	Q	V
0-5	9.43	37.56	0.25	1.00	0.10	0.11	1.05	0.67	0.04	0.08
5-10	11.00	19.19	0.26	1.13	0.00	0.10	0.79	0.92	0.09	0.18
0-10	10.15	29.21	0.25	1.06	0.05	0.10	0.93	0.78	0.06	0.13
10-20	12.01	17.28	0.22	0.91	0.46	0.14	1.15	1.22	0.13	0.26
20-30	11.05	16.85	0.44	1.73	0.26	0.38	1.92	0.96	0.26	0.55
30-40	13.00	20.52	0.39	1.70	0.90	0.22	1.79	1.23	0.21	0.68
40-50	14.30	20.91	0.43	1.67	1.04	0.20	1.80	0.53	0.29	0.87
50-60	16.14	25.46	0.39	1.59	0.38	0.17	1.50	2.05	0.29	0.70
60-70	15.67	24.01	0.34	1.45	0.96	0.20	1.63	1.24	0.28	0.68
70-80	14.41	21.53	0.37	1.45	1.09	0.27	2.63	1.78	0.28	0.78
80-90	16.24	26.80	0.46	2.07	3.26	0.24	2.01	3.09	0.33	0.99
90-95	16.58	23.34	0.42	1.59	2.94	0.32	3.14	1.18	0.41	1.04
95-100	21.11	32.65	0.88	3.36	5.44	0.44	3.96	1.78	0.57	1.67
90-100	18.78	27.87	0.64	2.45	4.16	0.38	3.54	1.48	0.49	1.35
All Classes	**13.95**	**22.98**	**0.38**	**1.56**	**1.13**	**0.22**	**1.80**	**1.40**	**0.25**	**0.66**

Table 16.2.5: Per capita monthly expenditure (Rs. 0.00) and quantity intake (Kgs) of major food items.

Urban Mahbubnagar — All Classes

Fractile Classes	Cereals		Pulses		Milk and Milk Products	Edible Oil		Meat, Fish and Eggs	Sugar	
	Q	V	Q	V	V	Q	V	V	Q	V
0-5	9.30	14.29	0.44	1.60	0.45	0.22	1.84	1.44	0.21	0.43
5-10	14.07	21.45	0.19	0.83	0.72	0.15	1.12	0.49	0.17	0.38
0-10	11.26	17.23	0.34	1.29	0.56	0.19	1.54	1.05	0.19	0.49
10-20	13.33	19.50	0.44	1.92	0.85	0.19	1.48	1.88	0.20	0.43
20-30	13.53	20.40	0.49	1.81	0.88	0.25	1.83	1.90	0.25	0.54
30-40	13.26	18.92	0.49	1.87	1.00	0.27	2.12	1.18	0.33	0.73
40-50	13.91	20.73	0.62	2.33	0.84	0.29	2.35	2.40	0.26	0.55
50-60	11.26	17.29	0.67	2.56	1.87	0.40	2.98	3.12	0.68	1.51
60-70	12.27	19.71	0.60	2.36	2.29	0.37	2.99	3.13	0.50	1.20
70-80	14.20	23.43	0.76	2.93	3.87	0.50	3.81	3.12	0.71	1.57
80-90	11.63	19.76	0.84	3.19	4.67	0.52	4.72	4.09	0.80	1.75
90-95	11.67	19.43	1.08	4.06	4.89	0.64	4.94	8.16	0.89	1.97
95-100	15.74	31.03	1.48	4.67	8.46	0.86	7.35	4.33	1.28	2.76
90-100	13.95	25.94	1.30	4.40	6.89	0.76	6.29	6.01	1.11	2.41
All Classes	**12.76**	**20.11**	**0.63**	**2.38**	**2.26**	**0.36**	**2.89**	**2.67**	**0.48**	**1.06**

NALGONDA

Table 17.1.1: Per capita monthly expenditure, average size of household and Household Operational Land Holdings (acres)

Rural Nalgonda — All Classes

Fractile Classes	Monthly per capita average total expenditure (Rs 0.00)	Average size of house-hold	Household operatio-nal land holdings (in acres)
0 - 5	27.71	5.48	1.59
5 - 10	34.53	5.05	2.62
0 - 10	30.98	5.26	2.10
10- 20	41.43	5.00	2.75
20- 30	47.88	5.17	3.51
30- 40	53.67	5.75	6.84
40- 50	59.32	5.05	4.85
50- 60	66.27	4.60	5.10
60- 70	74.25	4.33	5.03
70- 80	87.27	4.45	6.71
80- 90	105.96	4.79	9.14
90- 95	134.15	3.95	4.19
95-100	247.74	3.76	6.58
90-100	189.54	3.86	5.40
All Classes	**72.45**	**4.73**	**5.40**

Table 17.1.2: Per capita monthly expenditure, average size of household and Household Operational Land Holdings (acres)

Rural Nalgonda — Cultivators

Fractile Classes	Monthly per capita average total expenditure (Rs 0.00)	Average size of house-hold	Household operatio-nal land holdings (in acres)
0 - 5	31.21	5.75	5.87
5 - 10	39.84	4.38	8.62
0 - 10	34.94	5.06	7.24
10- 20	48.80	5.06	9.21
20- 30	56.28	6.06	10.25
30- 40	63.55	5.38	13.33
40- 50	70.88	5.12	7.78
50- 60	80.20	5.06	10.48
60- 70	90.73	5.13	11.00
70- 80	98.11	4.31	10.31
80- 90	115.89	4.94	14.07
90- 95	138.78	5.00	14.60
95-100	310.59	4.63	7.86
90-100	221.33	4.81	11.26
All Classes	**86.31**	**5.09**	**10.47**

Table 17.1.3 Per capita monthly expenditure, average size of household and Household Operational Land Holdings (acres)

Rural Nalgonda — Agricultural Labourers

Fractile Classes	Monthly per capita average total expenditure (Rs 0.00)	Average size of household	Household operational land holdings (in acres)
0 - 5	24.37	4.86	1.46
5 - 10	30.24	5.57	1.00
0 - 10	27.51	5.21	1.25
10- 20	37.12	3.86	1.12
20- 30	41.36	5.15	1.96
30- 40	45.28	5.15	1.08
40- 50	49.60	4.62	1.62
50- 60	54.36	4.23	0.85
60- 70	59.67	4.54	1.13
70- 80	66.70	3.38	0.41
80- 90	75.20	4.00	1.32
90- 95	88.81	3.29	0.49
95-100	183.21	3.00	0.51
90-100	133.86	3.14	0.50
All Classes	**55.85**	**4.32**	**1.12**

Table 17.1.4 Per capita monthly expenditure, average size of household and Household Operational Land Holdings (acres)

Rural Nalgonda — Others

Fractile Classes	Monthly per capita average total expenditure (Rs 0.00)	Average size of household	Household operational land holdings (in acres)
0 - 5	28.54	5.43	0.98
5 - 10	37.45	6.00	0.84
0 - 10	33.22	5.71	0.91
10- 20	43.28	5.67	1.53
20- 30	50.05	5.58	1.56
30- 40	54.04	4.75	5.94
40- 50	59.65	5.15	4.17
50- 60	66.11	4.75	2.38
60- 70	73.71	3.89	1.23
70- 80	88.36	3.50	2.00
80- 90	111.98	4.75	1.43
90- 95	135.75	3.71	0.48
95-100	186.71	3.14	2.42
90-100	159.11	3.43	1.44
All Classes	**69.47**	**4.71**	**2.26**

Table 17.1.5 : Per capita monthly expenditure, average size of household and Household Operational Land Holdings (acres)

Urban Nalgonda <u>All Classes</u>

Fractile Classes	Monthly per capita average total expen-diture (Rs 0.00)	Average size of house-hold	Household operatio-nal land holdings (in acres)
0 - 5	29.19	5.33	1.66
5 - 10	43.18	7.00	3.99
0 - 10	37.13	6.16	2.83
10- 20	54.45	5.25	13.86
20- 30	74.26	4.25	0.04
30- 40	79.88	4.00	0.12
40- 50	85.36	6.00	0.50
50- 60	98.68	4.75	0.05
60- 70	107.29	5.00	0.00
70- 80	126.14	4.50	0.00
80- 90	147.55	4.75	0.52
90- 95	183.11	4.00	0.00
95-100	246.74	3.75	0.00
90-100	213.54	3.83	0.00
All Classes	**98.44**	**4.74**	**1.42**

Table 17.2.1: Per capita monthly expenditure (Rs. 0.00) and quantity intake (Kgs) of major food items.

Rural Nalgonda — All Classes

Fractile Classes	Cereals		Pulses		Milk and Milk Products	Edible Oil		Meat, Fish and Eggs	Sugar	
	Q	V	Q	V	V	Q	V	V	Q	V
0-5	11.53	15.65	0.15	0.61	0.48	0.12	1.17	0.53	0.08	0.20
5-10	14.04	20.20	0.29	1.10	1.85	0.22	1.38	1.13	0.11	0.23
0-10	12.74	17.83	0.21	0.85	1.14	0.17	1.27	0.82	0.09	0.21
10-20	15.28	23.11	0.36	1.44	1.76	0.22	1.76	1.95	0.16	0.41
20-30	14.07	21.78	0.44	1.67	2.57	0.21	1.75	2.37	0.21	0.53
30-40	16.74	26.50	0.35	1.44	3.06	0.24	2.04	1.63	0.19	0.49
40-50	16.02	26.16	0.42	1.62	3.84	0.25	2.07	2.46	0.22	0.63
50-60	16.69	30.40	0.61	2.43	3.52	0.28	2.38	2.53	0.32	0.90
60-70	18.72	32.93	0.52	2.47	3.94	0.28	2.47	3.42	0.25	0.78
70-80	18.54	31.52	0.65	2.32	5.80	0.34	2.43	5.33	0.40	1.12
80-90	16.40	27.50	0.63	2.24	5.96	0.32	2.44	4.37	0.48	1.25
90-95	16.42	29.29	0.76	2.70	6.48	0.43	3.88	4.48	0.42	1.22
95-100	19.47	34.24	0.91	3.49	7.20	0.54	4.66	8.94	0.82	2.18
90-100	17.91	31.70	0.83	3.08	6.83	0.49	4.26	6.66	0.62	1.69
All Classes	**16.19**	**26.52**	**0.49**	**1.97**	**3.72**	**0.27**	**2.23**	**3.03**	**0.28**	**0.77**

Table 17.2.2: Per capita monthly expenditure (Rs. 0.00) and quantity intake (Kgs) of major food items.

Rural Nalgonda — Cultivators

Fractile Classes	Cereals		Pulses		Milk and Milk Products	Edible Oil		Meat, Fish and Eggs	Sugar	
	Q	V	Q	V	V	Q	V	V	Q	V
0-5	13.72	18.98	0.17	0.64	1.85	0.17	1.43	0.86	0.06	0.14
5-10	17.29	25.83	0.50	1.96	4.77	0.38	3.09	3.01	0.31	0.72
0-10	15.26	21.94	0.31	1.21	3.11	0.26	2.15	1.79	0.17	0.39
10-20	15.69	23.36	0.46	1.85	3.63	0.27	2.29	2.30	0.24	0.61
20-30	15.02	23.80	0.32	1.27	5.19	0.25	2.22	2.00	0.21	0.63
30-40	16.09	27.65	0.56	1.93	5.83	0.27	2.23	2.02	0.26	0.84
40-50	18.01	31.28	0.48	1.95	4.69	0.32	2.87	2.13	0.42	1.28
50-60	19.03	31.71	0.44	1.56	4.78	0.24	2.11	2.94	0.26	0.77
60-70	19.02	33.57	0.87	3.00	8.26	0.42	2.49	6.80	0.55	1.57
70-80	16.96	28.25	0.58	2.14	6.52	0.29	2.42	4.80	0.46	1.21
80-90	19.08	34.15	0.62	2.07	7.41	0.39	2.72	3.82	0.56	1.45
90-95	17.46	30.58	0.80	2.90	7.37	0.38	3.40	4.93	0.42	1.17
95-100	18.92	34.30	0.55	1.90	7.84	0.39	3.57	5.69	0.69	2.11
90-100	18.16	32.36	0.68	2.42	7.70	0.38	2.48	5.28	0.55	1.62
All Classes	**17.18**	**28.70**	**0.53**	**1.92**	**5.68**	**0.31**	**2.49**	**3.32**	**0.36**	**1.02**

Table 17.2.3: Per capita monthly expenditure (Rs. 0.00) and quantity intake (Kgs) of major food items.

Rural Nalgonda

<u>Agricultural Labourers</u>

Fractile Classes	Cereals		Pulses		Milk and Milk Products	Edible Oil		Meat, Fish and Eggs	Sugar	
	Q	V	Q	V	V	Q	V	V	Q	V
0-5	11.12	14.82	0.23	0.91	0.00	0.09	1.00	1.35	0.05	0.11
5-10	12.90	17.60	0.13	0.51	0.58	0.06	0.52	0.10	0.05	0.10
0-10	12.07	16.31	0.18	0.70	0.31	0.08	0.74	0.68	0.05	0.10
10-20	14.68	21.03	0.14	0.57	0.19	0.27	1.40	1.00	0.08	0.18
20-30	15.44	22.92	0.34	1.29	1.60	0.16	1.33	1.39	0.06	0.23
30-40	14.63	24.01	0.19	0.66	0.82	0.16	1.45	1.66	0.07	0.20
40-50	15.08	22.71	0.29	1.12	1.28	0.16	0.29	1.98	0.18	0.50
50-60	18.11	28.96	0.27	1.05	1.36	0.23	2.00	2.39	0.05	0.10
60-70	18.19	29.14	0.26	1.30	0.73	0.19	1.67	1.96	0.08	0.21
70-80	20.14	34.09	0.38	1.62	1.95	0.29	2.50	2.64	0.24	0.64
80-90	19.44	34.23	0.49	2.38	2.53	0.28	2.47	3.45	0.11	0.39
90-95	18.80	31.92	0.23	0.91	0.33	0.21	1.90	3.89	0.09	0.20
95-100	17.36	26.99	1.24	4.83	6.62	0.62	5.10	12.63	0.76	1.66
90-100	18.11	29.57	0.71	2.78	3.33	0.41	3.43	8.06	0.41	0.90
All Classes	**16.29**	**25.67**	**0.31**	**1.28**	**1.32**	**0.21**	**1.73**	**2.31**	**0.12**	**0.32**

Table 17.2.4: Per capita monthly expenditure (Rs. 0.00) and quantity intake (Kgs) of major food items.

Rural Nalgonda

Fractile Classes	Cereals		Pulses		Others: Milk and Milk Products	Edible Oil		Meat, Fish and Eggs	Sugar	
	Q	V	Q	V	V	Q	V	V	Q	V
0-5	9.87	14.18	0.13	0.59	0.59	0.18	1.66	0.17	0.12	0.36
5-10	14.76	20.71	0.62	2.69	2.14	0.20	1.60	1.76	0.14	0.32
0-10	12.44	47.61	0.39	1.69	1.41	0.19	1.63	1.01	0.13	0.34
10-20	13.99	21.63	0.46	1.56	2.17	0.22	1.63	1.99	0.24	0.58
20-30	14.37	23.44	0.54	2.30	4.19	0.25	2.03	3.21	0.31	0.72
30-40	15.26	25.38	0.51	1.82	2.99	0.24	1.96	1.31	0.38	0.91
40-50	15.25	26.00	0.42	1.79	3.85	0.26	2.18	2.92	0.22	0.71
50-60	15.08	30.87	1.01	4.07	3.18	0.28	2.29	2.67	0.36	0.97
60-70	15.84	26.90	0.68	4.00	4.04	0.27	2.36	5.68	0.34	0.94
70-80	17.51	30.26	0.71	5.59	3.47	0.31	2.75	5.25	0.36	0.95
80-90	13.11	21.95	0.77	2.73	3.52	0.33	2.69	5.29	0.37	0.96
90-95	14.50	25.75	0.81	3.12	3.62	0.54	4.61	7.20	0.66	1.87
95-100	18.82	31.45	1.02	3.91	9.57	0.66	5.78	6.07	0.89	2.35
90-100	16.48	28.36	0.91	3.48	6.34	0.59	5.12	6.68	0.76	2.09
All Classes	**14.71**	**24.65**	**0.62**	**2.70**	**3.37**	**0.28**	**2.36**	**3.32**	**0.33**	**0.86**

Table 17.2.5: Per capita monthly expenditure (Rs. 0.00) and quantity intake (Kgs) of major food items.

Urban Nalgonda — All Classes

Fractile Classes	Cereals		Pulses		Milk and Milk Products	Edible Oil		Meat, Fish and Eggs	Sugar	
	Q	V	Q	V	V	Q	V	V	Q	V
0-5	10.78	14.19	0.48	1.65	2.81	0.22	2.19	1.56	0.31	0.87
5-10	11.43	19.93	0.37	1.57	4.52	0.24	2.04	3.05	0.31	0.67
0-10	11.15	17.45	0.42	1.61	3.78	0.23	2.11	2.41	0.31	0.76
10-20	12.62	22.19	0.52	1.86	3.98	0.31	2.60	4.95	0.67	1.47
20-30	13.09	22.68	0.41	1.78	3.91	0.28	2.40	5.56	0.79	1.90
30-40	12.53	22.23	0.59	2.48	6.78	0.34	2.81	4.50	0.53	1.12
40-50	11.42	20.16	0.54	2.41	8.46	0.44	3.69	5.02	0.88	1.96
50-60	12.84	25.46	0.58	2.32	17.50	0.46	4.14	5.42	0.71	1.99
60-70	12.60	23.26	0.86	3.41	13.20	0.60	4.67	12.15	1.20	3.73
70-80	11.04	21.79	0.61	2.99	5.00	0.42	3.31	9.12	0.94	3.31
80-90	12.11	23.34	0.92	3.79	14.82	0.55	4.63	4.57	0.68	1.73
90-95	12.25	25.56	2.04	7.57	24.15	0.79	6.52	3.02	1.21	3.37
95-100	13.27	24.16	2.00	8.25	18.87	1.41	12.61	9.96	1.39	3.14
90-100	13.74	24.89	2.02	7.89	21.63	1.09	9.43	6.34	1.29	3.26
All Classes	**12.17**	**22.13**	**0.74**	**3.03**	**9.64**	**0.47**	**3.95**	**5.60**	**0.76**	**2.01**

WARANGAL

Table 18.1.1: Per capita monthly expenditure, average size of household and Household Operational Land Holdings (acres)

Rural Warangal — All Classes

Fractile Classes	Monthly per capita average total expenditure (Rs 0.00)	Average size of house-hold	Household operatio-nal land holdings (in acres)
0 - 5	19.94	5.05	3.17
5 - 10	23.92	4.37	0.71
0 - 10	21.79	4.71	1.94
10- 20	27.36	4.87	1.38
20- 30	30.07	4.11	0.86
30- 40	34.39	4.41	1.07
40- 50	39.08	3.89	2.07
50- 60	43.94	4.14	3.12
60- 70	48.04	3.76	2.33
70- 80	53.68	3.76	4.27
80- 90	61.92	4.38	5.73
90- 95	76.32	3.79	4.08
95-100	109.29	3.00	10.98
90-100	90.89	3.39	7.53
All Classes	**43.75**	**4.14**	**3.04**

Table 18.1.2: Per capita monthly expenditure, average size of household and Household Operational Land Holdings (acres)

Rural Warangal — Cultivators

Fractile Classes	Monthly per capita average total expenditure (Rs 0.00)	Average size of house-hold	Household operatio-nal land holdings (in acres)
0 - 5	20.72	6.38	6.16
5 - 10	24.72	5.00	4.38
0 - 10	22.48	5.69	5.27
10- 20	30.79	4.94	4.06
20- 30	36.82	4.88	8.27
30- 40	43.30	5.13	6.74
40- 50	46.09	4.31	4.94
50- 60	50.05	4.25	4.41
60- 70	55.09	4.40	5.21
70- 80	60.21	4.81	7.32
80- 90	68.67	4.50	8.50
90- 95	82.98	2.63	5.63
95-100	121.80	3.63	23.44
90-100	105.50	3.13	14.53
All Classes	**49.08**	**4.60**	**6.43**

Table 18.1.3: Per capita monthly expenditure, average size of household and Household Operational Land Holdings (acres)

Rural Warangal — Agricultural Labourers

Fractile Classes	Monthly per capita average total expenditure (Rs 0.00)	Average size of house-hold	Household operational land holdings (in acres)
0 - 5	18.40	4.17	0.17
5 - 10	22.30	3.33	0.25
0 - 10	20.13	3.75	0.21
10- 20	24.85	4.33	0.17
20- 30	26.20	5.09	0.16
30- 40	28.33	4.45	0.41
40- 50	29.89	3.42	0.33
50- 60	32.30	4.18	0.18
60- 70	34.55	4.27	0.45
70- 80	38.70	2.91	0.30
80- 90	46.21	3.00	0.21
90- 95	53.64	2.33	0.00
95-100	75.30	2.33	0.00
90-100	64.47	2.33	0.00
All Classes	**32.56**	**3.76**	**0.24**

Table 18.1.4: Per capita monthly expenditure, average size of household and Household Operational Land Holdings (acres)

Rural Warangal — Others

Fractile Classes	Monthly per capita average total expenditure (Rs 0.00)	Average size of house-hold	Household operational land holdings (in acres)
0 - 5	24.03	5.60	0.20
5 - 10	28.98	4.40	0.20
0 - 10	26.21	5.00	0.20
10- 20	31.48	4.20	0.50
20- 30	31.55	4.70	0.07
30- 40	39.47	3.40	0.30
40- 50	42.47	3.09	1.00
50- 60	45.74	4.10	0.35
60- 70	48.73	3.40	0.20
70- 80	54.38	3.50	5.68
80- 90	64.60	3.60	0.65
90- 95	80.06	4.20	0.30
95-100	104.34	2.80	0.42
90-100	89.77	3.50	0.36
All Classes	**46.22**	**3.84**	**0.93**

Table 18.1.5: Per capita monthly expenditure, average size of household and Household Operational Land Holdings (acres)

Urban Warangal <u>All Classes</u>

Fractile Classes	Monthly per capita average total expenditure (Rs 0.00)	Average size of household	Household operational land holdings (in acres)
0 - 5	23.64	5.71	0.43
5 - 10	28.30	5.14	0.00
0 - 10	25.84	5.43	0.21
10- 20	35.35	4.71	0.14
20- 30	40.60	4.64	0.31
30- 40	43.95	4.93	0.03
40- 50	46.93	4.38	0.00
50- 60	51.60	4.50	0.31
60- 70	55.85	4.21	0.06
70- 80	61.37	3.93	0.53
80- 90	72.72	3.50	0.00
90- 95	94.95	4.14	2.57
95-100	123.62	3.00	0.06
90-100	106.99	3.57	1.31
All Classes	**51.69**	**4.38**	**0.29**

Table 18.2.1 : Per capita monthly expenditure (Rs. 0.00) and quantity intake (Kgs) of major food items.

Rural Warangal

All Classes

Fractile Classes	Cereals		Pulses		Milk and Milk Products	Edible Oil		Meat, Fish and Eggs	Sugar	
	Q	V	Q	V	V	Q	V	V	Q	V
0-5	8.42	11.52	0.28	0.74	0.27	0.13	1.12	0.66	0.04	0.09
5-10	12.02	14.01	0.36	1.02	0.60	0.14	1.31	0.61	-	-
0-10	10.09	12.67	0.32	0.87	0.17	0.13	1.21	0.64	0.02	0.05
10-20	11.81	15.37	0.31	0.90	0.63	0.19	1.73	0.93	0.07	0.18
20-30	13.30	16.99	0.38	1.17	0.71	0.23	1.85	1.12	0.10	0.21
30-40	15.11	20.66	0.35	1.32	0.48	0.21	1.99	1.23	0.09	0.22
40-50	14.85	21.34	0.40	1.16	0.98	0.28	2.51	0.97	0.20	0.45
50-60	15.93	24.57	0.40	1.28	1.04	0.31	2.85	1.88	0.26	0.60
60-70	16.75	25.87	0.60	1.78	1.60	0.31	2.86	2.34	0.28	0.62
70-80	16.26	26.77	0.64	1.83	2.33	0.33	3.10	2.10	0.29	0.65
80-90	17.08	28.48	0.76	2.18	3.08	0.45	4.18	4.19	0.47	1.07
90-95	20.90	33.60	0.90	2.94	2.50	0.45	4.06	3.05	0.53	1.19
95-100	20.53	38.25	1.09	3.44	6.31	0.56	5.17	4.46	0.86	2.01
90-100	20.74	35.65	0.98	3.16	4.18	0.50	4.55	3.67	0.67	1.55
All Classes	**14.94**	**22.29**	**0.50**	**1.52**	**1.44**	**0.28**	**2.61**	**1.85**	**0.23**	**0.53**

Table 18.2.2: Per capita monthly expenditure (Rs. 0.00) and quantity intake (Kgs) of major food items.

Cultivators

Rural Warangal

Fractile Classes	Cereals		Pulses		Milk and Milk Products	Edible Oil		Meat, Fish and Eggs	Sugar	
	Q	V	Q	V	V	Q	V	V	Q	V
0-5	8.98	13.37	0.24	0.64	0.50	0.13	1.12	0.78	0.08	0.17
5-10	11.97	13.99	0.52	1.43	2.61	0.16	1.52	0.45	0.02	0.06
0-10	10.30	13.64	0.36	0.99	1.43	0.15	1.30	0.64	0.05	0.12
10-20	13.10	16.78	0.38	1.12	0.99	0.22	1.92	0.75	0.15	0.35
20-30	15.05	20.96	9.35	1.68	0.47	0.25	2.40	1.25	0.15	0.35
30-40	15.13	22.81	0.39	1.22	1.30	0.29	2.66	1.40	0.25	0.58
40-50	16.55	24.64	0.51	1.75	2.45	0.31	2.86	1.98	0.26	0.59
50-60	17.43	26.48	0.72	1.95	3.13	0.26	2.51	1.90	0.32	0.72
60-70	17.44	28.18	0.50	1.56	2.30	0.36	3.36	2.46	0.39	0.90
70-80	16.14	27.66	0.88	2.55	4.06	0.47	4.28	2.61	0.51	1.15
80-90	17.68	26.81	0.96	2.87	1.86	0.45	4.18	6.04	0.49	1.12
90-95	22.95	38.17	0.93	2.86	6.17	0.50	4.59	3.95	0.62	1.39
95-100	16.83	32.29	1.00	2.67	6.31	0.53	5.16	4.86	0.97	2.27
90-100	19.40	34.76	0.97	2.71	6.25	0.52	4.92	4.48	0.82	1.90
All Classes	**15.50**	**23.54**	**0.59**	**1.79**	**2.25**	**0.32**	**2.93**	**2.22**	**0.32**	**0.72**

Table 18.2.3: Per capita monthly expenditure (Rs. 0.00) and quantity intake (Kgs) of major food items.

Rural Warangal

Agricultural Labourers

Fractile Classes	Cereals		Pulses		Milk and Milk Products	Edible Oil		Meat, Fish and Eggs	Sugar	
	Q	V	Q	V	V	Q	V	V	Q	V
0-5	7.84	8.62	0.26	0.70	-	0.11	1.06	0.76	-	-
5-10	9.55	12.17	0.35	0.90	-	0.13	1.15	1.00	-	-
0-10	8.60	10.20	0.30	0.79	-	0.12	1.10	0.86	-	-
10-20	12.87	14.54	0.25	0.78	-	0.15	1.43	0.45	-	-
20-30	12.05	14.68	0.27	0.86	-	0.19	1.77	1.16	-	-
30-40	12.41	16.53	0.36	1.00	0.08	0.15	1.35	1.13	0.04	0.08
40-50	14.12	17.78	0.37	1.23	-	0.18	1.56	0.95	0.01	0.12
50-60	14.91	19.43	0.29	0.85	-	0.17	1.63	1.24	0.05	0.11
60-70	17.13	21.30	0.26	0.75	0.16	0.17	1.56	1.15	0.02	0.05
70-80	16.37	19.37	0.41	1.09	0.19	0.23	2.23	1.17	0.06	0.14
80-90	17.64	27.18	0.49	1.63	-	0.28	2.49	2.63	0.09	0.21
90-95	14.93	21.54	0.61	1.87	0.07	0.32	2.86	2.82	0.17	0.38
95-100	26.57	41.96	0.50	1.50	-	0.34	3.11	3.36	0.21	0.48
90-100	20.75	31.75	0.55	1.69	-	0.33	2.98	3.09	0.36	0.80
									0.29	0.64
All Classes	**14.23**	**18.50**	**0.34**	**1.02**	**0.04**	**0.19**	**1.73**	**1.28**	**0.06**	**0.14**

Table 18.2.4: Per capita monthly expenditure (Rs. 0.00) and quantity intake (Kgs) of major food items.

Rural Warangal

Fractile Classes	Cereals		Pulses		Others: Milk and Milk Products	Edible Oil		Meat, Fish and Eggs	Sugar	
	Q	V	Q	V	V	Q	V	V	Q	V
0-5	7.43	11.99	0.29	0.69	0.11	0.16	1.43	0.43	0.07	0.16
5-10	11.86	16.08	0.36	1.05	0.45	0.25	2.45	0.50	0.18	0.41
0-10	9.38	13.79	0.32	0.85	0.26	0.20	1.88	0.46	0.12	0.27
10-20	11.50	16.04	0.41	1.23	1.50	0.33	2.11	1.62	0.15	0.37
20-30	12.60	20.13	0.35	1.03	0.80	0.26	2.39	1.39	0.15	0.37
30-40	15.41	22.97	0.47	1.51	1.26	0.32	2.29	0.38	0.18	0.39
40-50	14.91	23.27	0.49	1.42	0.47	0.35	3.28	2.12	0.26	0.59
50-60	17.10	28.32	0.30	0.90	0.44	0.36	3.26	1.99	0.23	0.52
60-70	13.85	23.66	0.71	2.13	1.12	0.31	2.96	2.64	0.35	0.77
70-80	14.26	24.94	0.59	1.61	2.29	0.39	3.83	1.70	0.26	0.55
80-90	18.75	32.42	0.56	1.63	3.24	0.47	4.47	4.67	0.49	1.07
90-95	19.67	37.50	0.81	2.85	2.90	0.43	3.67	0.95	0.48	1.07
95-100	25.71	50.14	1.45	5.81	0.07	0.64	5.52	3.02	0.79	1.86
90-100	22.09	42.56	1.06	4.04	4.17	0.51	4.41	1.78	0.60	1.38
All Classes	**14.68**	**24.17**	**0.51**	**1.57**	**1.47**	**0.34**	**3.01**	**1.81**	**0.27**	**0.60**

Table 18.2.5: Per capita monthly expenditure (Rs. 0.00) and quantity intake (Kgs) of major food items.

Urban Warangal

All Classes

Fractile Classes	Cereals		Pulses		Milk and Milk Products	Edible Oil		Meat, Fish and Eggs	Sugar	
	Q	V	Q	V	V	Q	V	V	Q	V
0-5	8.52	13.01	0.21	0.67	1.50	0.17	1.59	1.37	0.13	0.27
5-10	8.69	11.87	0.28	0.69	1.33	0.24	2.29	1.46	0.39	0.81
0-10	8.61	12.47	0.24	0.78	1.42	0.20	1.92	1.41	0.25	0.53
10-20	10.92	16.35	0.38	1.31	0.68	0.22	2.04	2.94	0.26	0.56
20-30	11.92	19.81	0.35	1.25	3.94	0.30	2.60	2.05	0.37	0.81
30-40	11.42	20.23	0.50	1.68	2.17	0.26	2.46	2.72	0.33	0.72
40-50	12.05	21.46	0.43	1.52	2.02	0.21	1.99	2.37	0.46	0.98
50-60	14.08	24.13	0.54	1.85	3.20	0.32	3.00	2.68	0.46	0.99
60-70	12.63	23.03	0.57	1.44	4.67	0.40	3.90	2.42	0.63	1.38
70-80	13.51	24.94	0.69	2.11	5.81	0.50	4.87	2.77	0.58	1.28
80-90	16.08	31.83	0.78	2.68	6.73	0.50	4.66	4.29	0.67	1.46
90-95	16.90	31.38	1.07	3.36	8.62	0.64	5.83	4.46	0.90	1.96
95-100	17.00	32.33	0.90	3.08	7.35	0.69	6.40	4.19	1.00	2.21
90-100	16.94	31.67	1.00	3.24	8.09	0.66	6.07	4.34	0.94	2.07
All Classes	**12.54**	**21.88**	**0.52**	**1.71**	**3.62**	**0.34**	**3.20**	**2.71**	**0.47**	**1.02**

KHAMMAM

Table 19.1.1: Per capita monthly expenditure, average size of household and Household Operational Land Holdings (acres)

Rural Khammam — All Classes

Fractile Classes	Monthly per capita average total expenditure (Rs 0.00)	Average size of house-hold	Household operatio-nal land holdings (in acres)
0 - 5	25.71	5.46	0.55
5 - 10	30.26	4.38	0.92
0 - 10	27.73	4.92	0.74
10- 20	34.99	5.42	2.22
20- 30	42.02	5.27	1.58
30- 40	48.41	6.16	2.34
40- 50	54.15	5.23	2.09
50- 60	60.38	6.32	2.15
60- 70	66.61	5.68	1.82
70- 80	76.39	5.00	2.55
80- 90	94.25	3.88	2.14
90- 95	120.10	4.77	11.35
95-100	185.68	3.85	14.19
90-100	149.37	4.31	12.79
All Classes	**62.91**	**5.21**	**5.08**

Table 19.1.2: Per capita monthly expenditure, average size of household and Household Operational Land Holdings (acres)

Rural Khammam — Cultivators

Fractile Classes	Monthly per capita average total expenditure (Rs 0.00)	Average size of house-hold	Household operatio-nal land holdings (in acres)
0 - 5	30.20	5.80	2.73
5 - 10	34.18	5.40	5.07
0 - 10	32.12	5.60	3.90
10- 20	41.42	6.22	5.27
20- 30	48.54	7.12	6.70
30- 40	56.18	6.75	6.50
40- 50	63.30	6.62	6.20
50- 60	69.60	6.50	6.89
60- 70	77.88	5.12	3.20
70- 80	91.45	5.62	5.99
80- 90	113.19	4.44	12.72
90- 95	147.92	5.00	11.95
95-100	224.05	3.80	23.86
90-100	180.80	4.40	17.91
All Classes	**73.66**	**5.79**	**7.71**

Table 19.1.3: Per capita monthly expenditure, average size of household and Household Operational Land Holdings (acres)

Rural Khammam — Agricultural Labourers

Fractile Classes	Monthly per capita average total expenditure (Rs 0.00)	Average size of house-hold	Household operatio-nal land holdings (in acres)
0 - 5	25.39	6.20	0.74
5 - 10	27.52	5.20	0.62
0 - 10	26.36	5.70	0.68
10- 20	29.18	3.63	0.00
20- 30	33.39	5.11	0.61
30- 40	38.15	5.11	0.82
40- 50	42.40	4.89	0.00
50- 60	48.39	6.22	0.00
60- 70	52.02	4.22	0.42
70- 80	56.09	5.67	0.28
80- 90	60.86	5.50	0.99
90- 95	77.36	5.40	0.97
95-100	109.46	3.60	0.68
90-100	90.20	4.50	0.81
All Classes	**47.78**	**5.07**	**0.46**

Table 19.1.4: Per capita monthly expenditure, average size of household and Household Operational Land Holdings (acres)

Rural Khammam — Others

Fractile Classes	Monthly per capita average total expenditure (Rs 0.00)	Average size of house-hold	Household operatio-nal land holdings (in acres)
0 - 5	27.84	5.25	0.74
5 - 10	35.92	3.75	1.39
0 - 10	31.21	4.50	1.08
10- 20	42.71	6.00	0.42
20- 30	50.51	4.88	0.20
30- 40	57.00	5.25	1.05
40- 50	62.94	6.11	0.31
50- 60	67.40	5.75	0.69
60- 70	73.15	4.63	0.19
70- 80	84.96	3.88	0.27
80- 90	100.23	2.75	0.00
90- 95	119.98	3.00	1.26
95-100	157.70	4.25	8.76
90-100	142.09	3.63	5.00
All Classes	**66.92**	**4.75**	**0.90**

Table 19.1.5: Per capita monthly expenditure, average size of household and Household Operational Land Holdings (acres)

Urban Khammam All Classes

Fractile Classes	Monthly per capita average total expenditure (Rs 0.00)	Average size of household	Household operational land holdings (in acres)
0 - 5	28.00	6.60	1.52
5 - 10	41.04	5.60	1.79
0 - 10	33.99	6.10	1.65
10- 20	47.36	4.50	0.36
20- 30	56.02	5.75	0.46
30- 40	63.59	6.25	0.00
40- 50	71.32	7.25	6.02
50- 60	79.30	4.00	0.00
60- 70	88.75	4.38	1.88
70- 80	102.35	5.50	0.00
80- 90	129.91	4.38	0.00
90- 95	155.66	5.40	0.38
95-100	262.96	2.60	0.13
90-100	190.53	4.00	0.20
All Classes	**82.35**	**5.20**	**1.04**

Table 19.2.1: Per capita monthly expenditure (Rs. 0.00) and quantity intake (Kgs) of major food items.

Rural Khammam — All Classes

Fractile Classes	Cereals		Pulses		Milk and Milk Products	Edible Oil		Meat, Fish and Eggs	Sugar	
	Q	V	Q	V	V	Q	V	V	Q	V
0-5	13.52	14.73	0.04	0.18	0.06	0.11	1.86	1.02	0.09	0.22
5-10	12.74	16.54	0.24	0.99	0.39	0.18	1.57	0.87	0.11	0.27
0-10	13.17	15.54	0.13	0.54	0.21	0.14	1.29	0.96	0.10	0.24
10-20	14.15	18.09	0.24	1.06	1.58	0.23	1.85	1.37	0.17	0.39
20-30	14.25	21.29	0.37	1.51	1.61	0.25	2.04	1.55	0.21	0.47
30-40	14.70	26.51	0.45	1.71	2.93	0.25	2.18	1.46	0.31	0.76
40-50	15.30	25.60	0.52	2.20	2.14	0.30	2.52	2.03	0.43	0.95
50-60	16.22	28.24	0.50	1.89	2.09	0.29	2.55	2.66	0.39	0.95
60-70	16.62	28.99	0.63	2.47	4.39	0.32	2.81	3.17	0.71	1.59
70-80	16.95	32.94	0.62	3.22	3.44	0.35	3.04	3.67	0.55	1.32
80-90	17.02	31.11	0.91	3.76	6.03	0.42	3.72	5.52	0.73	1.60
90-95	19.61	33.38	1.10	4.69	7.65	0.65	5.19	5.18	1.11	2.77
95-100	20.62	40.68	1.06	4.60	10.35	0.68	5.89	4.79	1.28	3.61
90-100	20.06	38.64	1.08	4.65	8.85	0.66	5.50	5.00	1.19	3.14
All Classes	**15.74**	**26.23**	**0.53**	**2.21**	**3.15**	**0.31**	**2.67**	**2.61**	**0.46**	**1.09**

Table 19.2.2: Per capita monthly expenditure (Rs. 0.00) and quantity intake (Kgs) of major food items.

Rural Khammam

Cultivators

Fractile Classes	Cereals		Pulses		Milk and Milk Products	Edible Oil		Meat, Fish and Eggs	Sugar	
	Q	V	Q	V	V	Q	V	V	Q	V
0-5	13.45	16.90	0.17	0.83	0.48	0.14	1.17	0.79	0.03	0.09
5-10	15.00	18.09	0.30	1.32	0.83	0.28	2.24	1.76	0.06	0.14
0-10	14.20	17.47	0.23	1.06	0.65	0.21	1.69	1.26	0.04	0.12
10-20	15.54	20.48	0.29	1.24	2.25	0.25	2.07	1.86	0.23	0.53
20-30	17.37	23.70	0.54	2.31	4.28	0.25	2.00	1.93	0.29	0.65
30-40	16.19	27.36	0.60	2.62	2.69	0.30	2.52	2.42	0.33	0.73
40-50	18.49	29.26	0.60	2.33	5.15	0.28	2.31	2.68	0.62	1.30
50-60	18.98	34.32	0.54	2.40	4.50	0.28	2.42	2.33	0.48	1.14
60-70	17.44	32.49	0.56	2.30	3.61	0.37	3.15	4.98	0.63	1.49
70-80	18.82	34.27	0.93	4.13	10.13	0.31	2.80	4.78	0.63	1.40
80-90	21.62	34.74	1.05	4.46	9.47	0.67	5.15	3.57	1.17	2.73
90-95	19.40	39.22	1.08	4.86	7.54	0.56	4.74	7.28	1.16	3.07
95-100	23.42	44.82	1.42	6.37	18.68	0.95	8.50	4.00	2.05	6.09
90-100	21.14	41.64	1.23	5.51	12.35	0.73	6.36	5.86	1.55	4.37
All Classes	**17.78**	**28.89**	**0.63**	**2.71**	**5.19**	**0.35**	**2.91**	**3.01**	**0.56**	**1.34**

Table 19.2.3: Per capita monthly expenditure (Rs. 0.00) and quantity intake (Kgs) of major food items.

Rural Khammam

Agricultural Labourers

Fractile Classes	Cereals		Pulses		Milk and Milk Products	Edible Oil		Meat, Fish and Eggs	Sugar	
	Q	V	Q	V	V	Q	V	V	Q	V
0-5	13.55	14.23	0.06	0.26	0.15	0.13	1.10	1.21	0.11	0.26
5-10	13.65	16.15	0.04	0.17	-	0.10	1.14	0.88	0.04	0.08
0-10	13.60	15.11	0.05	0.22	0.08	0.12	1.12	1.06	0.08	0.18
10-20	12.93	15.97	0.22	0.83	-	0.19	1.59	0.48	0.11	0.26
20-30	14.02	17.96	0.21	0.89	1.25	0.18	1.47	1.02	0.14	0.30
30-40	14.78	20.25	0.30	1.32	1.58	0.20	1.61	1.33	0.20	0.38
40-50	15.16	21.77	0.37	1.43	1.82	0.23	1.97	1.35	0.22	0.48
50-60	15.15	25.37	0.32	1.30	1.58	0.21	1.97	0.79	0.22	0.50
60-70	12.91	21.96	0.56	2.16	2.68	0.27	2.21	2.50	0.24	0.55
70-80	14.84	24.75	0.27	1.16	0.65	0.21	1.90	1.51	0.30	0.67
80-90	16.37	30.30	0.52	2.09	1.02	0.31	2.73	2.57	0.32	1.08
90-95	15.30	33.70	0.19	0.74	1.33	0.20	1.72	2.45	0.20	0.45
95-100	17.17	34.88	0.67	2.59	0.17	0.29	2.83	7.11	0.41	0.83
90-100	16.04	34.17	0.38	1.48	0.87	0.24	2.16	4.31	0.28	0.60
All Classes	**14.65**	**22.87**	**0.31**	**1.26**	**1.15**	**0.21**	**1.86**	**1.68**	**0.21**	**0.50**

Table 19.2.4: Per capita monthly expenditure (Rs. 0.00) and quantity intake (Kgs) of major food items.

Rural Khammam

Fractile Classes	Cereals		Pulses		Others: Milk and Milk Products	Edible Oil		Meat, Fish and Eggs	Sugar	
	Q	V	Q	V	V	Q	V	V	Q	V
0-5	11.24	15.71	0.10	0.40	1.07	0.16	1.39	0.90	0.19	0.48
5-10	11.67	14.80	0.40	1.67	3.10	0.37	2.98	1.13	0.37	1.07
0-10	11.42	15.33	0.22	0.93	1.92	0.25	2.05	1.00	0.26	0.73
10-20	10.83	30.56	0.44	1.66	1.96	0.33	2.82	2.00	0.39	0.89
20-30	12.56	23.37	0.55	2.04	2.34	0.30	2.50	1.28	0.58	1.46
30-40	16.57	30.23	0.46	1.55	1.56	0.35	3.15	2.44	0.60	1.24
40-50	17.36	28.81	0.60	2.27	1.20	0.35	3.10	3.08	0.54	1.24
50-60	13.80	25.83	0.74	2.86	4.52	0.32	2.86	3.85	0.78	1.73
60-70	14.35	27.83	0.92	3.65	4.66	0.43	3.81	4.72	0.80	1.80
70-80	14.19	25.97	0.61	5.07	4.81	0.42	3.60	5.66	0.79	1.95
80-90	18.23	27.91	1.27	4.89	4.30	0.70	6.12	4.27	1.05	2.23
90-95	14.17	27.42	1.50	6.07	4.79	0.75	6.47	3.75	0.92	2.62
95-100	16.88	33.11	0.65	2.71	2.44	0.47	4.17	6.50	0.68	1.72
90-100	15.76	30.75	1.00	4.10	3.41	0.59	5.12	5.36	0.78	2.09
All Classes	**14.38**	**26.79**	**0.64**	**2.68**	**2.88**	**0.38**	**3.32**	**3.20**	**0.63**	**1.46**

Table 19.2.5: Per capita monthly expenditure (Rs. 0.00) and quantity intake (Kgs) of major food items.

Urban Khammam

All Classes

Fractile Classes	Cereals		Pulses		Milk and Milk Products	Edible Oil		Meat, Fish and Eggs	Sugar	
	Q	V	Q	V	V	Q	V	V	Q	V
0-5	14.85	20.55	0.39	1.58	3.64	0.42	3.39	0.45	0.38	0.86
5-10	14.29	16.21	0.50	2.09	2.95	0.23	1.86	0.71	0.23	0.48
0-10	14.59	18.56	0.44	1.81	3.32	0.34	2.69	0.57	0.31	0.69
10-20	12.78	22.90	0.33	1.48	3.35	0.29	2.33	1.88	0.35	0.74
20-30	13.13	25.90	0.54	2.33	3.29	0.32	2.67	2.40	0.49	1.28
30-40	12.04	23.42	0.64	2.53	3.94	0.47	3.98	3.28	0.49	1.10
40-50	14.00	24.87	0.95	3.92	4.28	0.53	4.43	4.98	0.51	1.32
50-60	11.75	23.31	0.89	4.13	4.68	0.55	4.43	5.64	0.61	1.74
60-70	14.37	25.69	0.76	2.74	8.23	0.34	3.03	4.80	0.70	1.89
70-80	12.56	25.62	1.13	4.71	8.43	0.57	4.63	3.77	0.80	1.75
80-90	16.83	33.21	1.56	6.41	11.10	1.06	9.70	8.61	1.04	2.61
90-95	15.37	33.22	1.63	4.97	12.50	0.83	6.56	10.44	0.98	2.38
95-100	17.46	35.43	2.08	7.77	9.15	1.04	9.12	8.62	1.12	2.44
90-100	16.05	35.59	1.77	5.88	11.41	0.90	7.39	9.85	1.02	2.40
All Classes	**13.80**	**25.17**	**0.87**	**3.48**	**5.89**	**0.52**	**4.38**	**4.29**	**0.61**	**1.48**

KARIMNAGAR

Table 20.1.1: Per capita monthly expenditure, average size of household and Household Operational Land Holdings (acres)

Rural Karimnagar — All Classes

Fractile Classes	Monthly per capita average total expenditure (Rs 0.00)	Average size of house-hold	Household operational land holdings (in acres)
0 - 5	17.63	5.24	0.67
5 - 10	20.11	5.00	0.73
0 - 10	18.84	5.12	0.70
10- 20	22.94	5.62	1.05
20- 30	26.87	5.33	2.04
30- 40	31.65	5.19	3.33
40- 50	35.76	4.61	2.28
50- 60	39.98	4.32	3.70
60- 70	43.74	4.22	4.30
70- 80	48.59	3.93	2.97
80- 90	56.06	3.95	5.25
90- 95	68.05	4.00	7.41
95-100	87.09	3.62	14.11
90-100	77.10	3.81	10.76
All Classes	**38.19**	**4.61**	**3.66**

Table 20.1.2: Per capita monthly expenditure, average size of household and Household Operational Land Holdings (acres)

Rural Karimnagar — Cultivators

Fractile Classes	Monthly per capita average total expenditure (Rs 0.00)	Average size of house-hold	Household operational land holdings (in acres)
0 - 5	21.39	6.43	4.76
5 - 10	26.53	6.00	6.30
0 - 10	23.87	6.21	5.53
10- 20	30.84	6.31	8.20
20- 30	34.64	6.00	7.20
30- 40	39.14	4.93	7.15
40- 50	42.20	5.20	10.04
50- 60	44.78	3.86	7.29
60- 70	50.72	4.29	10.11
70- 80	57.98	4.29	11.11
80- 90	68.85	4.57	13.39
90- 95	77.48	4.71	13.77
95-100	95.09	3.71	21.80
90-100	85.24	4.21	17.78
All Classes	**45.71**	**4.98**	**9.76**

Table 20.1.3: Per capita monthly expenditure, average size of household and Household Operational Land Holdings (acres)

Rural Karimnagar — Agricultural Labourers

Fractile Classes	Monthly per capita average total expenditure (Rs 0.00)	Average size of house-hold	Household operatio-nal land holdings (in acres)
0 - 5	16.39	4.50	0.23
5 - 10	18.19	5.13	0.46
0 - 10	17.35	4.81	0.34
10- 20	20.05	4.93	0.44
20- 30	24.33	5.87	0.65
30- 40	24.33	5.00	0.50
40- 50	26.60	5.14	0.67
50- 60	31.82	4.53	0.68
60- 70	37.32	4.00	0.52
70- 80	42.95	3.73	0.34
80- 90	48.47	2.93	0.38
90- 95	53.02	3.75	0.38
95-100	63.65	2.75	0.17
90-100	57.51	3.25	0.26
All Classes	**30.70**	**4.41**	**0.49**

Table 20.1.4: Per capita monthly expenditure, average size of houschold and Household Operational Land Holdings (acres)

Rural Karimnagar — Others

Fractile Classes	Monthly per capita average total expenditure (Rs 0.00)	Average size of house-hold	Household operatio-nal land holdings (in acres)
0 - 5	19.00	5.72	0.74
5 - 10	21.63	5.29	0.58
0 - 10	20.22	5.50	0.66
10- 20	24.86	5.25	0.63
20- 30	28.65	5.42	1.03
30- 40	32.20	4.75	0.62
40- 50	35.41	3.85	0.50
50- 60	38.92	3.92	0.63
60- 70	42.36	4.45	0.85
70- 80	47.24	4.33	0.13
80- 90	53.34	4.33	0.65
90- 95	62.78	2.71	0.49
95-100	86.18	2.86	0.37
90-100	74.78	2.79	0.42
All Classes	**37.56**	**4.44**	**0.62**

Table 20.1.5: Per capita monthly expenditure, average size of household and Household Operational Land Holdings (acres)

Urban Karimnagar

All Classes

Fractile Classes	Monthly per capita average total expenditure (Rs 0.00)	Average size of household	Household operational land holdings (in acres)
0 - 5	28.92	5.83	0.39
5 - 10	35.68	5.17	0.17
0 - 10	32.10	5.50	0.28
10- 20	40.46	4.64	0.41
20- 30	47.29	4.27	0.07
30- 40	53.65	5.80	1.85
40- 50	56.97	4.90	0.00
50- 60	62.24	5.20	1.80
60- 70	66.38	4.10	6.40
70- 80	76.43	4.55	4.73
80- 90	91.14	3.73	0.00
90- 95	115.40	4.17	0.00
95-100	173.96	3.33	0.00
90-100	141.43	3.75	0.00
All Classes	**63.91**	**4.73**	**1.49**

Table 20.2.1: Per capita monthly expenditure (Rs. 0.00) and quantity intake (Kgs) of major food items.

Rural Karimnagar — All Classes

Fractile Classes	Cereals		Pulses		Milk and Milk Products	Edible Oil		Meat, Fish and Eggs	Sugar	
	Q	V	Q	V	V	Q	V	V	Q	V
0-5	9.40	10.14	0.14	0.47	0.56	0.12	1.09	0.09	0.04	0.09
5-10	9.64	10.58	0.14	0.42	0.67	0.14	1.20	0.11	0.05	0.12
0-10	9.52	10.36	0.14	0.44	0.62	0.13	1.14	0.10	0.05	0.10
10-20	10.37	11.60	0.22	0.66	0.61	0.20	1.43	0.33	0.08	0.13
20-30	11.32	13.53	0.28	0.88	0.56	0.21	1.78	0.62	0.03	0.12
30-40	11.67	14.45	0.34	1.01	1.31	0.22	1.97	1.09	0.13	0.35
40-50	12.46	17.34	0.41	1.29	1.27	0.30	2.25	1.38	0.12	0.30
50-60	13.20	18.92	0.43	1.35	1.43	0.26	2.32	1.37	0.18	0.49
60-70	13.92	21.10	0.47	1.51	2.16	0.28	2.48	1.58	0.16	0.43
70-80	15.37	24.32	0.48	1.55	1.66	0.29	2.61	2.02	0.17	0.39
80-90	16.11	26.87	0.50	1.64	3.07	0.33	2.91	2.95	0.23	0.53
90-95	16.30	29.68	0.68	2.25	7.99	0.37	3.20	3.52	0.47	1.47
95-100	16.99	28.93	0.56	1.71	9.32	0.39	3.54	2.97	0.51	1.26
90-100	16.63	29.32	0.62	2.03	8.62	0.38	3.36	3.26	0.49	1.21
All Classes	**12.76**	**17.99**	**0.37**	**1.18**	**1.93**	**0.25**	**2.15**	**1.35**	**0.15**	**0.37**

Table 20.2.2: Per capita monthly expenditure (Rs. 0.00) and quantity intake (Kgs) of major food items.

Rural Karimnagar — Cultivators

Fractile Classes	Cereals		Pulses		Milk and Milk Products	Edible Oil		Meat, Fish and Eggs	Sugar	
	Q	V	Q	V	V	Q	V	V	Q	V
0-5	9.62	11.54	0.23	0.71	0.37	0.16	1.42	0.38	0.03	0.06
5-10	10.93	14.29	0.38	1.23	0.36	0.18	1.56	0.79	0.05	0.16
0-10	10.25	12.87	0.30	0.96	0.36	0.17	1.49	0.57	0.04	0.11
10-20	10.12	13.99	0.37	1.15	1.89	0.23	2.08	0.84	0.18	0.52
20-30	12.62	16.77	0.40	1.24	2.26	0.24	2.14	1.34	0.17	0.44
30-40	12.67	19.62	0.45	1.52	1.12	0.24	2.21	0.91	0.13	0.33
40-50	13.38	19.15	0.44	1.38	2.99	0.26	2.27	1.50	0.23	0.73
50-60	16.29	25.79	0.54	1.83	2.76	0.32	2.90	1.80	0.25	0.72
60-70	15.22	24.80	0.51	1.65	3.75	0.27	2.38	1.77	0.19	0.43
70-80	15.48	27.30	0.62	2.07	4.55	0.38	3.54	3.13	0.41	0.98
80-90	16.31	30.66	0.65	2.28	9.46	0.33	2.74	3.48	0.48	1.17
90-95	18.12	31.53	0.46	1.48	9.73	0.35	3.09	3.61	0.48	1.13
95-100	15.71	25.99	0.55	1.68	11.42	0.42	3.99	2.56	0.62	1.48
90-100	17.06	29.09	0.50	1.57	10.47	0.38	3.49	3.14	0.54	1.28
All Classes	**13.56**	**20.97**	**0.46**	**1.51**	**3.66**	**0.27**	**2.44**	**1.73**	**0.25**	**0.63**

Table 20.2.3: Per capita monthly expenditure (Rs. 0.00) and quantity intake (Kgs) of major food items.

Rural Karimnagar — Agricultural Labourers

Fractile Classes	Cereals		Pulses		Milk and Milk Products	Edible Oil		Meat, Fish and Eggs	Sugar	
	Q	V	Q	V	V	Q	V	V	Q	V
0-5	9.08	9.33	0.06	0.16	0.50	0.11	0.98	0.09	0.06	0.09
5-10	9.49	10.55	0.18	0.68	0.74	0.12	1.08	0.04	0.02	0.10
0-10	9.30	9.98	0.12	0.44	0.63	0.12	1.03	0.06	0.02	0.09
10-20	9.24	10.07	0.14	0.40	0.61	0.12	1.32	0.12	0.05	0.13
20-30	10.14	11.21	0.17	0.53	0.51	0.16	1.37	0.37	0.04	0.09
30-40	11.74	12.69	0.27	0.76	0.49	0.20	1.41	0.29	0.04	0.09
40-50	10.92	12.48	0.26	0.83	0.47	0.22	2.06	0.65	0.07	0.11
50-60	12.19	14.04	0.33	0.87	0.93	0.38	1.89	1.21	0.12	0.26
60-70	12.38	16.51	0.39	1.18	0.38	0.21	1.94	1.50	0.07	0.18
70-80	15.44	23.53	0.35	1.19	0.18	0.26	2.24	1.72	0.10	0.21
80-90	17.18	25.06	0.49	1.61	0.33	0.28	2.67	1.69	0.04	0.07
90-95	16.58	25.51	0.40	1.38	1.00	0.27	2.33	3.33	0.15	0.33
95-100	19.73	29.02	0.57	1.64	0.66	0.39	3.46	2.27	0.03	0.14
90-100	17.91	26.99	0.47	1.49	0.86	0.32	2.81	2.88	0.10	0.25
All Classes	**12.14**	**15.21**	**0.28**	**0.86**	**0.55**	**0.22**	**1.78**	**0.91**	**0.07**	**0.14**

Table 20.2.4: Per capita monthly expenditure (Rs. 0.00) and quantity intake (Kgs) of major food items.

Rural Karimnagar

Fractile Classes	Cereals		Pulses		Others: Milk and Milk Products	Edible Oil		Meat, Fish and Eggs	Sugar	
	Q	V	Q	V	V	Q	V	V	Q	V
0-5	10.11	10.70	0.14	0.43	0.75	0.14	1.05	0.13	0.06	0.13
5-10	9.59	10.87	0.18	0.56	1.00	0.35	1.27	0.31	0.18	0.16
0-10	9.86	10.78	0.16	0.30	0.87	0.24	1.15	0.22	0.12	0.14
10-20	10.41	12.60	0.21	0.67	0.86	0.19	1.62	0.16	0.07	0.17
20-30	12.47	14.43	0.24	0.76	0.83	0.20	1.76	0.55	0.07	0.14
30-40	12.58	14.93	0.36	1.06	0.65	0.24	2.04	1.42	0.08	0.16
40-50	13.75	19.90	0.44	1.43	0.60	0.27	2.43	1.87	0.09	0.20
50-60	11.72	17.68	0.44	1.22	0.93	0.27	2.58	1.03	0.22	0.59
60-70	13.32	19.99	0.41	1.22	1.86	0.23	2.17	1.96	0.11	0.27
70-80	12.38	20.19	0.54	1.69	2.60	0.32	2.89	1.71	0.25	0.56
80-90	14.65	24.81	0.46	1.42	2.03	0.31	2.66	2.89	0.16	0.37
90-95	16.58	27.35	0.62	1.95	2.99	0.41	3.79	4.15	0.29	0.70
95-100	16.15	27.15	0.66	2.11	4.77	0.45	4.13	2.90	0.45	1.16
90-100	16.36	27.25	0.64	2.03	3.90	0.43	3.97	3.51	0.37	0.94
All Classes	**12.49**	**17.51**	**0.37**	**1.13**	**1.40**	**0.26**	**2.21**	**1.38**	**0.14**	**0.32**

Table 20.2.5: Per capita monthly expenditure (Rs. 0.00) and quantity intake (Kgs) of major food items.

Urban Karimnagar — All Classes

Fractile Classes	Cereals		Pulses		Milk and Milk Products	Edible Oil		Meat, Fish and Eggs	Sugar	
	Q	V	Q	V	V	Q	V	V	Q	V
0-5	9.51	11.95	0.29	1.02	1.06	0.17	1.39	0.80	0.06	0.13
5-10	9.35	15.44	0.36	1.31	1.16	0.18	1.44	0.65	0.15	0.31
0-10	9.44	13.59	0.32	1.15	1.11	0.17	1.41	0.73	0.10	0.21
10-20	10.16	15.68	0.42	1.55	1.75	0.26	2.12	1.28	0.17	0.39
20-30	10.64	17.97	0.40	1.57	2.32	0.23	1.94	1.38	0.22	0.51
30-40	13.22	23.84	0.39	1.48	2.93	0.27	2.27	1.05	0.22	0.56
40-50	11.33	19.82	0.40	1.63	2.90	0.29	2.43	1.40	0.21	0.49
50-60	10.69	19.48	0.48	1.89	4.05	0.34	2.70	1.43	0.38	0.94
60-70	10.74	19.54	0.48	1.77	5.71	0.35	2.84	1.73	0.32	0.83
70-80	14.27	26.62	0.63	2.26	5.68	0.41	3.35	3.27	0.62	1.46
80-90	12.18	23.20	0.60	2.23	6.29	0.41	3.56	2.89	0.49	1.15
90-95	12.04	27.40	0.66	2.33	10.20	0.45	3.74	4.96	0.62	1.41
95-100	19.02	35.92	0.75	2.75	19.05	0.63	4.82	10.91	0.85	1.92
90-100	15.14	31.20	0.70	2.52	14.13	0.53	4.22	7.60	0.72	1.64
All Classes	**11.69**	**20.73**	**0.47**	**1.76**	**4.37**	**0.32**	**2.59**	**2.14**	**0.33**	**0.78**

ADILABAD

Table 21.1.1: Per capita monthly expenditure, average size of household and Household Operational Land Holdings (acres)

Rural Adilabad All Classes

Fractile Classes	Monthly per capita average total expenditure (Rs 0.00)	Average size of house-hold	Household operatio-nal land holdings (in acres)
0 - 5	19.94	5.71	0.04
5 - 10	25.07	5.36	1.04
0 - 10	22.42	5.54	0.54
10- 20	28.51	6.11	0.56
20- 30	31.84	5.89	5.29
30- 40	34.77	4.52	4.75
40- 50	38.99	4.26	4.76
50- 60	42.93	4.19	7.17
60- 70	48.45	3.30	4.27
70- 80	55.91	3.44	5.72
80- 90	67.49	3.70	5.41
90- 95	84.75	3.29	4.12
95-100	142.66	2.79	4.39
90-100	111.32	3.04	4.26
All Classes	**43.92**	**4.40**	**4.55**

Table 21.1.2: Per capita monthly expenditure, average size of household and Household Operational Land Holdings (acres)

Rural Adilabad Cultivators

Fractile Classes	Monthly per capita average total expenditure (Rs 0.00)	Average size of house-hold	Household operatio-nal land holdings (in acres)
0 - 5	26.67	5.67	8.73
5 - 10	29.01	5.67	10.31
0 - 10	27.84	5.67	9.52
10- 20	32.12	5.50	10.34
20- 30	34.74	4.92	10.68
30- 40	38.17	4.92	7.92
40- 50	41.82	4.67	10.03
50- 60	44.80	5.15	11.91
60- 70	51.58	3.83	7.74
70- 80	57.15	3.92	9.95
80- 90	67.39	3.92	9.87
90- 95	79.12	3.67	9.46
95-100	98.17	4.17	13.63
90-100	89.25	3.92	11.55
All Classes	**46.40**	**4.65**	**9.98**

Table 21.1.3: Per capita monthly expenditure, average size of household and Household Operational Land Holdings (acres)

Rural Adilabad — Agricultural Labourers

Fractile Classes	Monthly per capita average total expenditure (Rs 0.00)	Average size of house-hold	Household operatio-nal land holdings (in acres)
0 - 5	16.77	6.40	0.13
5 - 10	21.57	5.80	0.00
0 - 10	19.05	6.10	0.06
10- 20	24.55	4.20	0.00
20- 30	27.72	5.89	0.65
30- 40	29.72	5.44	0.00
40- 50	33.18	4.90	0.00
50- 60	36.01	3.78	0.04
60- 70	39.79	3.22	0.29
70- 80	43.22	3.11	0.12
80- 90	38.99	2.10	0.46
90- 95	55.93	2.00	0.00
95-100	80.38	2.20	0.40
90-100	68.73	2.10	0.21
All Classes	**33.09**	**4.07**	**0.16**

Table 21.1.4: Per capita monthly expenditure, average size of household and Household Operational Land Holdings (acres)

Rural Adilabad — Others

Fractile Classes	Monthly per capita average total expenditure (Rs 0.00)	Average size of house-hold	Household operatio-nal land holdings (in acres)
0 - 5	23.08	4.66	0.00
5 - 10	25.78	9.33	0.00
0 - 10	24.88	7.33	0.00
10- 20	30.04	6.00	0.36
20- 30	32.85	6.60	0.73
30- 40	41.65	3.50	0.00
40- 50	52.95	3.40	0.00
50- 60	59.33	3.00	0.30
60- 70	64.38	4.20	0.00
70- 80	76.61	3.00	0.00
80- 90	91.98	2.50	0.00
90- 95	132.53	2.67	2.00
95-100	249.09	3.00	0.00
90-100	194.24	2.83	0.99
All Classes	**55.26**	**4.45**	**0.27**

Table 21.1.5: Per capita monthly expenditure, average size of household and Household Operational Land Holdings (acres)

Urban Adilabao — All Classes

Fractile Classes	Monthly per capita average total expenditure (Rs 0.00)	Average size of household	Household operational land holdings (in acres)
0 - 5	29.74	6.00	0.00
5 - 10	32.02	5.71	0.29
0 - 10	30.85	5.86	0.14
10- 20	35.51	5.83	0.42
20- 30	39.58	4.92	0.00
30- 40	44.09	5.08	0.33
40- 50	49.88	4.25	0.67
50- 60	54.43	3.92	0.00
60- 70	59.67	3.42	0.33
70- 80	67.38	3.33	0.00
80- 90	80.69	4.42	0.00
90- 95	97.79	2.71	0.00
95-100	212.48	3.00	6.43
90-100	158.00	2.86	3.21
All Classes	**56.76**	**4.39**	**0.55**

Table 21.2.1: Per capita monthly expenditure (Rs. 0.00) and quantity intake (Kgs) of major food items.

Rural Adilabad — All Classes

Fractile Classes	Cereals		Pulses		Milk and Milk Products	Edible Oil		Meat, Fish and Eggs	Sugar	
	Q	V	Q	V	V	Q	V	V	Q	V
0-5	7.81	11.19	0.38	1.56	0.70	0.16	1.37	0.31	0.16	0.37
5-10	8.51	12.27	0.36	1.30	1.07	0.20	1.72	0.12	0.15	0.37
0-10	8.15	11.71	0.37	1.43	1.88	0.18	1.54	0.22	0.16	0.37
10-20	8.87	15.01	0.45	1.74	0.52	0.17	1.52	0.68	0.19	0.46
20-30	9.55	15.18	0.53	1.94	0.86	0.19	1.57	0.95	0.25	0.64
30-40	11.66	17.67	0.56	2.29	0.40	0.20	1.76	1.58	0.24	0.47
40-50	10.73	18.09	0.53	2.05	1.41	0.26	2.31	1.44	0.20	0.47
50-60	11.24	18.77	0.62	2.43	2.93	0.29	3.25	1.44	0.45	1.05
60-70	12.84	20.55	0.70	2.59	3.01	0.33	2.98	1.15	0.37	0.91
70-80	13.98	23.30	0.73	2.83	3.32	0.36	3.06	7.14	0.52	1.31
80-90	13.96	25.16	0.82	3.44	4.92	0.43	3.67	2.05	0.47	1.36
90-95	12.63	23.44	0.98	3.93	6.26	0.53	4.59	5.52	0.65	1.61
95-100	15.41	27.88	1.09	4.26	8.83	0.72	6.29	12.79	0.80	2.34
90-100	13.91	25.48	1.03	4.08	7.44	0.62	5.37	8.86	0.72	1.95
All Classes	**11.03**	**18.18**	**0.60**	**2.34**	**2.17**	**0.28**	**2.47**	**2.13**	**0.33**	**0.81**

Table 21.2.2: Per capita monthly expenditure (Rs. 0.00) and quantity intake (Kgs) of major food items.

Rural Adilabad

Cultivators

Fractile Classes	Cereals		Pulses		Milk and Milk Products	Edible Oil		Meat, Fish and Eggs	Sugar	
	Q	V	Q	V	V	Q	V	V	Q	V
0-5	8.38	13.79	0.50	1.94	0.76	0.18	1.50	-	0.21	0.51
5-10	8.09	13.79	0.47	1.88	1.03	0.19	1.62	1.74	0.26	0.50
0-10	8.24	13.79	0.49	1.91	0.90	0.18	1.56	0.87	0.24	0.50
10-20	9.77	15.94	0.58	2.21	1.08	0.19	1.48	1.20	0.29	0.64
20-30	11.90	18.53	0.61	2.75	0.17	0.20	1.79	2.15	0.25	0.42
30-40	10.51	17.74	0.56	2.12	1.78	0.24	2.12	1.81	0.22	0.49
40-50	11.20	19.09	0.56	2.28	2.84	0.30	2.57	1.05	0.39	1.01
50-60	11.27	18.51	0.68	2.63	4.16	0.28	3.63	1.48	0.49	1.14
60-70	13.72	23.70	0.72	2.56	3.61	0.35	3.07	0.96	0.49	1.14
70-80	13.98	21.88	0.70	2.77	4.14	0.36	3.13	2.41	0.53	1.56
80-90	14.30	25.85	0.72	3.43	6.97	0.40	3.43	1.91	0.56	1.67
90-95	11.36	20.09	0.72	3.19	5.16	0.55	4.68	4.95	0.64	1.60
95-100	13.88	24.58	1.32	5.00	8.80	0.64	5.64	4.88	0.60	1.44
90-100	12.70	22.43	1.04	4.16	7.10	0.60	5.19	4.91	0.62	1.51
All Classes	**11.51**	**19.27**	**0.65**	**2.62**	**3.04**	**0.30**	**2.69**	**1.79**	**0.39**	**0.96**

Table 21.2.3: Per capita monthly expenditure (Rs. 0.00) and quantity intake (Kgs) of major food items.

Rural Adilabad

Agricultural Labourers

Fractile Classes	Cereals		Pulses		Milk and Milk Products	Edible Oil		Meat, Fish and Eggs	Sugar	
	Q	V	Q	V	V	Q	V	V	Q	V
0-5	7.81	8.88	0.30	1.16	0.31	0.16	1.28	0.31	0.06	0.13
5-10	7.24	10.48	0.40	1.61	0.34	0.14	1.21	0.11	0.17	0.36
0-10	7.54	9.64	0.34	1.38	0.33	0.15	1.25	0.22	0.11	0.24
10-20	8.52	12.45	0.29	1.08	0.38	0.20	1.74	-	0.13	0.26
20-30	9.49	15.02	0.33	1.26	-	0.16	1.38	0.77	0.13	0.31
30-40	10.10	16.43	0.50	1.86	0.08	0.16	1.46	0.27	0.22	0.51
40-50	11.69	16.92	0.51	1.76	-	0.18	1.61	0.50	0.09	0.18
50-60	10.88	17.62	0.50	1.79	0.43	0.21	1.86	0.56	0.27	0.55
60-70	10.41	17.50	0.55	2.03	0.55	0.29	2.83	1.38	0.11	0.29
70-80	11.79	19.59	0.71	2.73	1.74	0.24	2.30	1.82	0.40	0.67
80-90	14.05	21.62	0.69	2.70	1.05	0.28	2.58	1.48	0.36	0.80
90-95	16.00	28.70	0.95	3.32	-	0.30	2.70	1.92	0.60	1.04
95-100	12.73	21.64	0.91	3.69	3.27	0.45	3.93	3.32	0.30	0.57
90-100	14.29	25.00	0.93	3.52	1.71	0.38	3.35	2.65	0.44	0.80
All Classes	**10.30**	**15.96**	**0.48**	**1.81**	**0.46**	**0.20**	**1.83**	**0.75**	**0.19**	**0.40**

Table 21.2.4: Per capita monthly expenditure (Rs. 0.00) and quantity intake (Kgs) of major food items.

Rural Adilabad

Fractile Classes	Cereals		Pulses		Others: Milk and Milk Products	Edible Oil		Meat, Fish and Eggs	Sugar	
	Q	V	Q	V	V	Q	V	V	Q	V
0-5	10.36	18.61	0.50	2.18	2.14	0.21	1.86	0.84	0.21	0.70
5-10	7.86	11.82	0.50	1.93	2.14	0.20	1.61	0.32	0.29	0.63
0-10	8.69	14.08	0.50	2.01	2.14	0.20	1.69	0.50	0.26	0.65
10-20	7.92	13.73	0.50	1.82	1.41	0.22	2,03	0.81	0.31	0.85
20-30	8.33	13.15	0.45	1.77	1.77	0.17	1.47	1.68	0.27	1.04
30-40	11.81	18.12	0.51	1.78	0.83	0.32	2.47	1.74	0.14	0.48
40-50	12.35	20.71	0.60	2.38	1.76	0.41	3.94	1.59	0.18	0.49
50-60	14.20	24.57	0.73	2.95	3.43	0.45	3.44	2.26	0.47	1.24
60-70	12.86	23.14	0.76	2.87	3.10	0.45	3.86	4.29	0.33	1.18
70-80	14.89	28.24	0.19	4.29	3.17	0.44	4.03	2.83	0.44	1.28
80-90	17.33	30.70	0.80	3.46	5.67	0.63	5.27	3.20	0.87	2.45
90-95	17.50	34.00	1.50	5.66	15.00	0.75	6.50	7.62	1.00	2.61
95-100	12.33	24.94	1.00	3.75	8.33	0.78	6.72	18.66	1.11	3.30
90-100	14.76	29.21	1.24	4.65	11.47	0.76	6.62	13.47	1.06	2.98
All Classes	**11.09**	**19.18**	**0.66**	**2.51**	**2.90**	**0.34**	**2.99**	**1.81**	**0.38**	**1.11**

Table 21.2.5: Per capita monthly expenditure (Rs. 0.00) and quantity intake (Kgs) of major food items.

Urban Adilabad

All Classes

Fractile Classes	Cereals		Pulses		Milk and Milk Products	Edible Oil		Meat, Fish and Eggs	Sugar	
	Q	V	Q	V	V	Q	V	V	Q	V
0-5	9.52	15.31	0.40	2.08	-	0.14	1.27	0.52	0.14	0.21
5-10	8.50	14.09	0.44	1.94	0.45	0.16	1.35	0.67	0.19	0.36
0-10	9.02	14.71	0.42	2.01	0.22	0.15	1.31	0.60	0.16	0.29
10-20	9.93	15.09	0.41	1.69	0.81	0.19	1.65	1.40	0.26	0.60
20-30	9.75	17.13	0.70	1.81	0.46	0.23	1.87	1.03	0.17	0.42
30-40	9.59	15.92	0.75	3.03	4.16	0.42	2.23	0.89	0.41	1.01
40-50	11.18	18.96	0.43	1.74	3.47	0.32	2.89	1.24	0.40	1.03
50-60	9.45	17.45	0.69	2.99	3.67	0.32	2.77	1.91	0.45	1.26
60-70	11.21	28.82	1.29	2.99	3.39	0.43	5.47	2.05	0.55	1.61
70-80	11.88	22.76	1.15	2.86	3.76	0.53	4.54	2.69	0.49	1.26
80-90	13.04	23.18	0.99	3.86	8.86	0.47	4.40	15.00	0.70	2.62
90-95	13.16	24.08	1.21	4.71	12.11	0.66	5.71	18.84	0.74	2.04
95-100	15.96	30.09	2.01	7.69	10.24	0.98	8.40	8.40	1.05	3.05
90-100	14.63	27.23	1.63	6.27	11.12	0.82	7.13	13.36	0.90	2.57
All Classes	**10.70**	**20.15**	**0.77**	**2.75**	**3.51**	**0.35**	**3.07**	**3.56**	**0.41**	**1.14**